A GUIDE TO
ARCHITECTURAL STYLES

A GUIDE TO
ARCHITECTURAL STYLES

Herbert Pothorn

PHAIDON · OXFORD

Originally published in German under the title
Das grosse Buch der Baustile

Translated from the German by James Ramsay

This edition published in 1983 by Phaidon Press Ltd,
Littlegate House, St Ebbe's Street, Oxford OX1 1SQ

Copyright © 1979 by Südwest Verlag GmbH & Co KG, München

English Translation copyright
© 1982 by Arnoldo Mondadori Editore S.p.A., Milano

British Library Cataloguing in Publication Data

Pothorn, Herbert
    A guide to architectural styles
    1. Architecture – History
    I. Title   II. Das grosse Buch der Baustile
    English
    722   NA200

ISBN 0–7148–2263–9

CONTENTS

INTRODUCTION

The word "style," in its normal figurative use, strictly speaking denotes the fashion or mode of creative expression, either written or spoken. Only in the last century was it extended to the figurative arts, replacing "manner," which had been current since the sixteenth century, and "taste," which had been in vogue in the eighteenth. It was used to indicate the recurrent characteristics and main distinguishing features of an artist or school. By extension it then came to mean the distinctive aspects of any one age, historical period, or even region.

Hence stylistics (the science of styles) has a twin function: it not only analyzes the historical sequence of eras, it also defines geographical areas in terms of clear cultural differences. Such definitions highlight the significance of time within the traditions of different parts of the world. In this respect East and West differ considerably. Pre-Columbian America is different again. The greatest differences are to be found, however, in parts of the world that are somehow cut off—by desert or ocean—from other communities, and that were able, so to speak, to set off through time at their own pace, undisturbed by perhaps more precipitate neighbours.

The history of architectural style is the history of man's compelling need for security and shelter, comfort, decoration, and individuality as manifested in different ways over the ages. The last of these imperatives is the most fundamental to our purpose, since it is from those individual details that characterize any given mode of being that we come to recognize style.

A fireplace with a roof and place to sleep evinces as little "style" as a sacrificial spot beneath an oak tree. It is with the emergence of the concept of sacral, aesthetic, and hierarchical necessity that we see the beginnings of the progress that has led through the great periods of the past to the styles of the present day. In this book a separate survey of Western stylistic traditions is followed by an examination of non-European cultures—including both some that disappeared centuries ago and others whose influence is still discernible today. Such an approach will show how the vast choice of building materials and architectural styles at the disposition of the present-day architect at once facilitates and complicates his job; at the same time it will be seen that nostalgia for past splendour and harmony is as out of place nowadays as in any period of doubt and universal change.

This change (by no means widespread yet, but in some areas quite firmly established) consists in a rejection of that approach to architecture that, accepting the feasibility of deducing human needs from statistics, believed it possible to suit everybody by following one or two standard norms. Despite the good intentions behind that approach, human beings cannot (fortunately!) be summed up in statistics. The reaction was predictable. The word "modern" or "modernistic," which only a couple of decades ago had a triumphant ring about it, has now lost much of its appeal. Those great building blocks we see around us every day—the linear austerity of which was hailed as being such a great advance, so bold, so functional, so concrete and geometrical—are no longer felt to be suitable models for future building projects, especially residential. Their monotonous façades betray a lack of architectonic imagination, critics now say. To build in this way is dangerous, they claim, since it creates a type of "residential man," living, not as he would wish to, but as his environment dictates.

It is of course possible to find people who belong to this species of "residential man," but their dwellings have little relation to what we generally imply in the word "architecture." We should not exaggerate, however. It would not be fair to think of these rationally conceived vertical developments as merely office silos or free-time prisons; yet suffice it to say that they encourage feelings of being boxed up, and that these in turn reduce neighbourly tolerance.

The following quote from an extremely celebrated architect will highlight the change of meaning that has come about in the word "modern": "We shall erect a skyscraper in the Île-de-France—a logically coherent, uncomplicated, unfussy, elegant, and respondent challenge to New York and Chicago." These somewhat grandiose words were spoken by Le Corbusier in 1922, when a certain number of architects quite unashamedly saw themselves as the builders of the community life of the future. This kind of "manifesto" now seems to have unpleasant overtones. There cannot now be many architects who would like to challenge New York and Chicago.

Those not entirely in tune with the present, and those who find it hard to imagine the aesthetic outlook (even in the most general terms) of the future, or who refuse to accept that architecture must necessarily continue to follow modern creative trends, will naturally look back and reflect on the past. Hence it is not only instructive, but helpful and salutary, in the face of such misgivings, to take an interest in the history of architecture.

Comparisons abound. Here we have contented ourselves with taking as many examples of building styles from the almost endless choice available as will illustrate overall similarities, different developments, and the various qualities that link up and differentiate one age or region from another.

Building Materials and Tools

Ready-made caves were soon not good enough for mankind. His first "home improvement" was to level the floor— digging here and there and laying down slabs of stone, then covering them with a layer of sand or clay, packed down hard. Thus man began to build.

For practical reasons, cavemen used to position their fireplaces in the front half of their cave or near the entrance. They would place stones together in a semicircle, and take note of the fact that one flat stone could successfully be laid on another. The gaps in between (the stones can hardly yet be said to be laid in any technical sense) were blocked up with clay. The fire remained alight, baking the clay astonishingly hard. Thus the first ovens appeared. The sleeping area was in the back of the cave, strewn with straw and skins. After a time the advantages of sleeping off the ground, on stones piled against the wall, began to be appreciated. These protected the sleepers from the dampness of the earth, and made a convenient place to sit during the daytime.

Considerations of defense and convenience were the conditioning factors of the first dwellings, which were still not exactly "buildings." No great sophistication was required to make use of the materials that lay ready to hand round and about. Bare hands sufficed, while the ground could be stamped down hard with one's feet. The one tool available was the digging stick. Leaving such a home for another cave in an area more

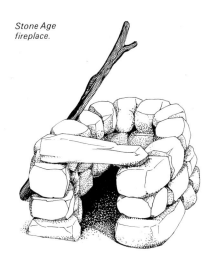

Stone Age fireplace.

abundant in game, on a sunnier hillside, or nearer a stream was no great hardship.

However, areas richer in wildlife and fruit did not necessarily always have natural caves (hollows or clefts worn out of the solid rock by water from melting ice and snow at the end of glaciations) in which homes could be made.

Perhaps those primitive stone fireplaces constituted the model for the first actual houses. The low walls of these fireplaces enclosed an area of about twice two hands' breadths. Built as tall as a man, above a hole in the ground, one arm's length wide and two deep, they could provide protection for the whole family. The roof would sometimes be made out of branches, twigs and straw. However, to begin with, or when not enough wood could be found, other roofing materials were used.

The earliest builders simply placed one stone on top of another, in such a way that after a certain point the walls started narrowing in towards each other, resulting in a sharp pointed vault. The shape of their construction was no doubt not of prime interest to such builders—the patterns vary from square to rectangular of different dimensions, even to circular. What mattered at first was merely fitting

everyone in. The shape of the roof developed as it were of its own accord, wall and roof making a single unit.

It was possible to erect this sort of construction with bare hands alone, as the stones did not need to be shaped. With time and patience each stone could be chosen according to suitability of natural shape. As the roof started to rise higher and a man standing on the ground could no longer reach to build farther up, a framework of branches could quickly be tied together to serve as a ladder.

Stone can be shaped, and even split, by stone. Tools came on the scene, and buildings became generally better, more beautiful and more regular in construction. As tools became more sophisticated, builders started to aim at more ambitious constructions, within the possibility of the materials available. Each course was laid as strictly horizontal as possible, while vertically (as became apparent in time) the stones were "displaced" from course to course in order to give the walls greater stability. As far as possible builders sought to construct walls free of irregularities. Sharp, jutting-out edges were carefully dressed, especially on the inside walls. Crudely built walls thus gave way gradually to relatively smooth ones.

Style without Design

Orderly arrangement of building materials was the result, not of preconceived design, but of the most elementary rules extrapolated instinctively during the process of construction. Starting from a square ground plan, the area enclosed decreases with each successive course. At the same time the square shape became increasingly circular from one course to the next. Hence a four-sided base had a conical top—although in fact the cone was truncated, as a hole was always left at the very top for smoke to escape through. Where there was no internal fire, the cone was finished off with either a flat slab or a clay cap in whatever shape the builder fancied: like a large knob, a simple rounding off, a pair

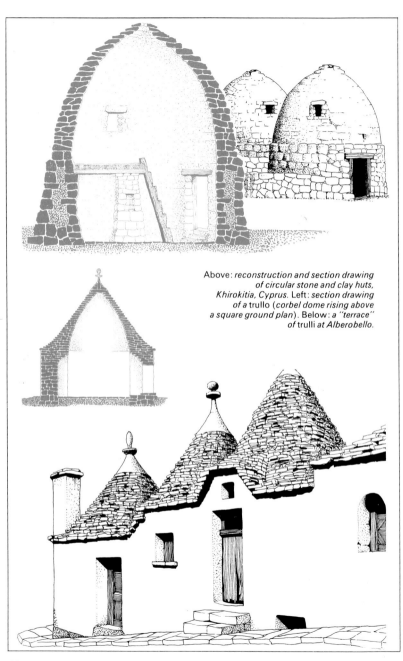

Above: *reconstruction and section drawing of circular stone and clay huts, Khirokitia, Cyprus.* Left: *section drawing of a* trullo (*corbel dome rising above a square ground plan*). Below: *a "terrace" of* trulli *at Alberobello.*

Right, top: *burial chamber at Megiddo, Canaan, third millennium B.C. Barrel vault structure built with unhewn stones. It has a covering of stones and earth. Vertical shaft entrance.* Right, center: *burial chamber beneath a dwelling, Ugarit, second millennium B.C. The stones are roughly squared. The visible surfaces of the corbels are slanted.* Right, bottom: *tomb built with unshaped stones on the island of Minorca, second millennium B.C. The covering slabs are supported by pilasters projecting from the walls as well as by free-standing pillars (early types of column).*

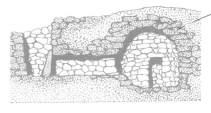

Below: *reconstruction of the interior of the nuraghe of Palmavera, near Alghero, c. 1000 B.C. The inset in the top left-hand corner gives an impression of the outside. The root of the word "nuraghe" is the ancient Sardinian nur, "heap." There was no question of economizing in stones in these buildings; their Sardinian architects evidently felt that the heavier the weight of stone, the safer would be the vault.*

of horns, a pine cone, or a (still roughly shaped) cross.

In this way there evolved one of the earliest styles. Developed *ad hoc*, it was indeed rudimentary, unpretentious, not even beautiful to look at; yet it already pointed the way to something that has survived, away from the mainstream of architectural history, down to our own day.

Of course, it does not appear to have much of a future now. Nobody in Alberobello today would go to a builder and say, "Build me a *trullo*." For his money he would expect a house with a solid cement base, complete with cellar, all built with "patented" cement blocks— something new and modern. The first person to want such a house there indeed did get something new and unfamiliar, since everyone around him was still living quite contentedly in *trulli* (albeit renovated countless times, modernized inside and out, plastered, and fitted with glass windows and electricity) passed down from generation to generation. Other additions to the original stone *trullo* cone roofs have been chimneys and television aerials.

About two hours' car drive northwest of the *trullo* villages in Apulia stands Castel del Monte, the Hohenstaufen prince Frederick II's hunting lodge, a curious but majestic medley of Romanesque, Oriental and Gothic styles. Compared with this the *trulli* are merely curiosities. Nevertheless they are strangely moving in their very crudeness of construction, and their great age inspires a certain sense of awe.

No *trullo* still standing in Apulia dates as far back as the Stone Age. However, their basic principle of construction was known then, and it recurs in many places around the Mediterranean and elsewhere.

Near Khirokitia on Cyprus the remains of forty-eight domed huts of definitely prehistoric construction have been discovered. Huddling together, some with interior sleeping platforms, they form a little village over 7000 years old.

The stone domes found in the Alps and in Provence are, despite appearances, much later. As one might expect, these constructions do not all share the same architectural characteristics. Widely differing basic shapes—from square, through oval, to circular—exist often side by side. Many examples of this type of building were discovered in fact by tourists, who would pass by, find them attractive and instinctively feel they were "very old." In appearance, indeed, they do evoke a very remote past. They can look almost prehistoric, especially when half ruined or in their original state, unaltered by later owners. Appearances can be deceptive, however.

Up in the mountain pastures of Sassal Masone, near the Bernina Pass, there are two handsome, solidly built domed huts which were at first thought to have been built in the early Middle Ages or even earlier. However, the Darmstadt architect Hans Soeder (1891–1962) was able to demonstrate that they could not have been built before 1870. He managed to trace the grandson of the man who had built them: as it turned out, they were the work of an Italian pastry cook and his assistant, originally from the mountainous area near Bergamo, who ran an inn in them. Apparently there was also a third domed building (somewhat smaller) in which milk was stored, but this proved too small for the business and was demolished.

Circle and Square

It is quite pointless wondering which of these two fundamental shapes is the more ancient, or whether the former developed from the latter or vice versa. Circular constructions are reminiscent of caves, but one cannot say that caves were actually the inspiration behind their first appearance. The preference for the circle can be accounted for by the fact that a circle allows maximum usable space to be created with the minimum of building materials. However, such a realization implies a certain knowledge of geometry. A more likely explanation is that the form derives from the round enclosure or the protective wall around the ditch.

The rectangle corresponds to the space taken up by a man lying stretched out on the ground. Two or more such spaces side by side always constituted a quadrangle, and as builders started to arrange one rectangular area next to another the angles at which the walls met remained constant. Thus the median lines (the axes of the four-sided construction) were vertical to each other, i.e. they crossed at right angles. This corresponded to a human being standing up about to move—looking in the direction in which he is about to go, his outstretched arms, at right angles to his line of vision, forming the second axis of the room.

Circular constructions (or geometrically related constructions with polygonal—hexagonal or octagonal—ground plans) were just as convenient to build with prehistoric building materials (i.e. undressed stone) as those with a four-sided ground plan.

Wood as a building material required straight walls, perpendicular to the ground. In other words they could not be curved in to form a dome. *Trulli* and Provençal shepherd's huts could not be built with wood. Wood is none the less

Small clay model of a house, to provide a dwelling for the souls of the dead; discovered with other funerary finds near Strelitz, Moravia; c. 2000 BC.

the most suitable material for the type of roof that rests on top of the walls of a house as an independent unit. This kind of roof can either straddle a supporting ridge beam or rise, gently or steeply, on four sides like a pyramid. It can project beyond the walls to protect them from rain and snow, or be extended at the front to form a sheltered veranda. From the

From left to right: *house with tent roof; house with side eaves; house with front veranda.*

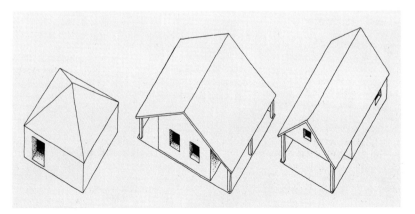

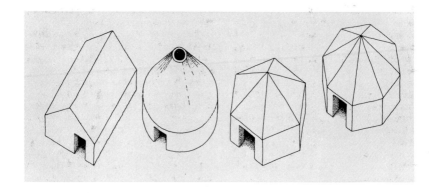

From left to right: *house with pitched roof;
circular house with a hole to allow smoke to
escape; hexagonal house; octagonal house.*

very start, however, working with wood
required more tools than working with
stone.

As tools improved in quality, so too the
possibilities of exploiting the available
materials expanded, in terms of both
technical mastery and stylistic awareness. With the increase of craftsmanlike
skills there emerged, together with the
ever greater precision of workmanship in
stone and wood, a desire to express and
satisfy personal taste. A clear idea had
entered the minds of those very first
architects: they had acquired a sense of
design. Of course this "design" was
never put down on paper, nor elaborated
in every detail. Yet something was formulated in their consciousnesses, prior to
the act of building. One or two lines
drawn in the sand signified, "Here's what
we'll do."

At this point we can at last begin to talk
about style—the expression of a certain
intellectual and spiritual state in the
formation of which magic, the notion of
an after life and general social attitudes
had played as great a part as mastery of
technical skills. Balance and harmony
raise the work above the ordinary run-of-
the-mill and give it an independent
coherence. The spark of creativity makes
it great.

Thus, in short, style is the end-product
of a certain harmony of intellectual,
spiritual, technical and economic forces.
Such a formulation may appear extremely
abstract; nevertheless, its very concise-
ness may provoke ideas. At this point we
begin to feel the lack of something—
some external element, some sense of
inspiration—that cannot be accounted
for by mere association of ideas or even
ideal models. Set expressions such as
"the spark of genius" or "creativity"
bring us closer to the heart of the matter;
yet these remain set expressions, and do
not explain how it is that sometimes the
creative spark seems to be lit by something "in the air" that defies rational
explanation. Ages that had living myt-
hologies at their disposal could talk
about muses and all kinds of other divine
agents. For us, "genius" has to suffice.

Yet this is the point. Were one to ask an
artist *how* he works, his answer would
clarify very little. Squares and rectangles,
polygons, circles, stone, wood, clay,
brick, burnt bricks, cement, metal and
glass, stucco and paint all make up the
ingredients of any given style. Yet without inspiration, when there is nothing "in
the air," when the creative spark is
missing, nothing can be done with those
ingredients.

Arches and Domes

All over the world, wherever man needed to protect his sleeping place and cooking hearth from the cold, from snow, from rain or from the heat, he built constructions similar to the huts on Khirokitia or to the cone-shaped dwellings in Apulia. They were not always built of stone. In the Sudan a mixture of mud and chopped straw was used. Eskimo igloos are still today built with blocks of packed snow. The Navaho Indians used to winter in dome-shaped huts made of pressed-grass bricks laid on a framework of wooden poles.

Numerous theories have been advanced as to why circular constructions should have appeared so early on, in such different places, independently of each other. Many of these theories enter somewhat deep waters: the need for a sense of security, fulfilled by the cave-like, egg-like or womb-like circle. Feelings of this nature were perhaps operating subconsciously. Essentially, however, it was simple that after much trial and error the circle proved extremely practical in its simplicity.

These constructions were not domes or vaults in the currently accepted sense. To distinguish them from the dome proper, we shall refer to them here as "step domes." They consist of rings or stones, one on top of the other, decreasing in diameter with each layer. The stones used were as flat as possible, preferably slab-shaped, and were laid as near horizontal as possible.

By contrast, a true dome is the product of delicate and complex calculations. The stones are cut into trapezoids, and are laid not horizontally but radially in relation to the central point of curvature. A true arch cannot be erected freely, as a step dome can: there has to be some form of internal scaffolding to hold up the stones during construction. In fact arches, vaults and domes are only safe and solid when completed. Once completed, however, they can reach heights and breadths which the old method could not possibly have attained. Accurate drawings and measurements are vital, though, since it is the geometrical precision of the vault—the regular flow of the curve—that makes the structure stable.

Arches and domes originated in the East. They were already widespread in the civilizations of the Middle East around 2000 BC, built to a remarkably high level of technical perfection. Yet neither the ancient Egyptians nor the Greeks displayed much interest in fine domes and arches. Both these peoples made their roofs with posts and beams laid on top of the walls. This technique, clearly deriving from wood-building procedures, soon came to be adapted in different ways for building in stone, as builders mastered and expanded their craft. Thus wooden posts were replaced

From left to right: *cross-section of a corbel vault; Roman masonry arch; incomplete arch, still with supporting scaffold.*

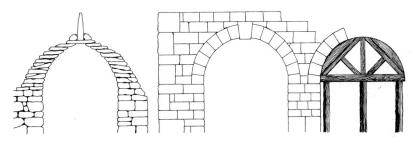

by columns, in all their many stylistic variants, while the beam evolved into the architrave.

Around 300 BC, the Romans adopted the dome, and ever since it has been one of the essential features of Western architecture. As well as stone and baked brick, the Romans also used a third type of building material, particularly suitable for arches and domes. At Palestrina (Roman Praeneste), east of Rome, are the ruins of the oracular shrine of Fortuna Primigenia (third century BC), a vast complex the most striking feature of which is the two-tiered series of parallel barrel vaults. These were built not in brickwork but in *opus caementicium*, a conglomerate of lime, pozzolana, fragments of tufa, and other materials cast over a framework. Volcanic ash, a sort of natural hydraulic cement, was used as a bonding material.

Contrary to what one sometimes reads, building with cement is no recent in-

From top to bottom: *frontal view, detail, and ground plan of the shrine of Fortuna Primigenia at Praeneste (Palestrina)*.

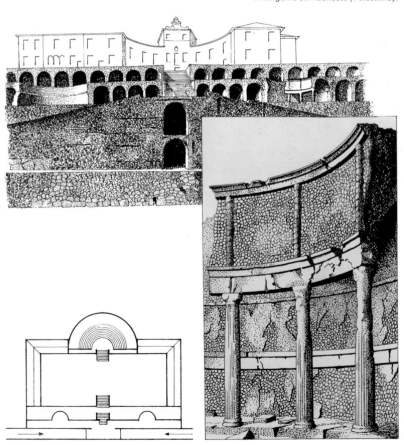

vention. Nor was the technique even invented by the Romans. It was commonly employed in volcanic regions at the very beginning of the historical era: in the Lipari Islands north of Sicily archaeologists have discovered the remains of concrete-type buildings dating from before 1500 BC, built with pebbles, volcanic ash and water. Some old books of art history make no mention of the use of volcanic ash as a cement. Ancient historians, too, paid scant heed to it, even though the remarkable ruins at Praeneste could hardly be overlooked. Their interest was mainly in artistic quality and pure form, rather than the level of craftsmanship and technical achievement of the past. Moreover, the cement walls on these volcanic islands were discovered rather late, and they were only able to be reliably dated some twenty years ago.

Praeneste
Although the shrine of Fortuna was finished (in a thoroughly Hellenistic style) in the time of Sulla, around 80 BC,

the ground plan dates from three centuries and more before. This ground plan consisted of terraces reached by two symmetrical ramps leading up from the valley. The impressiveness of the building testifies to the importance of this ancient Latin divinity, who not only brought good fortune but presided over every aspect of an agricultural people's existence. The ramps and walls leading to the first terrace are rudimentary in construction, built without mortar, with some very large polygonal stones. In some places, where necessary according to the plans, the builders cut into the bare rock. Both the vaulting and the walls of the second and third terraces are in *opus caementicium*, thickly plastered. Three columns and a niche still survive semi-intact, giving an idea of what this imposing monument must once have looked like. The vaults, which are so vital to the structure, were not originally visible. Around AD 1500, the Palazzo Barberini was built on the foundation walls of the amphitheater-shaped upper terrace.

ANTIQUITY

Egypt

The most ancient of all civilizations, that based on the Nile valley, only began to influence Europe after two thousand years and more—in its decadence, indeed, after the fall of the last dynasty. The Greeks and Phoenicians had trade relations with the Egyptians. Towards the end of the sixth century BC the Persians conquered the country and ruled over it for more than a century. In 332 BC, Alexander the Great included Egypt in his empire, claiming divine status for himself as the son of Ammon. There then followed the Ptolemaic dynasty, founded by Ptolemy of Macedon, despite six interfamily marriages of by no means pure Macedonian stock (in fact of equal parts Egyptian, Libyan, Nubian and Syrian). The last representative of this line, Cleopatra, literally fell, deviously draped in a sumptuous attire, at the feet of Caesar.

Rome made Egypt the granary of the Empire and received the Nilotic divinities into her own pantheon. During the Roman period, Egyptian art gradually ceased to influence that of the other Mediterranean civilizations, and the solemnly sealed doors of the royal tombs, which had withstood the ravages of time for so long, held no awe for the desert tribes who then and later overran the upper Nile valley. What archaeologists in more recent times have managed to preserve in museums is, notwithstanding its beauty and variety, only a partial record of splendours past. It is a testimonial to a faith, not devoid of terror, in a life beyond the grave.

In 1799, a lieutenant in Napoleon's army found, beneath the rubble of a destroyed house in the Delta area, the basalt slab that was later to become known as the Rosetta Stone. It bore the same inscription in three different forms of writing: hieroglyphs, Greek, and an ancient Egyptian demotic script. In 1822, the French archaeologist Jean François Champollion succeeded in partially deciphering the two Egyptian texts, using the Greek as a reference. This achievement represents the beginnings of scientifically conducted archaeological research in the Nile valley. The history of Egypt could now be properly recorded, and it was at last possible to gain some idea, more accurate than mere conjecture, of the purpose of ancient Egyptian monuments and their significance in relation to Egyptian concepts of the universe and the after life.

The, to us, daring size of Egyptian monuments was intended as an indestructible expression of royal might. For the peasant farmers along the river banks, as for all other subjects, these huge constructions affirmed the divine origins of every king since time immemorial. Who but a god could have shifted and raised so many stones—moved such mountains?

Apart from the irrigation system fed by the Nile, architecture was used exclusively in the service of kings, deities and the dead. There were indeed store-

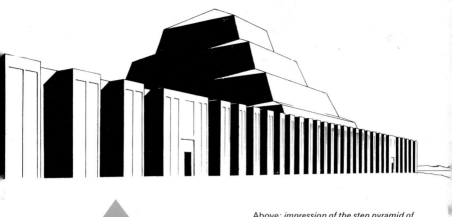

houses, archives and military buildings, but these were of little architectonic interest compared with the royal edifices. The king owned all the quarries in the rocky valleys, and kept an army of slaves. Yet the vast size of the buildings erected by the successive kings was dictated neither by this nor by some perverse whim. Rather, it reflects a desire to create a representation of the cosmos through a model of a spatio-temporal world having the Nile valley as its center.

In the third millennium BC, the star Alpha Draconis orbited the Pole, around which the fixed stars revolve night after night, with a deviation of less than three degrees. In summer in Lower Egypt this polar star of the pharaonic period stood thirty-three degrees above the horizon. The oblique shafts leading to the burial chambers are set at precisely this angle.

The sides of the pyramid of Cheops (each of which face one of the cardinal points) slope at an angle of fifty-two degrees—corresponding to the highest point of the brightest of the fixed stars, Sothis or, as we call it, Sirius. The perimeter of the base of the pyramid of Cheops relates to the length of the solar year: Egyptian architects used a unit of measurement which archaeologists call the "pyramid yard," equivalent to twenty-five inches (63.5 cm.). One twenty-fifth of a pyramid yard made one pyramid inch. In length, the base of the same pyramid measures about 251 yards (230 m.). Or course it is impossible to establish the exact length, as the outer facing slabs have disappeared. However, taking an approximate measurement of 252 yards (231 m.), that would make a total perimeter length of 36,524 pyramid inches. This figure corresponds to the exact length of the solar year (365.2422 days), at least to the fourth decimal point. Thus the dimensions of the pyramid of Cheops would appear to have both spatial and temporal connections with certain astronomical observations.

The mathematics of the pyramids is a

subject of controversy, as no contemporary documents or drawings exist to support any particular theory. Nevertheless, the astronomical and mathematical expertise of the period remains indisputable, together with the very considerable knowledge of geometry displayed by Egyptian architects.

Tens of thousands of workers laboured for some twenty years to dress, move and raise the two and a half million blocks of stone, each weighing about fifty hundredweight (2540 kg.), that go to make up the pyramid of Cheops (479 ft., 146 m., high).

Every ancient Egyptian building (whether cliff tomb, pyramid or temple) was conceived with astronomical concepts in mind as much as with aesthetic considerations. Finally, another determining element in the production of

Opposite: *the vast statues at the entrance to the cliff temple of Abu Simbel were carved out of the bare rock in the reign of Rameses II (1290–1223 BC). To save the complex from the rise in the level of the Nile when the Aswan Dam was built, it was removed to higher ground, above the original site. This operation took from 1964 to 1967.*

Below: *reconstruction and ground plan of a temple. The outer walls were perfectly flat, and the façade was covered with hieroglyphics. Temples of the same design were also dug out of cliffs, as at Abu Simbel. The rooms were always in succession one after the other, along an east–west central axis.*

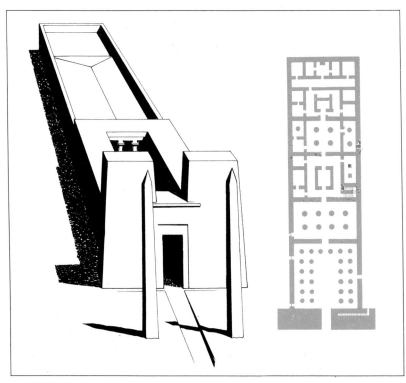

monuments of such vast size was the desire of the kings to express their own power. No wonder these gigantic works of architecture inspired a sense of wonder and awe. Huge flat façades stand guard before mysterious halls filled with forests of pillars. Only the elect could enter these halls, the walls of which were decorated with illustrated inscriptions, fully comprehensible to only a small minority. Common mortals could not begin to grasp the total scope of the Pharaoh's might.

Styles changed little throughout the long history of Egyptian architecture. Some temple façades, such as those at Karnak and Edfu, are built according to exactly identical principles and differ remarkably little in detail, although one was built over a thousand years after the other. The shape, once set, did not alter. The same was true of the style. Echoes

and repetition symbolized an eternal reality.

Building his future tomb was the center point of the Pharaoh's life. If Fate gave him a long, peaceful reign, the construction could reach gigantic size. Often it was enlarged even further by the next Pharaoh, when the various available chambers did not suffice for all the treasures that were to accompany the dead Pharaoh's soul on its journey through the afterlife. As is well known, death and the afterlife were constantly in the minds of the ancient Egyptians. However, there exist very few indications of the cult procedure for ordinary people when they died. Nor indeed is much known about the way of life of the masses. A secretly written text in one royal tomb allows us a glimpse of the divide between the nobility and *hoi polloi*: "Those who have cut the hard

Section of the Treasury of Atreus, Mycenae; corbelled dome vault built within a hillside.

stone, those whose fine work has produced a room in the pyramid, those who have erected a steep sloping obelisk—their places of sacrifice are as bare as those of the weary who die on the banks of the Nile unremembered by anyone." In a somewhat different vein, the inscription for the king reads: "The gate of heaven is open to you, the heavy fetters have been taken from you. The Sun god holds you by your hand, is guiding you and placing you on the throne of Osiris, lord of the underworld. You do as he does. You cause your house to flourish after you, and you keep your children from care."

In January 1960, President Nasser of Egypt pressed a button which set off ten tons of high explosives—and work started on the Aswan dam. Since the dam was completed, the level of the Nile has risen by about 330 feet (101 m.), overflowing roughly 250 miles (400 km.) of the old river banks. The necropolises and temples between Aswan (Philae) and Wadi Halfa would have been irretrievably lost had it not been for the intervention of Unesco, which organized a world-wide rescue operation that succeeded in saving all but a few monuments. Using all

Above, right: *a room in the palace of Knossos.* Right: *plan of the palace of Knossos made after Sir Arthur Evans's excavations.*

the available resources of technology and archaeological expertise, it was possible to dismantle and reassemble in safe places superb examples of ancient Egyptian architecture.

The Aegean

At a time when the Egyptians were building with precisely dressed stones, walls were being thrown up in the Peloponnese, on the Aegean islands and on Crete, using enormous blocks of stone piled crudely one on top of another. The excavated foundations of the first citadels indicate that they were laid *ad hoc* without any thought-out plan, with no considerations of prestige or self-expression in mind. But with the first colonnaded courtyards, conceived within the discipline of a four-sided surface area, with rooms all around, a certain rational element appears. Individual details reflect the influence of the Middle East and Egypt, yet the structural differences already constitute a style quite other than that of the vast structures of Egypt—a style (to our eyes at least) geared to human beings rather than to Sirius. And although built in honour of the gods, or to the specifications of those in the highest social positions (i.e. the priests and princes), these buildings seem closer to our own sensibility and to human reason. "Right" size and proportion became more important than sheer size for its own sake.

In the early stages of Aegean civilization, walls were still built to Cyclopean dimensions, as if by and for giants, and

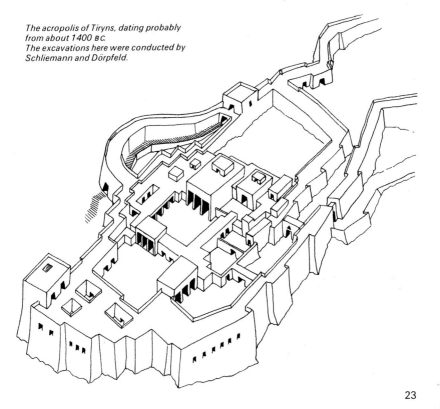

The acropolis of Tiryns, dating probably from about 1400 B.C.
The excavations here were conducted by Schliemann and Dörpfeld.

they have a kind of overbearing massiveness. The buildings erected on the islands to begin with resembled no others: they bear no architectural reference to any other style. Eastern influences came in, to a limited extent, later, but only in decoration, not in actual form.

The style that grew up in the Aegean and on Crete is known as Minoan, after the mythical king Minos, son of Zeus and the Phoenician princess Europa (according to the myth, Zeus assumed the shape of a bull and carried Europa off across the sea to Crete). Minos ruled over many islands—so the legend goes. The sea god Poseidon sent up a bull from the ocean, demonstrating his power. Minos was supposed to sacrifice this bull, but wishing to keep such a magnificent beast sacrificed a bull from his own herds instead. As revenge for this deception, Poseidon made the king's wife, Pasiphae, fall in love with the bull. Pasiphae then commissioned from Daedalus, an architect and sculptor based on the mainland (tributary lands of Minos), a hollow wooden cow, into which she climbed to have intercourse with the bull. The product of this union was the Minotaur, a man-eating monster with a bull's head and a human body, for whom Daedalus built the Labyrinth—a palace with endless rooms and corridors. Greek in origin, this savage legend perhaps expresses the revenge of Attica for the humiliations suffered under the Cretan domination: the Athenians under the Cretan yoke had every nine years to send seven youths and seven maidens to Crete as food for the Minotaur. In the end the hero Theseus managed to kill the monster.

In the *Iliad*, Crete is portrayed as a rich, powerful island with a hundred towns. This and other passages from Homer's epic provided Heinrich Schliemann with vital clues in his search for evidence of ancient civilizations. Schliemann (1822–90), from Mecklenburg in what is now East Germany, was a born archaeologist. A businessman by profession, he did so well in St Petersburg (Leningrad) and Amsterdam that he was able to spend the second part of his life living out his boyhood dream, immersed in early Greek antiquity—or more precisely in the prehistory of what we generally call classical antiquity. Homer was his guiding star. For him the old myths were history in poetic form.

In 1870 Schliemann began digging on the hill of Hissarlik in north-west Asia Minor, excavating the ancient city of Troy. With the help of Wilhelm Dörpfeld (who was to become his friend and who carried on the venture), he discovered one city on top of another in layers. The sixth, he concluded, was the Ilium of the Trojan legend. Some years later he went to Greece to search for the palace of Agamemnon, the attacker of Troy. He started digging at Mycenae and at nearby Tiryns, and in so doing unearthed another thousand years and more of Greek history. Schliemann had always maintained, almost as an article of faith, that the old legends were historical accounts written up in poetry, and his excavations bore him out.

In 1886 he sailed to Crete to look for the palace of Minos. He believed he would find it beneath an olive grove concealing a mass of ruins. However, he was unable to agree a price with the owner of the property, and was thus prevented from crowning his long career with the discovery of the Minoan treasures. He died in Naples in 1890.

Ten years later, the British archaeologist Arthur Evans (1851–1941) started excavating the town of Knossos, with its palace built by the legendary son of a mythical princess. He thought the work would last one year. After twenty-five years he was still digging, having unearthed some seven and a half acres of ruins. Archaeologists discovered foundation walls and the remains of large settlements, together with what must have been splendid palaces, some dating from before 3000 BC (i.e. the end of the neolithic era), along the southern coast of the island, as well as at Knossos in the north.

Little is known about early Aegean culture. No historical facts survive. Only through myths and legends are we able to guess the power of the overlords of these islands. Remnants of wall paintings still give a colourful impression of life at court there in the heyday of Aegean civilization. Scenes of acrobats with bulls depict activities midway between religious ceremonial and sport.

At first sight the ground plan of the palace of Knossos is confusing. It seems literally like a labyrinth, lacking any geometrical order. It is impossible to identify axes or lines of alignment. Ostentation appears to have been unimportant in the conception of the building. Essentially made up of corridors, all cutting across each other at right angles, there are few really big rooms. Even the throne room is of modest size. Many parts are illuminated by light wells. The narrow storerooms in the western section of the palace, where the *pithoi* (large pottery jars for the storage of oil or grain) were kept, were dark.

The massive columns in the courtyards are like enormous posts rammed into the ground by giants. The ponderous capitals appear as if squashed beneath the load they bear. The walls of the royal apartments were painted: slim figures walk through meadows strewn with lilies, within framework of wave-like lines and stylized floral motifs enclosed in turn in complex patterns of intertwining cuttlefish tentacles.

Around 1700 BC, disaster struck Crete—possibly connected with the invasions of the Iranian Hyksos. No legible records of this event exist, either on papyrus or on stone. Knossos was rebuilt later, but in 1400 BC was totally destroyed, burnt and sacked.

The downfall of Crete may possibly have been linked with the so-called Doric migration, although no corroborative evidence of this exists. The Dorians invaded the Greek mainland from the north and pushed right down to the Aegean. By the time they reached Crete, however, Knossos had quite probably already fallen.

We tend to think of the Dorians as a race of heroes, great conquerors and supreme creators of a new order. Certainly, the language they brought, or which they were responsible for spreading, Greek, that is, was the medium of this new order—a new mode of existence, no less, which came to fruition in the period we know as classical antiquity, and with which the concepts of beauty and harmony and perfection will forever be coupled.

After crude and barbaric beginnings (in certain aspects at least) a definite style emerged. This style, the first to exercise a fascination and formative influence on every successive age, is known, together with the order of temple architecture characteristic of it, as Doric. It is ironic that so little is known about the origins and early history of the race that gave its name to both the Doric style and the Doric order.

GREECE

"Classical" essentially means "perfect" or "complete." We use the word in various contexts: we talk of classical music, of the classical periods of great civilizations, of classical verse, of classical formulations, even of classical profiles. In conjunction with the word "antiquity" we mean the flowering of Greek art and every aspect of intellectual life in ancient Greece.

Classical antiquity did not begin immediately after the Doric migration around 900 BC. Time had to elapse before the newcomers became truly integrated with the indigenous populations. The Greek (as it was to become) mainland and the islands were only sparsely populated when the Dorians arrived. The native population was in all probability neither pushed out nor destroyed, but became subject to the new rulers. From modest beginnings there gradually evolved a rigorous style in statuary, represented by numerous stone figures—naked youths, probably either images of gods or funerary statues. Their faces are irradiated by a faint smile: they convey profound inner serenity. Temples also appeared, the ruins of which give us a glimpse of ancient splendour and still inspire a sense of wonder in us today, even though none have been spared the ravages of time, the corrosive effects of salt in sea air, earthquakes or war.

The basic model of the Greek temple was the cella, a four-sided area enclosed by walls and covered with a gently pitched roof. From the cella with pronaos (portico in front of the main temple area, the naos) there developed the pronaos *in antis*. The antae were the side edges of the pronaos, later becoming the end elements of a colonnade—usually pilasters at the end of the extended side walls of the naos. In larger temples, columns were placed between the antae to help support the pediment. Finally, a shady colonnade ran all round the temple.

The Doric order: entablature.
A: architrave; B: frieze (with
sculpted metopes); C: cornice.

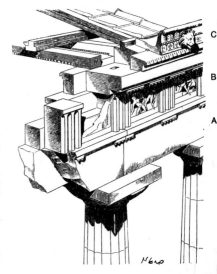

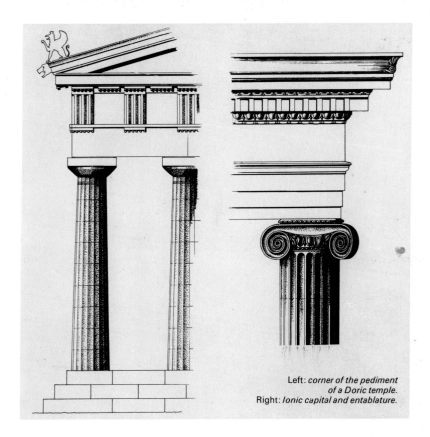

Left: *corner of the pediment of a Doric temple.*
Right: *Ionic capital and entablature.*

Though built entirely in stone, the constructional principle of this design derived from building in wood.

The Doric order in temple architecture is most effective on large, soaring structures. The columns are massive, as is revealed by the relation of diameter to height (1:4). The forms are simple. The column is stumpy, without a base. It narrows towards the top and has wide, sharp-ridged fluting, indicative of considerable technical skill, as it is more difficult to carve this type of fluting in stone than that separated by flat fillets as in the Ionic order. These columns are slightly bellied and thus do not appear too dumpy, despite their thickness. The capital is free of all sculptural decoration and consists of a kind of sloped cushion (echinus) beneath a slab-like abacus. Its very simplicity of form has a sober grace and dignity. When one considers, however, that these capitals—together with the statues that embellished the temples—were brightly painted in white, blue, red and gold, words such as "sober" and "dumpy" are no longer applicable. A Doric building, freshly painted, must surely have been a joyous as well as serene sight.

On the Ionian islands and in the settlements founded by the Ionians along the coast of Asia Minor there emerged in the sixth century BC new forms of temple

Left: *Corinthian capital and entablature (Hellenistic Age).*
Right: *capital from the portico of the Pantheon in Rome.*

architecture. The type of column used in this new style was known as "Ionic" even at the time of its spreading popularity. It did not replace the Doric order: in essence it was simply a new decorative form. However, although the basic structural forms did not change, new proportions appeared, dictated by the new order.

The Ionic style is richer and more refined than the simple Doric. The cornices and waterspouts are decorated with motifs whose origins go back to the very beginnings of Greek civilization, and which had become ever more sophisticated over the years. The entablature above the columns no longer included metopes (square spaces along the frieze), but featured an uninterrupted carved frieze instead. The slender columns seem all the slimmer due to delicate fluting. They stand on a base the outer profile of which forms an S. The

chief distinguishing characteristic of the style is the capital: beneath a thin abacus it flows sideways in broad scroll-like curls. This motif in fact appears sporadically in earlier ornamentation and probably comes from the East. It looks slightly like a blanket, rolled up at both ends, taking the weight off the shoulder of some human bearer. The optical effect of the capital enhances this impression—the heavy stone entablature somehow appears quite light. As has already been said, the Ionic order did not replace the Doric, the two existed side by side. In fact, in many temples the external columns around the cella (pteron) are Doric, while those inside are Ionic.

Around 400 BC, in central Greece and on the Corinthian isthmus, there emerged a third order, known as Corinthian after its native city. Credit for this new design is given to the Attic sculptor Callimachos. The extraordinarily detailed and complex decoration testifies to the wealth of the age, to the contemporary love of ostentation without heed to cost, and, last but not least, to the great skill of the stonemasons of the time. The characteristic feature of the Corinthian capital is the acanthus leaf, which was to become one of the most frequently used of all architectural decorative motifs— sometimes, indeed, even running rather wild. The acanthus is a thistle-like perennial, the long leaves of which lend themselves perfectly to stylization, fanning out flat or crisply curled up, according to aesthetic or functional requirements.

The Corinthian entablature and pediment are similar to the Ionic; at times, however, they are a little over-ornate for our tastes, especially in Roman examples. At the same time, the austere ornamentation of previous ages no longer reflected the concerns of those in power—ambition, authority and riches. Mass and, perhaps even more importantly, elaborate refinement were better vehicles of self-expression for the new rulers. Roman architects rethought the Corinthian capital on certain buildings, producing what is known as the Composite style: above the acanthus leaves (usually two tiers) are placed scroll-like motifs reminiscent of Ionic capitals.

From the very beginning the Corinthian style was indicative of a new age, already distinct from early Hellenic antiquity. The new Hellenistic period was typified by often florid art, which was nevertheless rooted in the ancient traditions. Properly "antique" elements were developed and modified. The severe earlier styles had, so to speak, to accept embellishments as though they were being dressed up for a party. The basically simple architectonic lines became festooned with rich, somewhat precious ornamentation—to the detriment of the

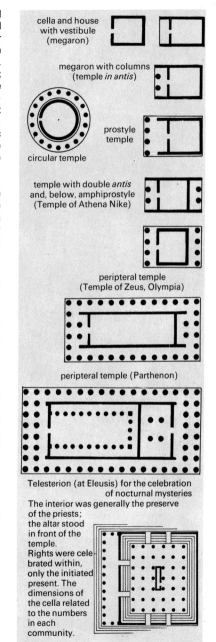

cella and house with vestibule (megaron)

megaron with columns (temple in antis)

circular temple

prostyle temple

temple with double antis and, below, amphiprostyle (Temple of Athena Nike)

peripteral temple (Temple of Zeus, Olympia)

peripteral temple (Parthenon)

Telesterion (at Eleusis) for the celebration of nocturnal mysteries

The interior was generally the preserve of the priests; the altar stood in front of the temple. Rights were celebrated within, only the initiated present. The dimensions of the cella related to the numbers in each community.

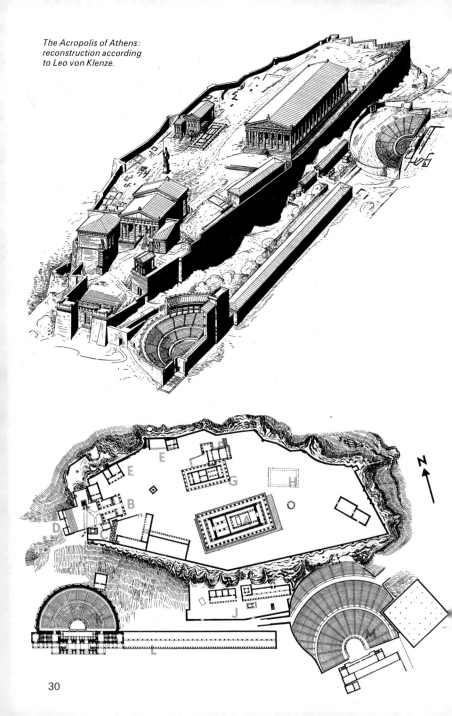

The Acropolis of Athens: reconstruction according to Leo von Klenze.

earlier nobility and austere splendour, it must be said.

Yet different ages see things differently. In fact what we now think of as pure classicism was often considered too simple, even too much like poor man's architecture. Buildings we consider to be "overdone" and affected today were once thought grand and in the only style fitting to complete expression of a certain *Zeitgeist*.

Thus the concept of "classicism," which is so central in the history of architectural styles, should be understood as an artistic current springing initially from the Ancients, tending to transform other basic styles—sometimes giving them greater refinement, sometimes merely prettifying them and watering them down. Classicism flourished, of course, in the Renaissance, and again during the period that saw a reaction against the capricious asymmetry of Rococo, with its love of illusion and broken architectonic order. All this will be dealt with later, however. For the moment we must stay with the Romans, who enriched the repertoire of architectural elements inherited from the Greeks with two crucially important features: the rotunda and the dome.

The Greeks had not succeeded in creating anything especially remarkable with these forms. They used arches and domes not at all, and circular temples were few and far between, perhaps because it was recognized that the principles of Greek architecture were not very well suited to round constructions. It is worth noting two examples, though: the circular Doric temple with domed roof near the seat of the oracle at Delphi, and the Ionic Philippeion in the sacred grove at Olympia, built by Alexander the Great in honour of his father Philip of Macedon.

Only in the building of theaters did the Greeks regularly diverge from their "classic" rectangular shapes to produce a truly successful architectural form. Rows of seats arranged in a horseshoe shape climbed up steeply around the circular or semicircular orchestra, giving every spectator a good view of the orchestra itself and the scene building with its proscenium for actors and chorus. The Romans continued the tradition of semicircular theaters, later going on to fully circular forms. Both these types of theater have provided models for future ages, down to our own day, and even their names have survived (amphitheater, arena, stadium, circus).

The Acropolis of Athens

According to legend, the first king on the hill of Athens was Cecrops, son of Earth. The Greek myths describe him as having the body of a snake. His daughters, Aglauros, Herse and Pandrosos, received from Athena, Zeus' daughter and protectress of the city, a box which they were to keep closed for ever. Curiosity overcame them, however. From the opened box issued Erechtheus, a chthonic creature similar to Cecrops, whom he succeeded on the throne. Cecrops' daughters were punished with madness for their curiosity, and hurled themselves off the top of the hill. The word "Acropolis" means high city. Situated on a plateau of grey-blue limestone about 500 feet (156 m.) above sea level, it was probably a fortified citadel and State sanctuary before 1000 B C.

Some of the foundations of the original buildings remain (the citadel was destroyed by the Persians in 480 BC). The

Key to the plan of the Acropolis at Athens (opposite):

A   Parthenon
B   Propylaea
C   Temple of Athena Nike
D   Roman fortifications
E   Foundations of minor temples
F   Erechtheion and Koreion
G   "Dörpfeld's Temple" (foundations of a temple predating the Persian Wars)
H   Foundation walls of a house dating from the Mycenaean period
J   Asklepieion
K   Theater of Herodes Atticus
L   Stoa of Eumenes
M   Theater and altar of Dionysus

reconstruction was completed under Pericles, the founder of the Attic Naval Alliance. The Parthenon (literally "Home of the Virgin"), the shrine of Athena Parthenos, was built in only fifteen years by the architects Ictinus and Callicrates. A Doric temple with pteron and prostyle porch, built throughout in Pentelic marble, it received its finishing touches in 432 BC. Tradition attributes the ornamentation of carved Attic marble to Phidias, a friend of Pericles. The eastern and western pediments depicted respectively Athena's birth from the head of Zeus and her struggle against Poseidon for Attica. The metopes are carved in relief with battles with giants (east), battles with Amazons (west), the destruction of Ilium (north), and Attic myths (south). The frieze around the cella shows the Panathenaic procession which took place in Athens every four years: men and women bearing sacrificial offerings, and in particular with the peplos for Athena, before the gods (east), then animals intended for sacrifice, and athletes in chariots and on horseback.

The Acropolis had only one entrance, to the east, where Mnesicles built the Propylaea, with two six-column Doric colonnades, between 437 and 433 BC. On the *pyrgos* below the Propylaea, Callicrates rebuilt the little temple of Athena Nike (the third on the site) in 420. The form of this temple is amphiprostyle, with two four-column Ionic porticoes.

To the north of the Parthenon stands the Erechtheion, built in about 420 BC in honour of Athena and Erechtheus. The design is untypical of Greek temples, and only on the east, in front of the cella to Athena, is there a typically Ionic six-column pronaos. To the north, a three-column Ionic porch leads to the shrine of Poseidon. The south-west corner is graced with a kind of loggia, accessible only from inside, the roof of which is supported not by columns but by six caryatids (or *korai*—statues of girls) looking out southwards.

The Acropolis has had an uneven history. The Romans left the shrines unharmed, and posterity has them to thank for copies of certain sculptures that have otherwise not survived. In the fourth century AD, the Christians "exorcised" Athena. The Parthenon was dedicated to Mary, and numerous reliefs showing pagan scenes were destroyed. The gold and ivory statue of the goddess was carried off to Byzantium.

When the Turks took Athens in the fifteenth century, the Parthenon was converted into a mosque and the Erechtheion into a harem. Later they turned the Parthenon itself and the Propylaea into gunpowder stores. The Propylaea was struck by lightning, setting off an explosion.

In 1687 the Venetians bombarded the temple, causing the roof and almost all the columns along both lengths of the building to collapse. The Venetians wanted to carry off the sculptures that still remained in good condition as booty, but most were broken during transport.

After the return of the Turks, Lord Thomas Elgin in 1800 obtained permission to remove to London all the freestanding sculptures and reliefs that survived. Today they are displayed in the British Museum as the Elgin Marbles.

The Turks used the stones of the temple of Athena Nike to construct fortifications. In 1835, the German archaeologist Ross endeavoured as far as possible to reconstruct the temple. Subsequently the insensitivity and rapacity of the Athenians reduced the Acropolis to a wilderness of ruins, exposed to all the ravages of the weather. Today not even the tiniest fragment of stone is allowed to be taken away, and archaeologists from all over the world are busy, together with the Athenians, restoring the damage and looking for missing fragments in a bid to save whatever still remains to be saved. The caryatids have been replaced by copies, and the orginals—which had begun to suffer corrosion from traffic and industrial pollution—are now safe in the museum of the Acropolis.

Opposite: *the Parthenon*.

ROME

Legend tells us of two brothers, Romulus and Remus, abandoned at birth, and adopted and suckled by a wolf. The shepherd Faustulus brought the two children up. Traditionally, Romulus founded the city and was the first king of Rome. He lived on the Palatine, one of the seven hills. The scholar Marcus Terentius Varro (116–27 BC) gave 753 BC (translated into our calendar) as the date of the founding of Rome, but there is no firm support for it. The names Romulus and Remus are Etruscan in origin, as are those of later kings (Numa, Tullus, Ancus, Tarquinius). The Etruscans were a race settled in central Italy,

Below: *impression of an Etruscan temple, similar in basic design to the Greek prostyle temple. A U-shaped wall creates an enclosed area in front of the building. The altar stands at the foot of the steps.* Opposite, above left: *clay model of an Etruscan house.* Opposite, center left: *plan of the basilica of Maxentius, Rome* (c. *AD300*).

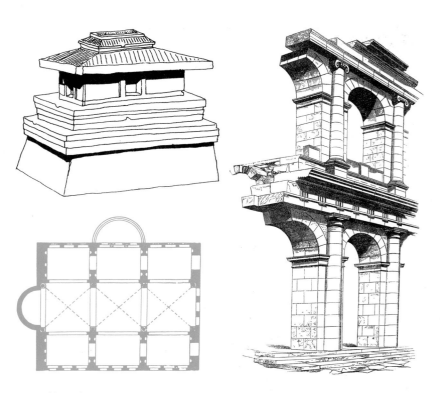

Above, right: *illustration of the construction of a typical Roman arch, with supporting pilasters, widely used, for example, in aqueducts and city gates, and in the Colosseum.* Below: *example of a Roman gateway integrated into an aqueduct—that of the Emperor Claudius, built around A D 50, and now known as the "Porta Maggiore."*

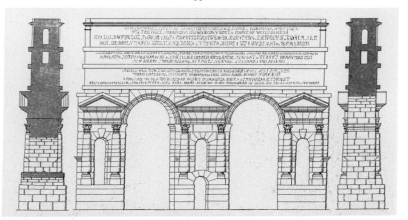

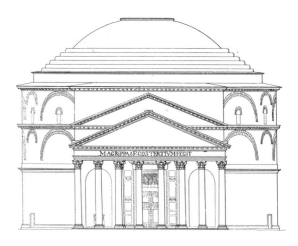

Above: *Corinthian
capital from
the Pantheon.*
Left: *façade
of the Pantheon.*

Left: *plan of the Pantheon.
The walls extending right
of the rotunda are part of
a baths complex.*
Below: *longitudinal section
of the dome and portico
of the Pantheon.*

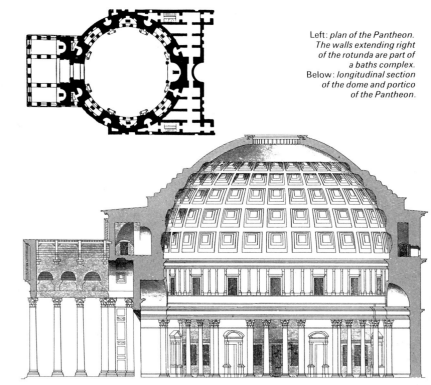

from Etruria (modern Tuscany, more or less) to Latium. With the ascendance of Rome they vanish from history. The Romans became masters of the entire peninsula, extended their power beyond the borders of Italy, and waged war and traded in every country of the Mediterranean, establishing themselves also in the ports founded by the Phoenicians and Greeks. Six hundred years later, Rome was "the center of the world." With a probable population of over a million at the time of Caesar, it was the first big city in the modern sense.

The square house form and the square city wall (*Roma quadrata*) are part of the Etruscan heritage. With gusto and admiration the Romans took over nearly all the architectural ideas and decorative motifs of Greek (especially Hellenistic) buildings. But increasingly, as time passed, colonnades gave way to arcades supported by pillars, with half columns as it were stuck on as a reminder of the Hellenic models.

As builders, and as creators of great arches and domes, the Romans developed their own distinctive style. As constructional engineers they surpassed the Greeks. On the artistic level, however, they ultimately remained imitators of the Hellenic genius, never managing to produce anything to rival the Acropolis at Athens. The Romans themselves had a different opinion, as we gather from Vitruvius Pollio's *De architectura* published in 25 BC and dedicated to Augustus. Rediscovered in the fifteenth century, this work became the most influential architect's manual of the Renaissance and early Baroque period.

Vitruvius considered that the style we call Hellenistic represented the high point of architectural creation. Modern taste is less favourable, seeing it as the adornment, as it were, of Roman imperialism—by no means always noble and sometimes downright vulgar.

The great creations of Greek architecture were in a sense offered in homage to the gods. Even theaters were sacred places, rather than merely clubs or entertainment centers. Greek domestic archi-

tecture, about which very little is known, was based on the simplest of principles: a square room with a fireplace in the middle, a smaller, undecorated structure in front (the megaron), and, though rarely, a colonnaded courtyard leading off to rooms without windows.

Roman architecture was geared to many different functions. The chief builder was the State, and, as Rome's might increased, so the need to give representational expression to that might grew. Even a purely functional structure such as an aqueduct had to be a prestigious building, with its own architectonic character. The arch was the universal motif, used for the most insignificant doorway and for great triumphal arches commemorating major political events alike.

Roman architects had a considerable range of building types to erect: temples, huge meeting halls, theaters, palaces, aqueducts and baths. In the construction of large concourses, the traditional colonnade principle gave way to a new form, the basilica. This word stems from the Greek and was used to denote the palace or official residence of the *Archon basileios* in the Athenian agora. In Roman times, any large-scale public edifice—public concourse, covered market or warehouse—was called a basilica. Today the word is used only for a certain kind of church, the interior of which is split lengthways into three or five naves, with rows of supporting columns. The side naves are always lower than the main central one. The roof may either be gabled, over wooden trussbeams, or domed. The columns support walls that rest either on horizontal stone beams or on arcading. Basilicas are decorated inside and on the short external wall where the entrance is.

The Pantheon

Less frequent, but always breathtaking in its creation of spatial effect, is the Roman circular domed building. The most outstanding example, the Pantheon, was erected by the Emperor Hadrian on the

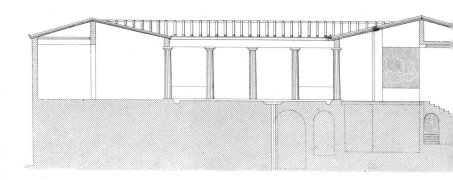

site of a temple to Mars, Venus and the deified Caesar which had been built by order of Agrippa and was later destroyed by fire. The vast area enclosed by the Pantheon is illuminated only by a round hole in the dome (the height of which — about a hundred and thirty feet (39.6 m.) — is roughly equal to its diameter).

It is better preserved than any other ancient Roman building. Only the outer layer of marble and stucco has been stolen, and this very theft allows us to appreciate the extraordinarily skilful masonry. The decorative changes incorporated inside over the years have not always been felicitous. Yet the overall effect of monumental grandeur has not been affected: the feelings the Pantheon aroused in the citizens of ancient Rome must have been very similar to those we feel today, almost two thousand years later. Another, less well-known example of Roman circular building is the great meat market, dating from the second century AD, transformed later into a church (San Stefano Rotondo), and several times restored.

Unlike Greek domestic architecture, about which little is known, the principles of Roman residential buildings are familiar to us. Essentially, they represent a development of the old Italic house with atrium. The atrium was a four-sided, partially covered room which constituted the nucleus of the home and off which all the other rooms (*cubicula*) led. In the

Above and below: Roman houses.
Above: section of a tradesman's house in Pompeii, incorporating a cellar. The upper part, the peristyle, is connected to the atrium by a stairway.
Below, left: house in the country, with staircase leading to bedrooms on the upper floor. Next to it (opposite, bottom), a baker's house in Pompeii. The oven and storage areas are to the left.
Opposite: bird's-eye view of a Roman castrum *(camp). These camps, built to a well-tried, functional design, were protected by walls (vallum) and ditches. The "streets" along the axes of the encampment created separate quarters, where the legionaries erected their tents. In the center were the administrative buildings, the private quarters of the commanding officer, and the drill yard. Castra formed nuclei for many Roman towns, and their basic layout is still discernible in several modern cities.*

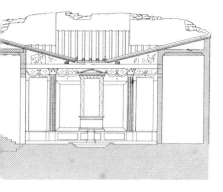

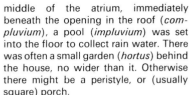

middle of the atrium, immediately beneath the opening in the roof (*compluvium*), a pool (*impluvium*) was set into the floor to collect rain water. There was often a small garden (*hortus*) behind the house, no wider than it. Otherwise there might be a peristyle, or (usually square) porch.

One should not imagine that all Romans lived in this type of house, however. Land in the city would have been too expensive for most people, especially in the days of the Empire. Less well-off citizens lived in rented accommodation in "tower blocks" (*insulae*), which were in effect nothing but the ancient Italian cellular type home, generally without any kind of entrance porch, multiplied endlessly and heaped one on top of another.

Development and Transition

As the world changes, thought changes with it; and this very change in thinking in turn changes the world. This applies not only to great moments of decisive development, when new eras begin, but also to our ways of interpreting and evaluating the past. Schoolchildren used to have to learn reams of dates by heart when studying history, and would often resort to mnemonics and rhymes of the "In sixteen hundred and sixty-six London town was burnt to sticks" variety. One vital date was always the fall of the Western Roman Empire: AD 476. But Rome was not destroyed in a day, to adapt the old saying.

In AD 475, the still-adolescent Romulus Augustulus was placed on the throne by his father, Patricius Orestes. He

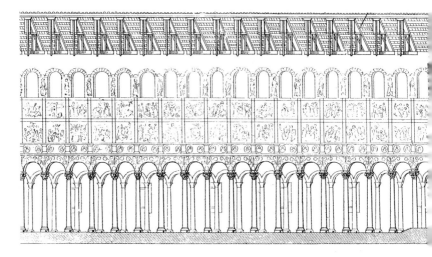

40

Below: *St Paul without the Walls in Rome (on the road to Ostia), built by Constantine in 314 over the tomb of St Paul the Apostle. The roof vaults are supported by four rows of twenty columns, forming five naves. In the ninth century the church was sacked by the Saracens. In 1823 it was almost totally destroyed by fire; with aid from all over the world, however, it was rebuilt, and eventually con-secrated in 1854 by Pope Pius IX.*

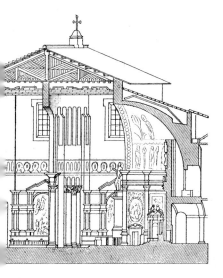

was toppled by Odoacer, king of the Sciri, from the lower Inn region. Augustulus' father was killed, while he himself was granted a pension. Meanwhile the Eastern emperor, Zeno (424–91), recognized Odoacer as king of Rome, although Odoacer preferred for a long time to hold his court on the Bosphorus.

Many crucially important events had occurred to fix the date AD 476 in the annals of history. In the hundred and thirty-two years between the death of Marcus Aurelius (AD 180) and the beginning of Constantine the Great's reign (312–37) there had been a new emperor almost every four years. In AD 330 the capital was transferred to Byzantium (the future Constantinople), and the time-honoured identification of the imperial throne with the Eternal City came to an end. The Roman empire was no longer governable from Rome, and for political and strategic reasons the official residence of the emperor moved to Byzantium.

Diocletian (AD 284–305) had a vast palace built for himself at Salona (modern Split), which for less than ten years served to all intents and purposes as the imperial residence, the capital of the Roman empire. But when the great and powerful ceased to inhabit such gigantic residences, the arcades and huge colonnades which had successfully withstood the devastations of time were walled up, arch by arch, and turned into homes for the poor.

Diocletian was the first Roman emperor to wear a diadem and Eastern finery. A new style emerged, deriving its decorative sense from the East. The work of Vitruvius was now forgotten. It should be stressed, however, that the architects of this period were far from imaginative. At the same time there was a distinct lack of good craftsmen, a result of the economic crisis that had affected the lesser bourgeoisie in the big cities—if one may use modern terminology to identify the class between the plebeians and the patricians.

Old buildings and monuments erected in honour of former emperors began to be

41

used almost as quarries: wall facings, precious marbles, friezes, columns and capitals all provided materials for new constructions which, while occasionally showing genuine sensitivity to balance of proportions, were for the most part devoid of architectonic vigour and aesthetic worth. The few true architects lived at court or moved in court circles, and were much too taken up in gratifying current appetites for ostentation and self-aggrandizement. What characterized the new, Byzantine style was experimentation with well-tried forms together with use of every possible detail of buildings that no longer served any purpose.

Christianity became the State religion. Constantine ordered numerous churches to be built, many of them very big. None survives in its original form, however. But after Constantine, and in the two centuries preceding the reign of Justinian I (527–65), there emerged alongside the State temporal buildings the first churches to have walls decorated with colourful, joyous and serene illustrations of the Scriptures—the first in what was to become a long tradition.

The word "Byzantine" conjures up for us visions of splendour, of gold and silk: we think of the monumental dome of Hagia Sophia, and of those sometimes almost indistinguishable portraits of emperors staring straight out at the observer. Yet we should not concentrate exclusively on the large buildings. Smaller, more modest churches sprang up all over the place as the new faith spread.

A new building type appeared beside the traditionally proven basilica design—a new standard plan for the house of God, with central nave, and dome alone reminiscent of the Roman rotonda. As architecture evolved over the centuries, innumerable modifications of this formula were elaborated; yet in the last analysis these were all decorative and did not affect the basic design, which was inherently very flexible. This basic design can be sketched in a few words: plumb below the very center of the dome, the two main axes which determine the

overall shape and orientation of the building cross at right angles. The size of the central area, i.e. the space covered by the dome, is dictated by equal (or nearly equal) lengths along both axes.

The dome rests on walls, arches or pillars which together form a square, a hectagon or even sometimes an octagon. If the dome is raised above a square, an intermediate constructional storey is introduced above the supporting base structure: this transitional section itself employs the dome technique, using fan-shaped pendentives. Hexagonal and octagonal structures similarly have pendentives, but they are less noticeable as they are less markedly curved.

The central expanse of open space can be increased on all sides, for instance with semicircular domed niches set lower than the main dome, or with other squares roofed with regular domes. In this way the cruciform layout of the principal axes can be extended. Thus the transverse nave, or transept, appeared, while lengthwise churches once again began to look almost like community halls.

This variability in the shape and dimensions of the secondary sections of the church led in the Baroque era to a highly imaginative rethinking of the crossing.

Technically the crossing represents a very remarkable achievement. Absolute precision in the dimensions and expert craftsmanship were required to erect a lasting building. It is thus hardly surprising that the simpler old-fashioned basilica was never supplanted. At the same time, especially in Italy, ancient Roman buildings were turned into churches. Churches were often erected over former secret underground places of worship dating from the persecutions. The subterranean structure then became the crypt—the final resting place for the bodies of the faithful.

Many of the most sumptuously decorated Byzantine churches are quite small and in no way exceptional from a technical point of view. Yet the exquisite mosaics and paintings in them put them in a class of their own, and despite

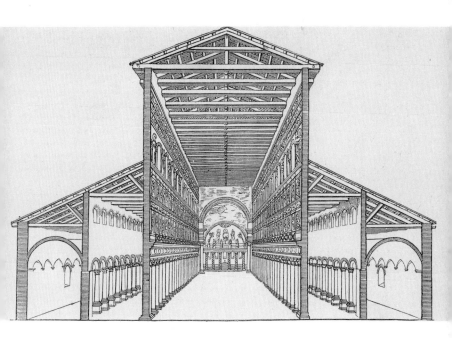

The first basilica of St Peter, in which Charlemagne was crowned emperor by Pope Leo III in AD800, was erected above the tomb of St Peter (crucified upside down in the reign of Nero, AD64 or 67). A five-nave church, it was built at the time of Constantine, and was consecrated by Pope Sylvester in 326. For a thousand years it remained undamaged by either fire or earthquake; finally, however, it became structurally unsound.
It underwent restoration in the fourteenth century. A hundred years later, Pope Nicholas V conceived plans for a new church.

numerous later alterations they have lost nothing of their original simple beauty. Their modest splendour—if one may put it so—honours no earthly prince, nor does it provoke gasps of admiration from the visitor as the Pantheon or Hagia Sophia do. It tends rather to inspire in believers, and in art lovers, a sense of quiet awe—without recourse to all the lavish paraphernalia of a golden age now long past. For, notwithstanding the extravagance of the Eastern Roman potentates, the early Middle Ages were hardly golden.

Byzantine ornamentation borrowed much from the East, but in the sixth century new elements appeared. The new style of writing, and the long, serpentine floral motifs that now began to figure in decoration came from the North.

A Germanic race, the Lombards, from the middle Danube region, had migrated down into Italy, settling in Lombardy (named after them) and pushing on right down to the south. The new decorative

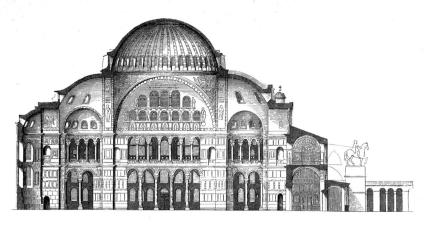

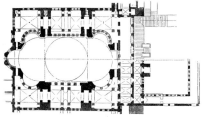

Emperor Justinian I left two monumental achievements behind him: the Corpus juris civilis *(or* Codex Justinianus*) and the church dedicated to* Hagia Sophia, "The Holy Wisdom," *in Constantinople (above: longitudinal section and plan of St Sophia). Work began on the building in 532.*
The architects were Anthemius of Tralles and Isidorus of Miletus. The domes were ready after five years; however, the central one collapsed twenty-five years later, probably due to earth tremors.
In fact the new dome—which has stood proudly in place now for almost fifteen hundred years—is only slightly more solid than the first. The actual dome vault itself is shallow, measuring 105 feet (32 m.) across, and approximately 184 feet (56 m.) in height. The church was designed with a central plan, and gives an impression of a vast, elongated room. This effect is created by the two semidomes that spring from the main piers, east and west respectively.
The interior is sumptuously decorated with stone inlay and mosaics. For a long time it was thought that these figurative decorations had been lost for ever, when the church was converted into a mosque after the fall of Constantinople to the Turks in 1453. No major

structural changes occurred, however, although four minarets were added to the exterior, and the interior decoration was covered over with painted plaster. In 1837 Sultan Abdul Mecid commissioned the Swiss architect Gaspare Fossati to restore the mosque; Fossati gained permission to uncover all the mosaics and copy down the designs. They had to be plastered over once again before the mosque was reopened, however. Kemal Atatürk declared Hagia Sophia a Byzantine museum, and it ceased to be a mosque in 1932. The mosaics are thus visible again.

Opposite: *interior of Sant'Apollinare in Classe, near Ravenna. This church, built between 536 and 549 under the direction of Giuliano Argentario, is virtually all that remains of the ancient port of Classe. The apse is typically Byzantine—circular inside, and polygonal outside. The capitals are heavily carved with acanthus leaves blowing in the wind, a frequent late fifth-century motif.*

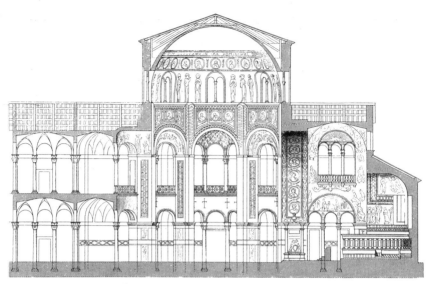

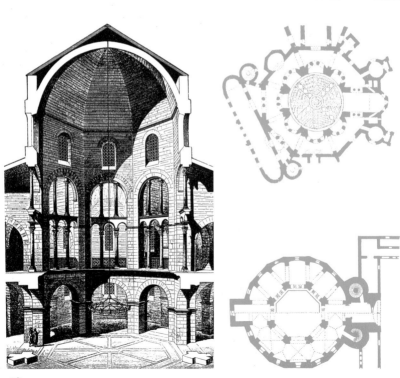

Opposite, above: *longitudinal section of San Vitale, Ravenna.*
A central plan, octagonal structure, it is externally austere and richly adorned with mosaics internally. It was erected during the reign of Theodoric the Great and consecrated in 546. Center, right: *plan of San Vitale. On the left, the pincer-shaped narthex forming a porticoed courtyard at an angle to the centralized body of the church.*
Below, left: *longitudinal section of Charlemagne's Palatine Chapel at Aachen (Aix-la-Chapelle), modelled on San Vitale, designed by the imperial architect, Odo of Metz, and completed in 805.*
Below, right: *plan of the Palatine Chapel. The bottom half of the figure shows the ground floor, while the top half represents the upper story, with pairs of columns between the arches springing from the main pillars.*

forms, initially quite foreign to the Byzantine aesthetic, probably derived from the Lombards. This is not to say that the invaders had brought with them a new style or new type of art. During their long journey south, fighting and skirmishing on the way, they could not have had much leisure or inclination to contemplate capitals and the different ways in which they might be decorated. But, as they became more settled, their natural fierceness and roughness of character began to find expression in their new buildings. In fact certain types of domestic roof and wooden porch can be traced back to them. Many surviving metal locks and bolts bear their stamp, as does a certain type of stone wall in which courses of smaller stones, set at an angle, are interspersed among the regular layers of stones.

The church of San Vitale in Ravenna, built between 527 and 546, has delicate columns with white marble capitals whose decoration—intricately intertwining vine tendrils—in no way recalls either the Ionic scroll, the classical acanthus leaf, or even Eastern arabesques. It is

perhaps most reminiscent of northern inlaid woodwork.

The Lombards soon became Christians, but, as they were not especially well disposed towards Rome, Pope Leo III was grateful for the friendship of another Germanic race, the Franks, who had likewise become converted to Christianity, albeit without necessarily very profound conviction. On Christmas Day in the year 800, Leo placed the imperial crown of the Caesars on the head of the Frankish king, Charlemagne, and it was not long before the Eastern emperor was calling the new ruler crowned by the Supreme Pontiff of all Christendom his "dear brother."

Unlike the Lombards, the Franks had not migrated as a people to Italy, but had arrived as an army. They had no intention of settling in southern Europe—and indeed they soon returned home.

Charlemagne had already been to Italy four times before his coronation, carrying to the other side of the Alps new concepts of architecture (except for the buildings remaining from the days of Roman rule, there were no stone buildings in these countries at that time). With him, and after him, and supported by the spreading faith of Christianity, a new urge to learn began to grow in areas that for years had been suffering from the unending battles of migrating races. Now there was a cultural and spiritual heritage, however slight still, to be cherished.

Definite borders were settled on, and with the advent of a certain degree of security of both life and property the ground was prepared for the seeds of a new civilization coming from the South. The *Pfalzen*, or residences of the German kings, gradually became proper courts, at first along Roman lines, but then soon along lines more appropriate to the different climate and the peculiarly Frankish need for unassailable security.

Carolingian archetypes evolved from Byzantine models, and these in turn paved the way for the Romanesque style—so called in memory of its first origins. Charlemagne, whom Wolfram

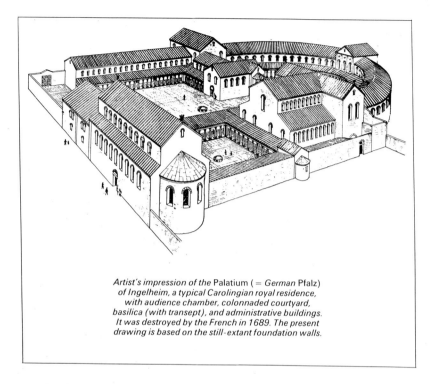

Artist's impression of the Palatium (= *German* Pfalz)
*of Ingelheim, a typical Carolingian royal residence,
with audience chamber, colonnaded courtyard,
basilica (with transept), and administrative buildings.
It was destroyed by the French in 1689. The present
drawing is based on the still-extant foundation walls.*

von den Steinen called "the beacon of Europe," not only imported new ideas but also encouraged trade and barter: books, relics, silk, yet more books, the treasure of the Avars, and ancient columns for the *Pfalz* chapel at Aachen (Aix-la-Chapelle) in exchange for Saxon horses. He was also given, as a present from the Abbasid sultan Harun-al-Rashid, a white elephant—which, however, died of cold at the imperial residence of Lippeham on the lower Rhine.

ROMANESQUE

Medieval Europe was a vertiable hive of political activity. Charlemagne's great vision of an empire embracing central and southern Europe foundered with his grandchildren. The temporal and ecclesiastical princes did not always see eye to eye, but sometimes they pretended to be friends. All was by no means sweetness and light, however. There existed a German national empire, calling itself both holy and Roman, which paid scant heed either to *pietas* or to the civic ideal which had fired the Romans.

Yet we ought not to indulge in too much lugubrious contemplation of the self-centerdness, the thirst for power and the fake piety of what we refer to as the Romanesque period, since, despite the warring of rival power factions, from the point of view of style, at least, there was considerable unity. In fact the first truly Western style had been created. This was especially so in central Europe, where it was as if every craftsman and architect had served his apprenticeship with the same great master. The spread of the new style was due largely to the monasteries—centers built up around small missionary settlements dating back as far as the fifth century. To begin with, these consisted of modest buildings erected on land cleared for farming around the church. Soon more ambitious structures arose, though along proven architectonic lines and according to the rules of the individual order.

Monasticism first appeared in the East, based on the idea of the monk's cell. The word "cloister' comes from the Latin *claustrum*, "closed." It signified a place where men lived communally, praying together, shut away from the world around them.

Already in A D 529, Benedict of Norcia had formulated a precise rule of monastic life with the founding of the monastery of Monte Cassino: liturgical prayer (*opus Dei*), work, especially in the fields (*ora et labora*), meals and rest, all conducted communally. Charlemagne, and after him Louis the Pious, raised the Benedictine Rule to the status of a general model and instituted monastic schools—the only kind of school that existed in the Middle Ages. All later Rules are essentially variations of this model, never departing far from the basic intentions of St Benedict. And it would seem that these far-spreading Rules were responsible for the stylistic unity of the period. Despite arguments about borders and privileges, and despite the political confusion, Christianity was in the end the ordering and unifying element both of aesthetic style and of the major works of architecture of the age.

The term "Romanesque" was coined much later, and only became common in the nineteenth century. Previously, different names were used to designate the period we are now looking at, but none corresponded entirely with the reality. "Byzantine" was correct only for the period during which contacts with Constantinople were lively and influential. Now and again "neo-Greek" was

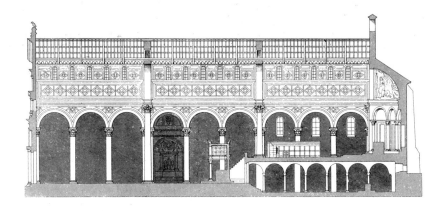

Above: *San Miniato, Florence. Three-nave basilica without transept, dating from the eleventh century. The central nave is split into three sections by two arches springing from pillars. The floor of the choir is raised, to give greater height to the crypt, which is only steps lower than the level of the body of the church. The apse windows are closed in with transparent slabs of alabaster.*

Below, left: *plan of a Cistercian monastery built along the lines established by St Bernard of Clairvaux (1091–1153), an energetic advocate of the crusades. The essential basic shape is a simple rectangle, and there are no unnecessary luxuries—no figurative decoration, and not even a bell tower. Only in* the Gothic period was this severity somewhat relaxed.

Below, right: *plan of a charterhouse for twelve monks and their prior. St Bruno of Cologne (1032–1101), founder of the Carthusian Order, left no written Rule. Later Carthusian houses were closed, self-contained communities, like that of the first hermits. Only the prior had any contact with the outside world.*

Opposite: *San Zeno, Verona, dedicated to the first bishop of Verona. This triple-nave basilica was built around 1200, and restructured in the fourteenth century. The famous bronze reliefs on the doors are close in style to those of Hildesheim Cathedral.*

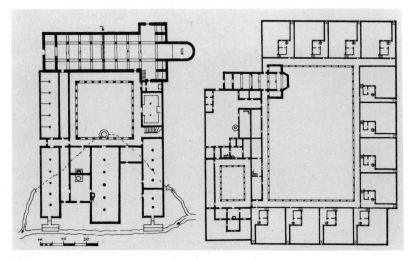

used, but this was as misleading as "old German," since the style so referred to was neither German, nor Greek, nor Roman, nor typical of any one area, but was authentically European.

"Romanesque" thus seems most appropriate, recalling as it does the origins of the main elements of the style: the basilica, the round masonry arch and space defined by arcades. Used for the first time by the French historians De Gerville and Arcisse de Caumont in 1820, the name quickly passed into other languages.

All buildings constructed between the late tenth and the thirteenth centuries are Romanesque in style; in some respects, however, it may be permissible to say that already in the twelfth century in France totally new architectonic principles began to be born, anticipating Gothic. At first the stylistic idiom of Romanesque continued to be Carolingian. The thirty years before and after the year 1000 are known in Germany as Saxon-Ottonian Proto-Romanesque. This stage is often extended to stretch from 936, when Otto I was crowned, to 1024, when Henry II, founder of the bishopric of Bamberg, died. From a purely stylistic point of view, however, it is not possible to give such exact date limits for Romanesque.

Most Romanesque buildings are church buildings—the traditional models for ecclesiastical architecture becoming ever enriched. The basilica had, so to

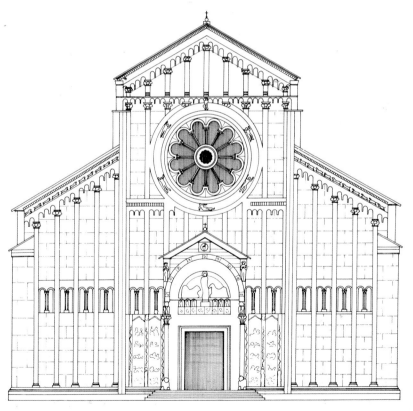

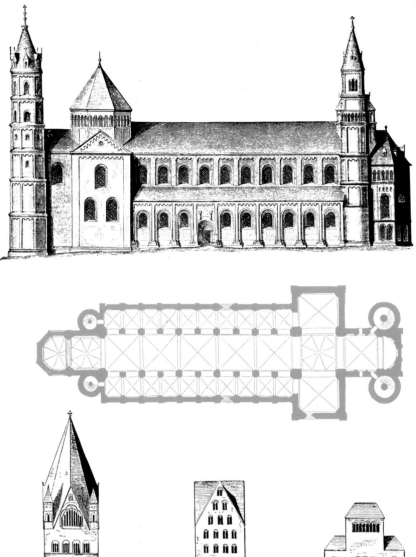

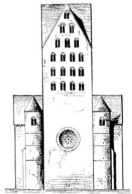

speak, a face-lift with the increased importance of the west elevation, where the entrance was. Towers flanked the façade, often projecting beyond the width of the main body of the building. The so-called westwork, or towered apse, appeared at the west end.

These towers were frequently named after the archangels Michael and Gabriel. Such architectural nomenclature derived from atavistic echoes of Germany's pagan past: it was from the west, where the sun sets, that the demons of darkness came, and the *Westwerk*, conceived and built as a protective bulwark against such evil spirits, acquired extra strength if it was dedicated to the archangel who carries a sword and slays dragons. Another important development from the old-style basilica was the crossing, that is the place where the transept cuts across the main nave at right angles. To make more of this section, the nave was extended eastwards. Thus the choir or chancel was born, at this point ending in an apse that took in the whole breadth of the central nave. The floor of the choir is always higher than that of the main body of the church, even if by only a few steps. Usually the entrance to the crypt was situated in the choir ("crypt," from Greek *cryptos* "hidden," has its origin in the underground burial places used by the early Christians during the persecutions). Typical of German Romanesque

Opposite, above: *Worms Cathedral. This drawing does not feature the chapels and sacristies that were added later. Incorporating two choirs, this church was built on pre-existing foundations towards the end of the twelfth century. The western choir (on the right) was finished in 1230. Notable architectural elements are the four circular towers and the two octagonal "domes" (rib vaults beneath tent roofs) above the crossing and the west choir.
Center: plan of Worms Cathedral. Below: three examples of Romanesque church façades. Left to right: Soest, Paderborn, Minden.*

churches is the double choir (e.g. at Mainz and Worms), a choir at the west end balancing that at the east.

Tunnel vaults and domes are rare in early Romanesque architecture. The main nave has a ceiling suspended from the framework of the gabled roof. After the year 1000, however, the central nave and the transept were roofed with barrel vaults, intersecting to form the crossing. As well as this groin (or cross) vault, one more solution to the problem of the crossing was found. The barrel vault of the central nave ended at the crossing bay. The crossing itself then rose higher and was roofed with a separate barrel vault or a dome—from which there later derived the ribbed groin vault. From the outside one has to imagine the vaulting over the crossing, as it is concealed by a gently pitched tent-roof to fit in with the gabled roofs over nave, transept and westwork.

The decoration of Romanesque buildings had a rich store of motifs, and in these (though not in their figures) classical decorative elements are often to be found. Eastern and Byzantine ornamentation also seems to have exercised an influence. In Western Europe there then also appear northern influences, which were possibly brought in by the eternally bellicose Normans, or which they perhaps developed, still in their own characteristic style, on the spot.

Romanesque church styles undoubtedly influenced secular buildings. However, barely a single such building has come down to us in its original state. Those that did not burn down or at least partially collapse were restructured and altered repeatedly over the centuries. It is, of course, only natural for architects to express themselves through the structural idiom of their own times.

The Moorish Style in Spain

In the seventh century, the Arabs started their process of expansion north and south, leaving their native desert territory to fulfil the duty imposed on them by the Prophet—world jihad. They destroyed

Above: St Mark's Basilica, Venice, from
an eighteenth-century print. Built in 830,
St Mark's was ravaged by fire in 976.
In the eleventh century the Venetians rebuilt
it along Byzantine and Oriental lines.
The façade contains some Gothic elements.

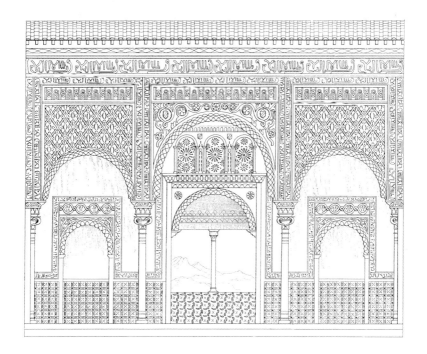

Above: *harmoniously subdivided walls and
arches in the Court of the Myrtles
in the Alhambra (in Arabic "red rock,"
because of the colour of the walls),
the palace of the Moorish kings at
Granada. Thirteenth century.*

Below: *longitudinal section and
plan of Sultan Hassan's mosque
in Cairo (fourteenth century).
Attached to the mosque are
a school, a library, facilities for
the sick and an almshouse.*

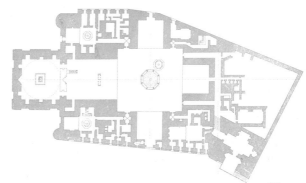

the Persian Sassanid empire and took the provinces of Syria and Palestine from the Eastern Roman Empire. In 641 they conquered Egypt and founded the city of Cairo. Seventy years later, the great warrior Tarik occupied the spit of land between the Iberian peninsula and the rock named Gebel al-Tarik (Gibraltar) after him, and in a seven-day-long battle on the Guadalquivir utterly defeated the Visigothic king Roderick. In 755, the Umayyad Abdurrahman created the caliphate of Cordoba.

The Arabs ruled Spain for seven centuries, but their architecture, which came to evolve a unique style there, is not to be found in all parts of the Iberian peninsula. The Tajo, on the banks of which Toledo stands, represents more or less the frontier of their influence. The most northern Moorish city was Calatayud in Aragon, where the famous golden pottery of Toledo was produced. In 731 an Arab army reached Tours and Poitiers, where it was finally halted by Charles Martel.

The Arabic word "*islām*" means "submission to the will of God," and this consciousness of man's relation to the divinity had a decisive effect on Islamic civilization, which indeed in a sense developed through its religion, embracing many very different peoples— Iranians, Turks, Syrians, Kurds, Egyptians and Berbers.

Islamic philosophy, natural sciences and mathematics had a lasting influence on European thought. By contrast, Islamic architecture was confined to those areas actually governed by the Arabs, i.e. the south of Spain and the Balearics. Building in brick and the art of the arch came from the East, and their decorative motifs stemmed entirely from the Near East. Decoration was often enriched by calligraphy—monograms of Allah and the Prophet in unbroken succession beautifully filling up spare space. Graceful to look at, and almost illegible in its elaborate complexity, Arab calligraphy in a sense replaced the anthropomorphic representation of God and the depiction of the human form,

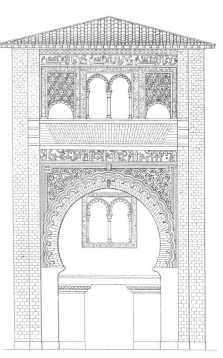

Above: *horseshoe-arched doorway, entrance to a house in Granada.* Below: *trefoil arch transformed into double multifoil arch.*

both forbidden by the Prophet.

Islam—at least in so far as it follows the book of laws known as the Sunna ("Customs") as well as the Qur'ān—allows no figurative images. For the Shi'ites (i.e. "the separated"), who do not go on pilgrimage to Mecca, the Sunna has no authority, and thus it is that the enchanting genre of the Persian miniature came to be born.

Islamic architecture learnt much about articulation of space from the Byzantines. The Christian church of Hagia Sophia became the model for innumerable mosques. The arcaded courtyard around a well as the entrance to a mosque parallels the Christian cloister—if not culturally, at least structurally.

The most distinctively Islamic architectural feature is the minaret. Five times a day, from the top of the minaret, the muezzin calls the faithful to prayer.

Arches of all kinds exist side by side in Islamic architecture. Arab architects delighted in combining round arches and capitals: the result was the horseshoe arch. They then felt the need to make the height of the arch independent of its span, and pointed and often very wide arches were evolved. Arab arches do not always have an unbroken line of curvature. Often the sides start off curved, then change to lead up in a straight line to a more or less pointed center. The so-called ogee, common in late Gothic buildings, is rare. Trefoil arches are very common, however, and are often bewilderingly intricate. Late Romanesque architecture also makes use of this type of arch. From it the Arabs elaborated the multiform arch, a purely decorative form, open to endless variation.

However, since such an arch could not carry any great weight, there was always an old-style round arch with it. The trefoil is the main decorative motif in the Great Mosque at Cordoba, where it is duplicated over and over again between the delicate columns, giving the building an extraordinary sense of lightness.

All the architectonic forms and decorative motifs evolved for the greater glory of Allah in mosque architecture reappear, somewhat modified and on a smaller scale, in secular buildings. Superb carved wooden screens were set in gates and windows, while the ceramic tiles on walls and floors were sometimes so skilfully decorated that the lines between them could not be seen.

The Moorish occupation of Spain ended in 1492, when the Catholic kings Ferdinand and Isabella conquered Granada for Spain and Christendom. Boabdil-Abdallah, the last Moorish ruler, was forced to withdraw to Africa.

Islamic architecture never became fashionable in Europe, although the odd eccentric would occasionally put up a Mooresque folly. Its decorative style exerted a considerable influence, however, which still makes itself felt in pottery, printed fabrics and wood carving. Finally, of course, there is the arabesque—that stylized, gracefully meandering decorative line, plant-like yet abstract, which has always enjoyed popularity in various fields.

GOTHIC

St Denis (feast day 9 October) is one of the patron saints of France. He is sometimes known as St Dionysius of Paris. In 1144, Abbot Suger dedicated a church to him; the choir of this church had been five years in the making. Suger wrote a book about the building process, in which he says:

In the middle we have twelve columns corresponding to the number of the Apostles, and the same number in the side naves to signify the number of the prophets; they soar to the upper superstructure, echoing the words of the Apostle who builds in the spirit. Thus you are no longer merely guests and strangers, but citizens together with the saints and the household of God, raised *in spiritu* on the ground of the Apostles and prophets, because Jesus is the cornerstone, joining up the walls, by which every edifice, spiritual or physical, grows and becomes a holy temple in the Lord.

In many other sections of the book emphasis is placed on the symbolism of the architecture. Numbers acquire meaning; intentions are declared and promoted; technicalities, problems encountered during the building, as ways for realizing the plans were thought out— all are dealt with in long Latin periods. Yet one piece of information is missing: the name of the architect. From the text it is apparent that the church was not the Abbot's own work. Somehow it sounds strange to say that the unknown architect of Saint-Denis was the inventor of Gothic. Nevertheless, to all intents and purposes it is true. This anonymous master builder did in fact create a totally new technique of construction. His use of masonry was revolutionary, and the way in which he broke up walls into pillars and bays allowed great shafts of light to stream into the building through windows as tall as the height of the choir would permit. The choir of Saint-Denis— at least the ground floor—is well enough preserved for us to be able to appreciate the extent of the whole building. The fact that its architect did not invent the pointed arch or the buttress, the main elements of Gothic, in no way detracts from his achievement. Nor is it in any way belittling to describe the ground plan or horizontal projection of his Gothic "temple" as being basically five naves, with those on the sides surrounding the choir in a semicircle.

The first pointed arch known to us dates from the early seventh century and looks almost exactly like a Gothic arch, except that it is somewhat heavier. It is part of the decoration of a building in the urban area of Cairo, on the Nile island of el Rôda, where the level of the river used to be measured. Buttresses for supporting the lateral stress of arches and vaults were already in use in Roman times, and ribbed vaults had appeared already before the twelfth century.

Yet the choir of Saint-Denis is revolutionary in the way it combines different technical and aesthetic innovations and fuses them into interdependent unity. Technical brilliance was not the only important feature or innovatory factor in Gothic. Nor, even, was it the most

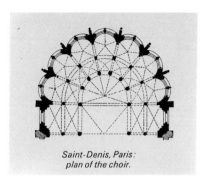

Saint-Denis, Paris:
plan of the choir.

Right: *two types of Gothic church.*
Above, the "normal" Gothic basilica. The
side naves are distinctly lower than the
central one, and the roof level is split,
creating three or more separate roofs. The
buttressing (piers and half arches) is
visible externally.
Below, a Hallenkirche *(Gothic hall*
church). Both nave and aisles are the same
height, and there is a single pitched roof.
There are no flying buttresses (as
described above).
Both illustrations here are section
drawings; the section plans are in bold.

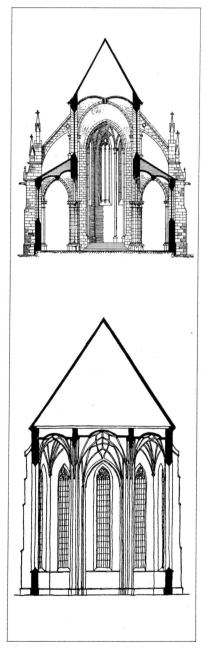

spectacular aspect of the style. Architectonic form was the truly vital point. Space
could now be used differently. No longer
was it necessary to have rows of regular
arches, as round arches must be. Pillars
no longer had to be placed in a square, as
rib vaults with pointed arches could
safely be raised above an elongated
rectangular ground plan, because their
height could remain the same even if they
were differently spaced. Finally the tracery, which is so characteristic of Gothic,
became almost formally systematized
into a decorative replica of structural
principles—as it were, a long-
reverberating echo of the larger forms.
What in the foundations was the result of
technical planning recurs in ornamental
tracery, buttresses, spandrels, pinnacles
and turrets, and along the angles of spires
shooting up towards the clouds: a sym-

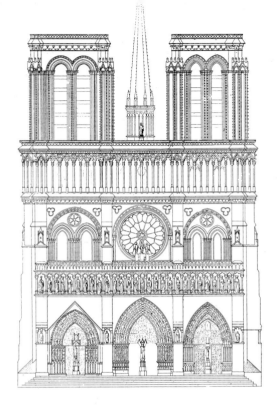

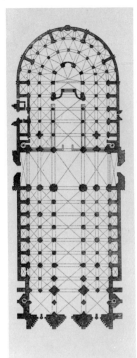

phony of stone orchestrated by a master builder and his assistants.

The great counterweight to all this upward movement, appearing in splendour above the great west door, is the rose window, symbolizing the sun, the world and the constellations, and capable of infinite variation. Gothic is indeed much more than pure technical display and geometry.

It is hard for us today to realize that at first Gothic was a regional phenomenon of "cathedral country," and that in Italy, for example, it was ignored for a long time, only later, in the fourteenth century, coming into vogue for a brief hundred years or so. It then disappeared before the impetus of the great Humanist, classical revival we now call the Renaissance.

The word "Gothic," now unfortunately tinged with a certain sentimentality, was coined in Italy during the Renaissance as a derogatory term. The painter, architect and art historian Giorgio Vasari (1511–74) used it to describe something barbaric, that is, nonclassical. It kept the same overtones until the late eighteenth century, and was used of buildings that were clumsily designed, over-ornate or tasteless. With the rise of Romanticism (from around 1820), however, the Gothic style began to be judged differently, and the word began to acquire its present sense.

Goethe's universal genius allowed him to appreciate Gothic before his time. When he went to Strasbourg he was expecting the cathedral to be, as he wrote, "an ill-shapen, straggling, bristling monster." He describes his impressions on seeing it for himself in his essay *Von deutscher Baukunst*

Opposite, left: *Notre-Dame, Paris. West front. Building work began in 1160, under the auspices of the highly cultured Bishop Maurice de Sully, in the early stages of his episcopacy. By 1225 the choir, main nave and west front had been completed; 1270 saw the completion of the north and south transept elevations, with their respective doors.*
Opposite, right: *plan of Notre-Dame. The transept cuts almost across the middle of the five aisles making up the body of the building. The side aisles also extend right round the choir. Around 1300 a series of chapels was constructed between the bases of the flying buttresses. Dimensions: length 420 feet (128 m.); width of west front, discounting the buttresses, 125 feet (38 m.); height inside 115 feet (35 m.); height of the towers (though these were never finished) 226 feet (69 m.).*
Below: *Bourges Cathedral, begun around 1190 and consecrated in 1324. This church has five aisles, intersected by a transept.*
A particularly striking feature is the projection of the flying buttresses right up to the roof.

("German architecture") (1771), in which as his final word he declares: ". . . es ist gut."

In the mid nineteenth century, records dating from the age of the cathedrals came to light, and were translated and printed. Those who admired Gothic art were thus given a closer glimpse of the motives and feelings of those who had erected such daring, miraculous structures. Robert de Mont-Saint-Michel wrote in 1144:

This year for the first time we saw at Chartres believers harnessed to carts laden with stones, wood, grain, everything needed for building the cathedral. As if by magic the towers rose into the air. This was not only happening here, but all over France and Normandy, and elsewhere. People everywhere were performing acts of humility, doing penance, and pardoning their enemies. Men and women could be seen dragging heavy loads through bogs, singing of the miracle of the Lord taking shape before their very eyes.

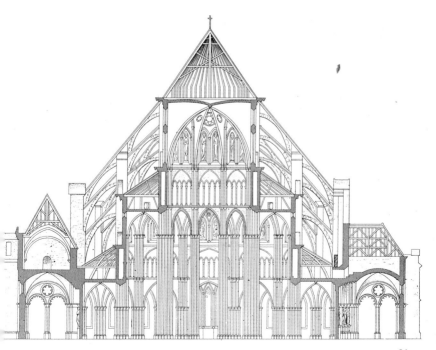

Left: *a "wimperg"
(decorative gable
over a Gothic window),
Sainte-Chapelle,
Paris. 1248.*

Opposite: *Strasbourg Cathedral.
Top left: the choir and transept (in
bold) rest on eleventh-century
foundations. A church had already
existed on this same site since 510
which was traditionally said to
have been founded by King Clovis.
A Romanesque church had then
replaced the first.one, only to be
itself destroyed in the early
decades of the twelfth century.
Bottom left: the west front as
originally intended (above) and as
it actually is (below). Right: the
west front, by Friedrich Adler.*

A few years later, Abbot Aimon of Saint-Pierre-sur-Dive wrote:

Whoever saw or heard the like? That is, powerful lords and princes of this world, blown up with riches and honours, and women of noble birth bending their proud heads and yoking themselves to carts like draught beasts to take wine, grain, oil, lime, stones, and wood to people building a church? And although many more than a thousand people are all working together, there is silence, not a word or even a whisper can be heard. As they go along with trumpet blasts, with their blessed banner, nothing could stop them, not mountain nor water. You might imagine you were seeing the ancient Israelites crossing the Jordan. God

Himself seems to be guiding them. The waters of the sea withdraw before them. Many eyewitnesses from Sainte-Marie-du-Port testify to it. Once the pilgrims reach the church they want to help build, they make a great square of carts and watch and sing psalms through the night. Candles and lanterns are lit on each cart, and relics are carried to the sick who have been brought along, and the whole company forms propitiatory processions for their restoration to health.

The names of many of the first Gothic architects have been lost. Abbot Suger of Saint-Denis fails to mention his, but such an omission should not be seen as being

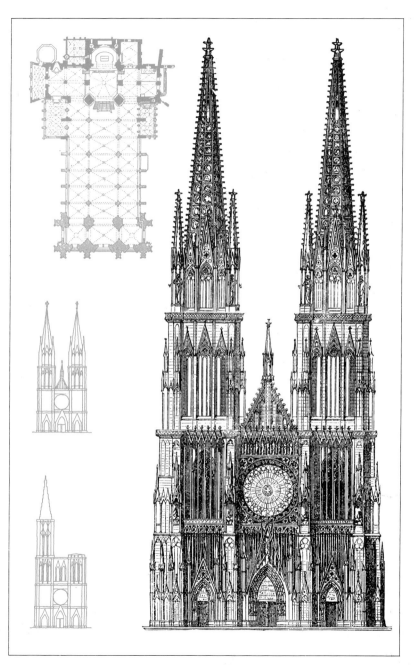

63

negative. At that period it would not have seemed of great import to give the architect's name. Attitudes later changed radically: master builders acquired reputations that spread well beyond the area where they worked; their names were passed from mouth to mouth; they were offered tempting conditions to help out on sites that had been abandoned because work on them had stretched on too long.

At Canterbury the monks worked on the main nave of their future cathedral; in 1174 the choir burnt down. The monks, in despair, did not know whether to pull down what was still left standing or to continue building on from it. William of Sens was invited over from France, and he supervised the work on the choir for over five years. The monk Gervasius records:

... at first he did not tell us what he thought had to be done, for fear that, depressed as we were already, the truth would be too much for us to bear. Meanwhile he himself, with help from others, started preparations, and only when he saw that the monks were recovering their morale did he reveal that it would be necessary to demolish the damaged pillars together with all the masonry supported by them if they wished their church to be completely safe and

flawless. In the end the monks agreed to the demolition of the remains of the choir. William had stone sent over from abroad. He invented the most wonderful machines for loading the materials on board, and for disembarking and transporting them. At the same time he gave the stonemasons carved wooden models to guide them in their work.

In his fifth year at Canterbury, William fell from some scaffolding, receiving such severe fractures that he was immobilized. He then entrusted the work to a skilful monk who had already been supervising. From a bed he directed "what ought to be done first and what afterwards. But as the doctors could not heal him, William returned to France to die in his native country."

In 1235 the French architect Villard de Honnecourt wrote a manual for those working under him which he copiously illustrated and which still survives. From his instructions it appears that Gothic builders took little account of exact dimensional order. A basic dimension

Above: *Brunswick town hall, fourteenth century.* Opposite: *part of the west front of Siena Cathedral—a combination of Gothic and traditional Tuscan elements.*

Opposite: *the main door in the west front of Cologne Cathedral. The first stone of this building was laid in 1248. The names of some of the architects involved are known to us: Meister Gerhard (d. 1279), Meister Arnold (d. 1308) and Johannes (d. 1331), Arnold's son. The choir was completed in 1322. The last great medieval architect was Konrad Kuyn (d. 1469). However, building did not cease with the passing of the Middle Ages: this cathedral was to have been even bigger and more magnificent than its models at Reims and Amiens. The end of the fifteenth century saw completion of the east choir and part of the main nave; meanwhile work had already started on the towers. However, there remained a great gap between the two finished sections. Perched on the southern tower, which had been built up to half its planned height, was a crane that for years was almost a symbol of Cologne. Work was suspended for three centuries.*

Then in 1842 the first stone of the new building was laid; and by 1880 the whole structure was complete. Ernst Zwinner (1802–61), the architect in charge, employed over a hundred stonemasons to work in exactly the way their Gothic forebears had. Cologne Cathedral is a triumph, and a supreme example of respect for the past; nevertheless, it reveals the intrinsic limitations of restoration work. Whilst architecturally an undeniable success, the sculptures fail to recapture the vitality of genuine Gothic.

During the Second World War the building was severely damaged by fourteen bombs: nine of the main nave arches collapsed. Rebuilding started a year after the war ended, and was finished in 1956. As a memorial to these latest ravages of war, the sculptor Ewald Mataré designed a work showing the city in flames for the south doors.

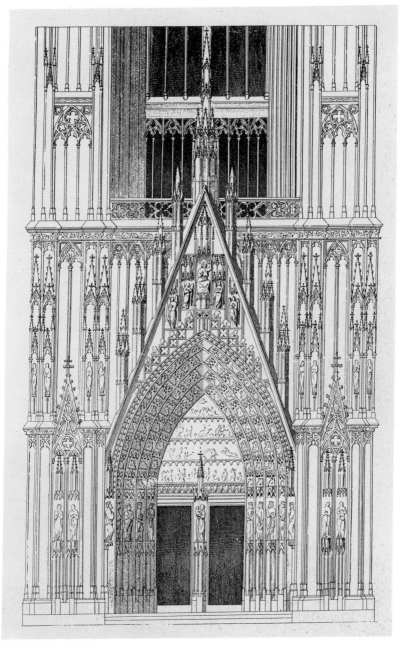

was decided on, and both the building as a whole and the individual sections were then determined by simple multiplication or division respectively. Many drawings were made, but few calculations. Scholars agree that architects had barely any understanding of statics, or the strength of materials. Nevertheless, they did have an instinct for proportions of dimensions, for how walls should be strengthened, for the thicknesses of pillars, and for the types of stone needed to bear a given load. Geometry was the key to their technical achievements, using basic artisan forms—the square, the half square, the circle and the curved arch—as starting points. The two vital tools of the builder's trade were a pair of compasses and a plumb line. For all their lack of arithmetical expertise, these architects managed to create works of almost miraculous beauty—works that a handful of self-important Humanists later did their best to belittle with the word "Gothic."

In their modest way, shunning the "bubble reputation," they yet bore out in their actual work the words of Solomon to the Creator of all things: "Thou hast ordered all things with degree, number and weight."

At this point it seems appropriate to devote a few lines to the historical background of this period: to the great river of time along whose banks the spires of cathedrals and abbeys point heavenwards. What was it that prompted architects to adopt such dramatically new structural forms, raising the house of God well above the roofs of the houses tight-packed, higgledy-piggledy, within the city walls? Was Christianity perhaps in some way in danger, and was it felt necessary to erect visible signs as encouragement to flagging faith? In fact Christianity was not endangered, only the church that Helen, the mother of Constantine the Great, had built on the Holy Sepulcher in Jerusalem. Since the Moslem Fatimids and, after them, the Seljuks had gained control of Palestine, pilgrims had found travelling in the Holy Land difficult.

In 1095, Pope Urban II had called a crusade. Godefroy de Bouillon and six other knights had set off for the Holy

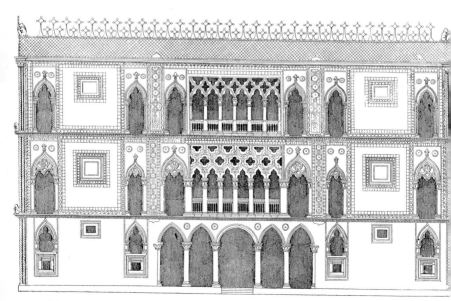

Right: *Santa Maria da Batalha, in Lisbon, built in 1385 by King John of Portugal.*

Opposite: *the Cà d'Oro, on the Grand Canal in Venice. Dating from the fifteenth century, this building is highly idiosyncratic in all respects, forming a delightful blend of Gothic and Byzantine styles. Though the main façade was perhaps originally intended to be perfectly symmetrical (as in this drawing), in fact only the central and right-hand sections were built. The Cà d'Oro was restored at the beginning of the present century.*

Land. Via different routes they brought a French and Norman army two hundred thousand strong to Constantinople. Though often on the verge of exhaustion, they destroyed the Islamic residences in Syria, stormed Jerusalem, and, after fearsome massacres, took the church of the Holy Sepulcher.

This triumph, won at the cost of so much blood, was short-lived, however. Despite papal exhortations for crusades throughout the twelfth and thirteenth centuries, and despite various expertly led military expeditions to the Near East, the hard fighting was in vain: the holy places remained in Muslim hands.

Religious zeal, a certain asceticism, and sheer natural belligerence had united both great and small in the crusades. Many men lost their lives for their faith — and also, it must be said, for the satisfaction of their own instincts of aggression. Yet, despite all the losses and bloodshed, the crusades had many positive results in Europe. Towns experi-

enced a new era of prosperity due to overseas trade; closer contact with Arabic civilization brought new horizons to philosophy and the natural sciences; and new religious orders were founded (Carthusians, Cistercians, Premonstratensians, Dominicans, Franciscans, Carmelites and Augustinians — all between 1086 and 1244). Scarcely less important were the curiously spiritual orders of knights, which persisted after the crusades, such as the Knights Templars, the Knights Hospitalers (future Knights of Malta) and the Teutonic Knights.

From the south of France right up to the Baltic countries, it was the religious and knightly orders that used the Gothic style of building. Gothic was the most widespread style in Europe at the end of the Middle Ages; at the same time, each country had its own form of Gothic, corresponding to the temperament of its people and the building materials available, as well as to the purposes for

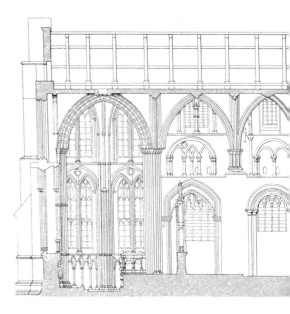

Section through the center nave of Durham Cathedral. On the left is the choir; in the middle, the crossing, with the base of the tower. Romanesque in conception, it was begun around 1100; alterations and enlargements then took place in the thirteenth and fifteenth centuries.

which new buildings were constructed— for, as trade expanded and cities became larger, these purposes were soon no longer solely religious, as had been the case at first, for instance in France. Castles and rich townsmen's houses, town halls, cloth halls, and storehouses all shared the same style and overall stamp: thin walls with strong pillars, pointed arches, and stone (sometimes marble) tracery in windows and on façades.

French Gothic perhaps developed more steadily than any other. It reached its peak around 1250, but that is not to say that it started to decline after that. The original plans of the great cathedrals were often altered during building, which would go on for many years. There was certainly a slackening of the tremendous building fervour of the early days, as we see by the stumps of never-completed towers. The cathedral at Chartres, for instance, was initially intended to have nine towers: in fact only two were built, and even then one has a distinct "poor relation" look about it. Elsewhere seven

towers were not uncommon at the planning stage—two at the west end where the main entrance was, two at either end of the transept, and one (the largest) over the crossing. Many towers remained incomplete not because of lack of manpower or money, but because of the danger of overloading the foundations. Hence the ideal cathedral as conceived by Viollet-le-Duc was never actually built, and the multi-tower format was superseded by the two-tower model. Alternatively, the west end superstructure known as the westwork, a single tower above the main entrance, was also a viable proposition. In Italian churches the bell tower (*campanile*) is usually a completely independent structure, set to one side of the main body of the church, rather than forming an organic part of the actual church building.

German Gothic began around 1250. The most beautiful early example of the style is the Elisabethkirche in Marburg (1235–83), the towers of which were, however, not completed until 1360.

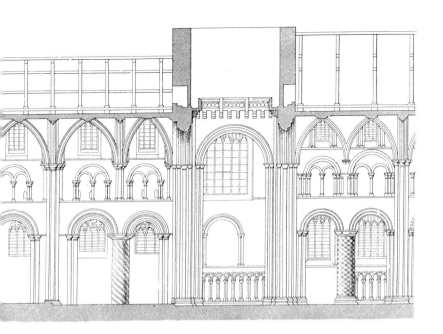

In some places, especially in the north, due to the unavailability of sandstone or good limestone, brick had to be used. However, brick is not suitable for flying buttresses. The result was the hall church (*Hallenkirche*) in which the walls are supported by pillars projecting internally. It is this that gives German brick Gothic its characteristic compactness and that dictates the articulation of the nave into one bay for each window.

German architects and patrons were quick to adopt the Gothic style. Bamberg Cathedral, finished in 1220, is Roman-esque, while the Gothic Elisabethkirche in Marburg postdates it by only fifteen years.

Northern Gothic is a perfect counter-balance to French Gothic, which seems to get bigger and grander the farther it is from the Rhine.

Strasbourg is where the mood changes. Apart from the Romanesque choir, the transept and the dome above the crossing, the style of the cathedral is entirely French. It was to have had twin towers and an impressive westwork.

Whether the architect was German or French is not known. However, Erwin von Steinach (d.1318) supervised the actual building work, taking control in 1284. A hundred years after his death, the north tower was finished by Ulrich von Ensingen, and the façade above the rose window was raised by one storey, thus closing the gap between the northern tower and the base of the southern. This later work was considered to spoil the effect of the west elevation. We have now become accustomed to this somewhat whimsical asymmetry, and the imbalance which once aroused such criticism has now become "a notable feature."

Gothic came to Italy later than to other countries in Europe, and there are few pure French-style Gothic buildings there. Italian architecture of this period is strongly influenced by Roman, Romanesque, and Byzantine elements. The architectonic decoration is rich and exuberant and highly inventive, partic-ularly in Venice, where it appears in magnificent profusion especially on secular buildings.

Examples of English Gothic window tracery.
From left to right: Early English, 1150–1300 (first two windows);
Decorated, 1250–1400 (corresponding to the French flamboyant); Perpendicular, 1350–1550.

The *duomo* in Florence, begun in 1286 following an initial plan by Arnolfo di Cambio, and commissioned by the wool weavers' guild "in honour of the republic and people of Florence," was to have been wholly Gothic. Yet when completed in the first half of the fifteenth century it had heavy cornices both inside and out, which stressed its horizontal orientation. It also featured a dome raised over a central octagonal—the first large dome built in Italy since the Pantheon, and one of the first masterpieces of the Italian Proto-Renaissance. Milan Cathedral is an excellent illustration of what happens when Italian, German and French architects work and compete together for too long. Despite everything, though, Italian Gothic stands as one of the most charming of all architectural styles.

It is often said that England is the land of late Gothic. This is not strictly true, since English Gothic was almost contemporary with French. Prior to the thirteenth century, Gothic structures had already been raised on Romanesque foundations at Canterbury, Durham, Norwich and elsewhere. A distinctive English Gothic style soon emerged, differing from the classic French in its arch structures, which were more idiosyncratic and often technically bolder. Figurative decoration in English cathedrals is austere, while their rib vaulting, with all the variants of tiercerons and liernes (secondary and tertiary ribs), and their developments into net and fan vaulting, reveal supreme inventive genius and technical mastery.

Looking upwards in an English Gothic building, one has the impression of looking up into a tree, so elaborate are the geometrical ramifications of the vault ribs. Another striking feature of English Gothic is the love of huge windows. The closely positioned mullions in these tend to emphasize their perpendicularity, creating a curiously two-dimensional effect, and allowing light to stream through but without creating a sensation of greater space. Sometimes these windows are too wide to be contained within a standard-size pointed arch: thus the Perpendicular style appears, similar in its basic conception to the Moorish arch, though worlds apart as regards tracery.

England had more difficulty than any other country in weaning itself off Gothic. British architects almost missed the Renaissance boat completely. The late Gothic phase, Tudor Gothic, is probably the most idiosyncratic of all Gothic styles, yet it developed into a clearly thought-out, systematic genre. The names of the various periods of English Gothic are particularly appropriate. The early, plain phase, Early English, lasted up until about 1250, after which the following hundred years saw the Decorated style—a name indicative of the essential characteristic of English Gothic: tracery became more elaborate and inventive; plain walls virtually disappeared. The next phase, Perpendicular, derives its name from the effect of the division of pillars, wall surfaces and windows into rectangular panels, which lend structures a decidedly perpendicular character (a feature also of Tudor architecture). New forms then developed out of Perpendicular: the classic pointed arch became modified into lancet arches, ogee arches and the typical wide Tudor arch. Finally, the Elizabethan style forms a sort of prelude to English Renaissance, mixing old and new in bewildering combinations.

English Gothic drew to a close eventually around 1600, at least in important buildings. Vernacular architecture continued in the old tradition, the "honest English" gentry refusing to incorporate the new "Italian" style into their country houses. A somewhat bizarre style developed, and it is hardly a surprise to find it, after a long and vigorous life, influencing nineteenth-century neo-Gothic.

Romanticism, with its love of the past, resulted in construction of Gothic-style town halls, private houses and artificial ruins both on the Continent and in England. Gothic railway stations and factories appeared in the second half of the last century. The fashion was short-lived, however. Despite one's inclination to dismiss neo-Gothic as the symptom of a certain decadent romanticism, the buildings themselves were designed and built with considerable skill and sensitivity. Gothic "revisited" seemed the most suitable style not only for the sublime but also for the sense of civic dignity of the nineteenth-century bourgeoisie, based on the austere virtues of "the good old days." Thus innumerable churches were either built in Gothic or acquired Gothic towers; Gothic civic buildings sprouted—the Munich *Rathaus*, for instance, which no doubt thousands of tourists have mistaken for a fifteenth-century building; in 1836, the British houses of Parliament began to rise on the bank of the Thames; and even in New York neo-Gothic made its mark in St Patrick's, which, from the vast Rockefeller Center that towers about it, looks like some millionaire's toy "imported" in honour and memory of a great-grandfather from Freiburg im Breisgau.

THE RENAISSANCE

In 1453, Sultan Muhammad II took the city of Constantinople, the capital of the Eastern Roman Empire. Those Greek scholars who escaped being killed fled to Athens, which was occupied and sacked in its turn three years later. The Greeks fled again, to Italy, settling in Rome, Florence and Bologna, where they began to teach philosophy. They brought with them a great store of learning acquired from ancient books—knowledge which in Italy at that period had been partly forgotten, partly distorted and falsified through exegeses and reworkings.

The new teachers and their disciples called themselves Humanists (from the Latin *humanitas*, translatable as "action, way of life worthy of a man"). Basing their thinking on the rediscovered works of antiquity, the Humanists sought to formulate a new ideal of cultural training, and intellectual and spiritual activity, free of constricting rules and rigid formulae established through a narrow, one-sided interpretation of ancient texts. However, they encountered serious problems due to the hostility of Church dogmatists, and were obliged to elaborate what they called "the double truth," by means of which they expressed their own opinions on the one hand and paid homage to the Church Fathers on the other.

Yet despite these problems there was a veritable explosion of intellectual life. Many universities were founded at this time. Art and literature received a huge stimulus from the new cultural climate. People celebrated the rebirth of antiquity.

In architecture, Hellenistic forms began to supplant everything "Gothic." Hence the adoption of the concept of rebirth (*renaissance*) in describing the new style. Antonio Vasari was reponsible for first introducing the word into art historical terminology, although his *rinascita* did not yet apply to style so much as to a manner of thinking and seeing things and creating. The word "Renaissance" itself only became widely used after Jakob Burckhardt published his *Die Kultur der Renaissance in Italien* (The Civilization of the Renaissance in Italy) in 1860.

The roots of the Renaissance go back to the Middle Ages. The enormous success which the Humanists enjoyed is less astonishing when one realizes that the ground had already been prepared and was ready for the seeds of change: medieval culture had lost all its vitality and shrank in fear from new ideas. Indeed, thinking of something new could cost one one's life.

Renaissance is a far-reaching, complex concept. Much more is contained in it than simple rediscovery of ancient Hellenistic remains—columns, Corinthian capitals, Roman arches, and half columns abutting on to pilasters. It involves also the rebirth of personality, and the liberation of the artist from rules which had come to seem overrigid and outworn.

After an uncertain start, strong encouragement began to come from the Church. Pope Nicholas V did not hesitate to assert that he would gladly have spent

Right: *San Zaccaria, the oldest Renaissance church in Venice, begun around 1450 by Antonio Gambello. Façade by Mauro Coducci, c. 1515.*

Below: *Palazzo Strozzi, Florence, begun in 1489 by Benedetto da Maiano and continued by Cronaca. Work was completed only in 1533. The capitals and dosserets of the columns blend together in a harmony typical of early Florentine Renaissance architecture. The Strozzi were a patrician family frequently at odds with the powerful Medici.*

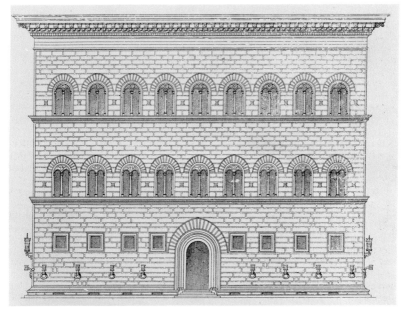

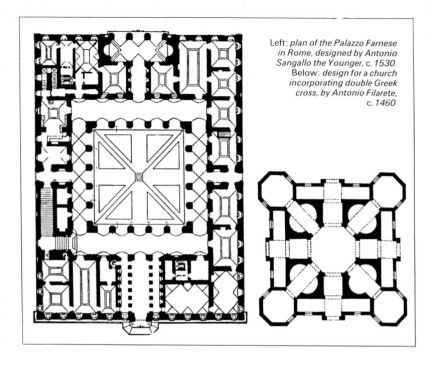

Left: *plan of the Palazzo Farnese in Rome, designed by Antonio Sangallo the Younger, c. 1530.* Below: *design for a church incorporating double Greek cross, by Antonio Filarete, c. 1460*

all his money on books and buildings. Founder of the Vatican Library, he it was, too, who decided that the old basilica of St Peter's had become insufficient. He was responsible for the plans for the enlarging of the building (drawn up around 1450, but revised several times fifty years later).

New patrons—princes, rich merchants, and last but not least the heads of the Italian Republics, especially Venice—made a decisive contribution to the flowering of arts and sciences.

It should also be said that artists and architects met with less resistance than thinkers. Clear expression of one's own ideas about the new developments of civilization could be extremely imprudent in the sixteenth century. The trials of Giordano Bruno and Galileo—one the prophet of a new world vision, the other the champion of a new astronomy with untold numbers of suns—occurred not at

the beginning of the Renaissance but towards the end. Giordano Bruno went to the stake in 1600, after a long term of imprisonment; Galileo was forced to retract his "heresies," on pain of execution, in 1633. The Renaissance was not just one momentary episode, but a gradual awakening, often "underground," in the menacing shadow of the Inquisition.

The melting pot of the new style was Italy. The new age began around 1420 with a firm rejection of everything that came later to be called "Gothic." Yet the adoption of Roman and Hellenistic building modes did not lead to pedestrian imitation of antiquity. A new feeling for space, a new "taste," evolved with the

Opposite: *Brunelleschi's dome on Santa Maria del Fiore in Florence, with Giotto's campanile on the right.*

Below: *golden proportions of the human figure.*
Left: *five "golden rectangles," achieved by joining up the points of intersection of two pentagrams placed one on top of the other in such a way that the perpendicular of each vertex intersects the corresponding side of the other pentagram.*

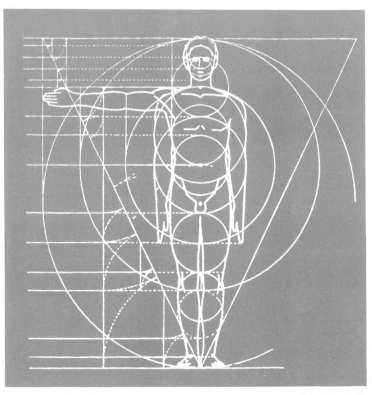

revival of the central plan and the self-contained, closed façades. The guiding principle of patronage was: show off your wealth, your pride, your vanity, as long as the new building is totally suited to its purpose and is in every way functional. Build yourself a house where, if people want to get away from you, they do not have to climb tortuous spiral staircases into gloomy rooms with narrow slit windows. Arrange the windows in a way that reflects your own inner order and your own way of thinking. Put up soundly structured walls, well designed in relation to each other in such a way that they need no buttresses. All houses have several floors one on top of another: build your house so that from the outside the various structural levels are clearly discernible. Run cornices above and below the windows to highlight them. The roof cornice should be particularly imposing, so that people will not think you ran out of money before the building was finished.

These or similar principles dictated the design both of *palazzi* (palaces, town houses), whether large or small, and of middle-class houses of the Renaissance. Decoration was modest at first, but then ornamentation became richer (even over-ornate); pilasters and half columns emerged from the façades, accentuating the vertical axes of the building, yet without detracting from the effect of the horizontal cornices. Thus the façades of Renaissance buildings reveal an ordered rhythm of horizontal and vertical lines, with due respect paid to proportion.

There are numerous examples of both ecclesiastical and secular buildings: *palazzi*, town halls and other public edifices. In attractive contrast to the massive town buildings there are the country villas, for which architects had ample room to design much more spacious buildings with very substantial wings.

At this point it is worth making mention of the "golden section," by means of which a network of geometric lines and compass-drawn curves could be woven over pictures not only of figures and buildings, ground plans and façades but also of natural things such as leaves and flowers, inspiring in the viewer a feeling of magical, scientific revelation. These drawings also included highly detailed observations. Of course the *sectio aurea* was often vested with a sort of mystery which was nothing but detrimental. "Golden proportions" were shown to be present in certain remarkable works of art in which the artist had merely used his natural sensitivity to harmonious proportion rather than ruler and compass.

The golden section is found by dividing a line in such a way that the total length of the line has the same relationship to the longer section as the longer section has to the shorter. There are various ways of making this division. The simplest is to imagine the line one wishes to divide as being the long side of a right-angled triangle, the second side of which is half the length of the first. A circle is then drawn with a compass, having as its center the apex opposite the long line and having a radius equal to the length of the short side. The curve of the circle intersects the third side (hypotenuse). A second curve is then made, centered on the apex opposite the short side and having a radius extending to the intersection on the hypotenuse. The long side is thus in turn divided, into two unequal sections, known respectively as the major and the minor: and these two sections stand in golden ratio to each other. In other words, the minor section is to the major what the major is to the sum of both.

There is also a mathematical method of achieving the golden section. After lengthy calculations one arrives at the equation $x = 0.61803 \ldots$ recurring. All we need to know here, however, is that a triangle with sides in a ratio of 3:5 (i.e. whole numbers) to each other can be considered roughly as a "golden triangle"; of course mathematically it is not, but it is close enough to deceive the eye. The error is tiny, and becomes ever tinier as the series continues: 5:8; 8:13; 13:21; 21:34; 34:55; 55:89; 89:144 and so on. The trick is obvious: the sum of two numbers in the correct ratio gives the

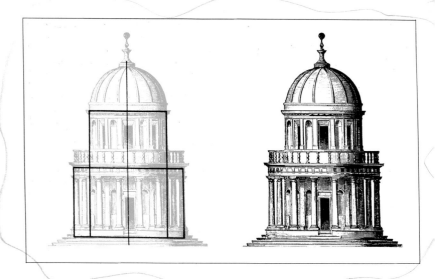

second figure for the next golden ratio.

The golden section was not a discovery of the Renaissance. It has cropped up throughout the history of architecture since the age of Euclid (c. 300 BC), to whom is also attributed the construction of the pentagon—a geometrical figure related in several ways to the golden section. The sides of the five-pointed star (pentagram or pentacle) intersect in golden ratios. Certain other surprising ratios and relationships led to the adoption of the pentacle as a magic sign to ward away witches and nocturnal spirits, and as a secret identification symbol for clandestine groups.

Golden ratios can be found in many buildings, in the geometrical make-up of façades and walls, and even in three-dimensional compositions. Yet one should not set too much store by the interplay of numbers and circles. Pleasing dimensions, harmony and proportion are not achieved with numbers alone. Mathematical formulae can at best arrive only at an approximation to the grandiose or subline. The Renaissance saw what was almost an obsession with the idea of the need to formulate a theory of perfection; but the quest for this theory

was merely an accompaniment to the creative process.

Europe began to feel the effects of the Renaissance when it was coming to its close in Italy. It reached France at the beginning of the sixteenth century, and a little later crossed east of the Alps. In Germany the new style was called the *Welsche Manier* (the "Latin" manner). In England, as has been said already, the Renaissance very nearly did not happen at all.

Naturally the Renaissance did not spread to these countries in its pure, original forms, but rather in its later, more florid manifestations. These might occasionally be accused of being somewhat "too much of a good thing"; but at the same time it was often judiciously pruned, in order to make it less typically Italian and closer to native German or Dutch styles. It became the favourite style of international trade, and especially in Germany and Holland the façades of commercial branch buildings and the two or more pediments of town halls bear witness to a flourishing merchant class, in an age when the wars and misery of the seventeenth century were still in the unforeseen future.

Opposite: *"golden proportions" in Bramante's
Tempietto (1502).
The rectangles traced over the drawing of the
circular temple are "golden rectangles." The
centralized-plan Tempietto stands in the
courtyard of the Convento di San Pietro in
Montorio, Rome.*

Below: *Palazzo Valmarana, Vicenza, by
Andrea Palladio; finished in 1566. Palladio
was the father of the late Renaissance style
("Palladian Neoclassicism") that led to the
Baroque. He used almost exclusively
Hellenistic-Roman architectural elements,
freely adapting them to create effects of
greater opulence and splendour.
A frequent feature of his work is the so-called
"colossal order," where a single elevation is
broken by a series of huge columns or pilasters
rising at least two floors high.*

The final phase of the Renaissance is
known as Mannerism. In art history the
term implies a highly personal mode of
expression; it also indicates the adoption
of the specific idiom or *manner* of a
certain artist by others, or by a whole
school. Yet this does not fully explain the
concept: it also entails a love of exaggeration and artificiality, obtained by any
means possible. Mannerism tends towards excess, towards distortion of
perspective for theatrical effects. This is
still not all, however. By its very nature, it
escapes precise definition. It was the
product of a spiritually uncertain age—an
age caught between the Reformation and
the Counter Reformation, seeking for
new certainties, and attempting to guide
itself through all this insecurity with the
help of fantasy, pushing familiar, already
lovingly developed forms and techniques
to their extreme, perhaps with the aim of

preserving them from decadence. Like any other "-ism," Mannerism cannot be confined within a precise chronology. In the same way as classicism, archaism and historicism, it was by no means free and spontaneous, for its allegiance was to a type of reality that had already long ceased to exist. And yet in its very insecurity it was innovatory.

The word "Mannerist" can be applied to architects as diverse as Palladio, Vignola, and Borromini: these, and many others, created masterly effects of per-spective. In painting, the names of Pontormo, Tintoretto and El Greco immediately spring to mind. And this same basic sensitivity has persisted—albeit with certain interruptions—down to our own day, producing a wealth of ideas, different effects of light and shade, and often startlingly intense visions of chaos. Mannerist painting was as it were a forerunner of Surrealism, i.e. that trend or movement of ideas that aimed to re-establish the unconscious, freeing it from the tools and formulae of reason.

The arsenal (Zeughaus) at Danzig, built around 1600 and destroyed in the bombings in 1945.

BAROQUE AND ROCOCO

The Portuguese used to describe a pearl that was not perfectly round as *barroco*. In French, Italian and German (*baroque*, *barocco*, *Barock*) the word came to mean odd, strange, bizarre. During the nineteenth century it came to be used to identify the style that began to replace that of the Renaissance around 1600. First used of architecture, it was soon applied to all the arts, becoming a sort of metaphor for a certain way of seeing the world, expressed, for example, in broad, expansive movements (take the Spanish formalities of greeting, for instance), voluminous clothing and general extravagance, and in a love of curved forms (even to the point of distortion) and rich ornamentation (even to excess).

One might characterize the three successive styles of Gothic, Renaissance and Baroque symbolically with the goddesses Diana, Juno and Venus. Diana, the huntress, goddess of the moon and patroness of virgins is tall and slender, with delicate limbs; chaste, despite her athletic build, she is reserved almost to the point of being affected. Juno is more statuesque, is both sensual and calm, conveys a sense of the sublime, and by this very sublimity is perhaps less seductive for men than Diana or the third goddess, Venus, in whom we find a complete, harmonious fusion of femininity, beauty and sensuality. In a different way one might also say that Gothic sees life in terms of Fate, the Renaissance in terms of Task, and Baroque in terms of Joy. However, this is all rather whimsical.

Such neat formulae may illustrate certain phenomena, but they do not quite express their essence.

The Baroque period stretches from 1600 to 1760. However, these dates (especially the first) should not be taken as rigorously precise time limits. The Baroque grew out of the Renaissance through Mannerism. There is really no strict chronology. Already existing basic forms began to move towards a new harmony, a new fusion of one with another; obviously structural elements became concealed; the functional disappeared behind an apparently effortless gaiety. The boundaries between the arts vanished, so to speak, spontaneously. Architecture became sculptural, sculpture became part of architecture, and painting was now no longer just two-dimensional interior decoration, but contributed to the overall riot of perspective values. Domes, barrel vaults and ceilings became tents, heavenly pavilions and cloud sets for allegorical subjects, for which even the largest areas would have been too small without *trompe-l'œil* enlargement.

This working together of architecture, sculpture and painting resulted in the distinctively Baroque features of pathos, magnificence and intoxicating crowding of both subject matter and purely formal line.

The architectural history of the basilica of St Peter's gives a good idea of the way in which the Baroque emerged out of the Renaissance.

In 1450, Pope Nicholas V planned an enlargement of the old basilica, entrusting the work two years later to Bernardo Rossellini, who built a new apse. Later, under Pope Julius II, Bramante totally demolished the old church, together with Rossellini's apse, and started a new building on a Greek-cross plan with a central dome, secondary domes, and barrel vaults above the naves. In 1515, under Pope Leo X, Raphael took over the planning and direction of the works. The first (south) arcades of the transept were roofed with domes. But Raphael was only to be employed on the project for five years—at the age of thirty-seven he died, and was solemnly buried in the Pantheon. In 1520 Antonio da Sangallo was appointed to supervise the work. During the twenty-six years of his direction, the apses were built and the floor was raised by about ten feet (3 m.). A new design for the dome was discussed, but nothing was finalized.

Paul III ascended the papal throne, and in 1547 Michelangelo was given the job of supervising the building process. The surface area was reduced and the southern apses were demolished. A new façade was erected and a third design for the dome drawn up. After Michelangelo's death in 1564, work proceeded roughly as he had envisaged until 1573. For the next twelve years all progress ceased.

In 1585, Pope Sixtus V entrusted the work to Giacomo della Porta and Domenico Fontana, who together modified the design for the dome and extended the building eastwards to join it up with the Vatican Palace. In 1592, after completion of the dome, work started on the interior. From 1607 to 1629, Carlo Maderno was in charge (under the papacy of Paul V). Maderno, who had trained under Fontana, was already a representative of the new Baroque era: nevertheless he followed Michelangelo's

From a design by Borromini for the façade of the College of Propaganda Fide, in Rome.

Palmi. 10.

Pal. 6.

Pal. 7.

Palmi. 10.

Pal. 15. e. Minutti. 30.

Pal. 3.

Pal. 15. e. Min. 30.

Min. 30.

Pal. 7.

Pal. 7. e. M. 30.

Pal. 6.

Palmi 6.

Pal. 12.

Palmi 7.

Palmi 32.

Palmi 26.

Palmi 10.

Pal. 12. e. Min. 40.

Pal. 22. e. Min. 40.

Palmi 7.

Pal. 35. e. Min. 50.

20   30   40   50   60

plans more scrupulously than his predecessors. The Pope asked him to provide two extra chapels, and in order to do this he had to alter the exterior. Two frontal towers were planned in front of the central nucleus of the building, thus extending the ground plan lengthways. In 1626, after completion of the interior decoration, the new basilica was consecrated. Twenty years later, Lorenzo Bernini took up the plans for the towers

Above: *Sant' Agnese, Rome (Piazza Navona), built between 1652 and 1677 by Girolamo and Carlo Rainaldi. Borromini also worked on the building during the first five years. The front elevation is elegant in line and richly inventive, with five main axes of balance.*

Opposite: *the Trevi Fountain, Rome. In its present form it is the work of Nicola Salvi and (to a lesser extent) Giuseppe Pannini.*

again; however, the foundations proved insufficiently stable. Bernini was responsible for the design of the great piazza, with, at its outer end, two vast colonnades forming a broken circle. Work on the piazza ended finally in 1667.

Numerous problems faced Bernini when he was designing this square, recognized as a masterpiece of its kind. Maderno's much-criticized façade of 1614 had to be integrated with it. Then the center of the square had already been fixed by the obelisk commissioned by Sixtus V and erected by Fontana after a great deal of thought in 1585. Bernini's colonnades reach out like arms to embrace and guide the hordes of pilgrims as they approach—not the most beautiful, but without doubt the most impressive and biggest church in all Christendom. When one is flying over Rome, the sight of this vast architectonic monument is unforgettable: composed essentially of two squares, it forms a sort of vast pair of pincers, which almost force the visitor on, between its solemn arms, preparing him for the splendid interior of the basilica itself.

The Baroque was the art of Catholic countries; the style of the revitalized Church of the Counter Reformation. Secular Baroque architecture was, so to speak, symptomatic of worldly absolutism. It was an art form worthy of great monarchs. Indeed, the sheer cost of Baroque edifices often imposed an intolerable burden on the finances of lesser sovereigns. The Rococo, which one might describe as one variant of the last stage of Baroque, preferred smaller, prettier forms, and was thus—at least as far as size was concerned—more accessible to monarchs and aristocrats of modest resources; it was also more suited to the requirements of the bourgeoisie, the member families of which reflected on a lesser scale the same absolutist sensitivity and way of thinking.

The new word in artistic circles, "Rococo," was an amusing and alto-

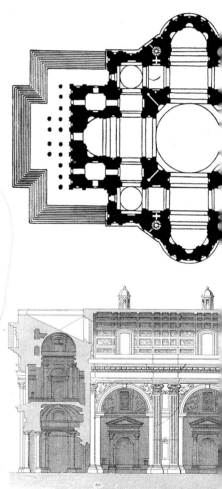

Right: *St Peter's. Longitudinal section, showing clearly the construction of the dome and the barrel vaulting. To the left is the entrance portico.*
Above: *Michelangelo's design for St Peter's, 1547, borrowing from that of Bramante. This design was altered in the seventeenth century, the main entrance being set farther out, to achieve greater space inside.*

gether appropriate bastardization of the French *rocaille* ("rock-work"), a common ornamental motif which appears in various forms in both stucco and painted decorative work. Hence Rococo is above all an interior style.

The exponents of the new style worked along the lines of Baroque architecture, but on a reduced scale. Building plans often only consisted of ovals, with flat, elliptic, three-centered basket-handle vaults for roofing. The curvilinear forms of Rococo buildings seem more ornamental than structural. Domes often appear to be there purely for show— decorative metal and plaster nets (*Rabitz*) hiding the roof beams.

Just as the early Renaissance was Italian, so Rococo was French. The French do not often use the word,

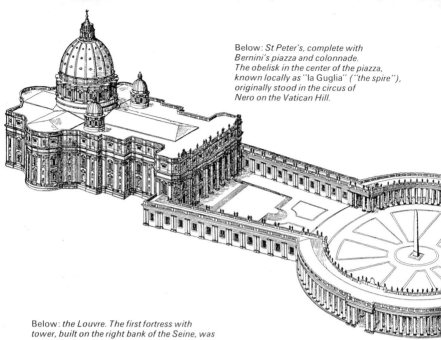

Below: *St Peter's, complete with Bernini's piazza and colonnade. The obelisk in the center of the piazza, known locally as "la Guglia" ("the spire"), originally stood in the circus of Nero on the Vatican Hill.*

Below: *the Louvre. The first fortress with tower, built on the right bank of the Seine, was that of Philip II Augustus in the thirteenth century. Charles V (1338–80) then demolished this to make way for a proper royal residence. Subsequently the court moved down to the Loire valley.*
In 1527, however, François I returned to the Louvre, and in 1546 commissioned Pierre Lescot and Jean Goujon to adapt the existing building (the tower was removed) and build a new palace. In the seventeenth century the work continued under the direction of Jacques Lemercier. The elevation shown here was designed and constructed in Louis XIV's reign. Louis had invited Bernini to Paris, but then had soon started to disagree with him. At this point Claude Perrault drew up a

Neoclassical (Palladian) design, which was realized between 1667 and 1674. The dominant feature of this elevation is the sixteen pairs of Corinthian columns. The center section lends subtle emphasis to the horizontal dynamic of the two wings. During the French Revolution, the treasures of the Louvre were declared national property, and the museum was opened to the public.

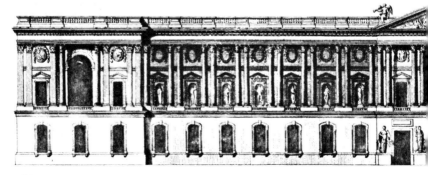

Right: *the church of SS. Martina e Luca,*
built on the foundations of an
old Roman building in the Forum.
The work of a contemporary
of Borromini, Pietro da Cortona.

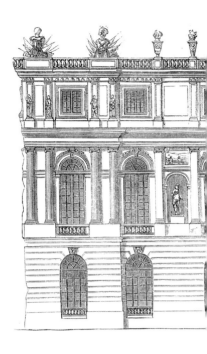

Above: *detail of the façade of the Château de Versailles, built in 1668 under Louis XIV, in a park where previously there had only been a little hunting lodge. Initially François and Louis Le Vau were the architects; however, in 1676 Jules-Hardouin Mansart took over.*

Two buildings by Sansovino, in Venice. Top: *façade of San Giorgio dei Greci (1532);* above: *side elevation of the Biblioteca Marciana (1553).*

Opposite, right: *the Benedictine monastery of Melk, on the Danube. The abbey is perched on a precipitous granite cliff, dominating both town and river. The Tyrolean Jakob Prandtauer was the architect. Begun in 1702, work was completed ten years later. Along with Fischer von Erlach, Prandtauer is considered one of the most important architects of Danubian Baroque. Melk is rightly famous not only for its magnificent position, but also for its wonderfully light, lofty interior, and the effortlessly graceful exuberance of its main façade—as seen here, with its twin towers and high dome set back behind them.*

however. They like to be more precise. Their Rococo is divided into three separate stages: *Régence*, that is the period of the regency of Philippe d'Orléans (1715–23); the short, brilliant period of Louis Quinze, so-called after king Louis XV; and the later phase of Louis Seize, after King Louis XVI, the grandson and successor of Louis XV (although this last style is already becoming Neoclassical). The career of Louis XVI fits ill into the carefree framework of the Rococo. Without any outstanding talent, he yet recognized his predecessors' mistakes and was ready to approve reforms for the benefit of his people. All to no avail, however. He died under the guillotine in 1793.

German Rococo affected the outsides of buildings more than its French parent. The façades of buildings constructed in the new manner in Germany often have delicate, slender lines and are free of oppressively heavy sculptural elements; the decoration tends to be in fine stucco. The little châteaux in the Nymphenburger Park in Munich and at Sanssouci in Potsdam (the residence of Frederick II) are examples among many of the exquisite beauty of this style. German patrons often invited in architects from France or Italy, although native German architects were by no means inferior to their foreign colleagues.

Southern German and Austrian churches are proof that even a style like the Rococo, for all its profane joyousness and openness to life, and despite the often exceedingly "worldly" poses of its innumerable little putti can still in its own way be solemn and render glorious praise in the clearest of accents.

NEOCLASSICISM

There is much controversy over the extent to which, and the date at which, the first period of English Neoclassicism (in the seventeenth century) began to exert an influence on the Continent. Germany was in the throes of war at the time, and absolutism held sway in France. Contact with England was either nonexistent or very rare. Italy was in the process of losing its position as torchbearer of European civilization and culture, resting on the laurels of its great past.

In 1600 a young Englishman called Inigo Jones (1573–1652) visited northern Italy, bringing back with him on his return numerous sketches made on his trip and a copy of *Architettura* by Andrea Palladio—the great late-Renaissance architect, who had perhaps studied Vitruvius in more depth than any of his peers. To Palladio (1508–80) history must give credit for the so-called "colossal order"—columns or pilasters rising several stories high, with an enlargement either of the base up to the level of the whole of the first floor, or of the bearing block.

At the same time as Inigo Jones, yet quite independently, a young German architect, Elias Holl from Augsburg (1573–1646), also went to Italy to study Palladian architecture. In 1602, having been appointed principal town architect of Augsburg, Holl built his masterpiece, the *Zeughaus* (arsenal); ten years later he produced the boldly designed town hall, the façade of which has characteristically clean, severe lines—a not unoriginal adaptation of designs he had seen in Italy. These two buildings are among the most beautiful examples of Renaissance architecture in Germany.

Palladio's influence on Inigo Jones was altogether different. Through his work, Jones managed to anticipate certain elements of design that appeared elsewhere in Europe only after the Baroque and the last, delicate, airy phase of Baroque: Rococo.

Comparison of Jones's masterpiece, the Queen's House at Greenwich (begun in 1616), with English buildings constructed a hundred and fifty years later will reveal only variations of style, not of basic conception. Inigo Jones put an end to the confusion of styles that had typified the Tudor period; yet English Neoclassicism does not, properly speaking, begin with him, although he was the supreme model of the style.

England in the first half of the seventeenth century was not sufficiently trouble free to devote its energies to building—to "translating Palladio into English." Charles I, grandson of Mary Queen of Scots, had appalled his subjects (both Scottish and English) by his decision to govern alone, without Parlia-

ment. It was an impossible ambition: any such policy was totally unrealistic. After a few decisive victories against the Royalist troops, Oliver Cromwell proclaimed a republic. In 1649 Charles was beheaded. Cromwell's republic failed largely because of the Puritans' inability to sort out internal political problems. The Stuarts returned, only to show that they had not learnt a great deal in the interim. London was struck by the Great Plague in 1665, then in 1666 by the Great Fire. Only when the Dutch William of Orange and his Stuart wife Mary ascended the throne together did times start to improve in Britain. During the great period of the eighteenth century she began consolidating her overseas territories (India, Canada and Australia) and establishing bases and trading stations at strategic points on the seaways. A new age opened in England—that of enlightened rationalism. Human relations improved, and it was no longer considered that violence was the natural way of reacting to those of different beliefs.

After the destruction of London by the Great Fire, Christopher Wren (1632–1723) achieved the prodigious feat of building some fifty new churches, the most notable being St Paul's Cathedral. The dome of this magnificent

Above: the Queen's House, Greenwich. The earliest Neoclassical building in England, designed by Inigo Jones in 1616.

Right: Aston Hall, Warwickshire, built by John Thorpe around 1630, in the Elizabethan style.

structure is generally agreed to be fault-less; however, like the Hôtel des Invalides in Paris (1706) the actual body of the building seems as it were to hestitate midway between Baroque and "Palladian Neoclassicism."

Neither of these buildings is in the end as successful as the brilliantly inventive Karlskirche in Vienna, built in 1739 by Fischer von Erlach (both father and son), or Georg Bahr's Frauenkirche in Dresden (1743).

German and Austrian architects were still not yet interested in Neoclassicism, the advent of which occurred only towards the end of the century. Then, however, the transformation was rapid and far-reaching.

In 1791 there appeared the Brandenburg Gate, designed by Carl Gotthard Langhans (1732–1808), which became the symbol of Berlin; built with Doric columns, it has five gateways, extending out from the center in carefully balanced proportion.

Neoclassicism might be said to have begun on the Continent in the last quarter of the eighteenth century. In France there was revolution. Now, according to a later Russian opinion, a revolution is "the sudden collapse, within a few years, of centuries-old institutions that appear so solid and impossible to budge that even the most courageous reformers dare not attack them in their writings. Revolution means the collapse or disintegration of everything that previously constituted the very substance of a nation's social, religious, political, and economic life." Compared with the situation in France, Germany was relatively stable at the end of the eighteenth century. At any rate, far less bloodshed occurred. The Seven Years War had been concluded. Resistance had grown up against the petty princes who, wishing to emulate the Sun King, squandered the money they raised in taxes and then, when the coffers were empty, sent out recruiting officers to enlist young men—either by persuasion or force—into military service, only to sell them off in whole companies. In his play *Kabale und Liebe*, Schiller has an old

Below: *St Paul's Cathedral, the most important of Sir Christopher Wren's numerous London churches. The left-hand section of this drawing is a transversal cutaway view, showing the sloping colonnaded gallery on which the interior dome rests. Rising above this inner dome is a protective brick cone, which in turn supports the wooden scaffolding bearing up the exterior dome. Surmounting the whole structure is a double lantern. The top of the cross stands about 345 feet (105 m.) above the ground.* Right: *Bath, the baths, with colonnaded wings. Walter Ison, c. 1740.*

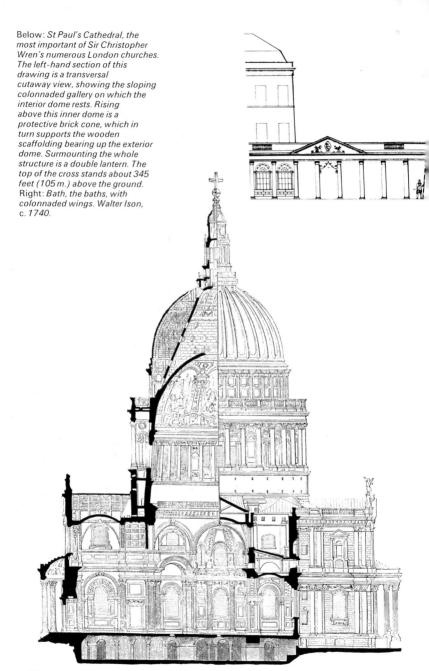

servant tell his mistress about the young men of their own land shipped out to America.

During this period, new ideas came not from politics but from literature. The new school of poetry was soon known as *Sturm und Drang* ("storm and stress"). This was the title of a play written in 1776 by a young "hothead," Friedrich Maximilian Klinger (1752–1831), who, it should be said, did not end his adventurous life with quite as much of a bang as he had begun it. He became an officer and served under various commanders, finishing his career as a general and head of the Russian cadet corps.

Sturm und Drang marked the beginning of Romanticism, a cultural, spiritual, literary and artistic movement that accompanied classicism and led it, through "Gothick," to historicism.

Classicism is referred to in Goethe's *Von deutscher Baukunst* ("German Architecture"). In fact Goethe did not use the term to describe the new movement, and what he thought of it was undoubtedly affected by the startling impression Strasbourg Cathedral had made on him.

He was not at first impressed with Neoclassicism. His youthful *Sturm und Drang* enthusiasms had taken him far back in time; he wrote fiery, passionate verses and sentences in which he flew back down the ages to the very beginning, when a house was a house, with four solidly built walls, not columns and fancy masonry. He disliked the idea that sections of temples should now be used in the construction of middle-class dwellings. He had too great a respect for antiquity to watch it being profaned with equanimity. Aware of the profound changes that were taking place during his lifetime (and to which he was contributing), he must have realized that the rediscovery of classical models was not a starting point for new ideas and new goals, but was itself the consequence of a new understanding of the world and of an urgent inner need to do away with the preciousness of Baroque gone to seed. *Sturm und Drang* is the perfect description for the new poetic impulse of the time.

What Goethe objected to, and what later critics of Neoclassicism were to point out, was mainly that the exponents of this style had adopted the formal idiom of a noble, long-past age, and that it was unseemly that classical designs intended to represent the sublime should be used for buildings that were far humbler than, say, a temple to Zeus.

The front door of a modest suburban house would be graced with a miniature Doric, Ionic or Corinthian porch, through which would pass not priests or believers rapt in mystical fervour but vulgar members of the petty bourgeoisie. The essential difference was that classical styles were not concerned with the dimensions of the building in which individuals lived from day to day, whereas Neoclassicism

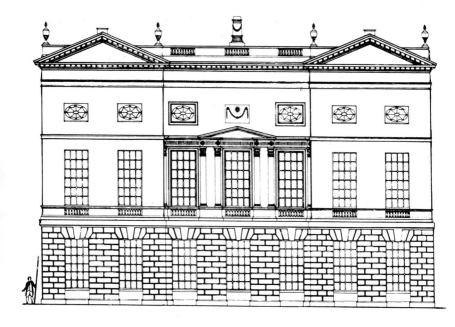

was—and, moreover, with a view to personal aggrandizement.

The best German Neoclassical architect (and painter) was Karl Friedrich Schinkel (1781–1841), from Neuruppin. A pupil at the Berlin Academy of Architecture, he was taught by Friedrich Gilly, one of the great theorists of Neoclassicism (though none of his buildings—of which there were never many—survives). Schinkel visited France and Italy in his youth; in 1815 he was appointed senior architectural advisor to the king of Prussia. A proud, reserved man, he had a fine sensitivity to form and an excellent feeling for proportion. His favourite order was the Doric, which he used in all kinds of building, from the Königswache in Berlin (1818) to the Charlottenhof in the country outside Potsdam (1826). Of his numerous works it is worth citing the Schauspielhaus (1821), which has a Doric portico, and the Altes Museum (1828), both in Berlin; and the Nikolaikirche in Potsdam (1837). His projects included a new royal

castle on the Acropolis in Athens, a *Schloss* called Orianda, in the Crimea, for the empress of Russia, and churches in various styles—Romanesque, Byzantine and Gothic.

Already the historicism of the second half of the century had emerged. However, in Schinkel's buildings what was later to run riot in florid superabundance was still contained within very precise limits. He was not concerned with ostentation and opulent display, but with his own brand of calm, measured solemnity. He was an aesthete, a Prussian Greek, in an age when all formality had to be borrowed from old traditions, in which he could express himself only through the forms and dimensions of the past, adapting them with masterly skill to new needs.

When still Crown Prince, Ludwig I of Bavaria decided to build a classical-style forum on the west side of Munich, where he lived. The result was one of the most superb examples of what happens when Greek and Hellenistic architectural con-

Opposite: *the Guildhall, Bath, by Thomas Baldwin (1740). Like the baths and colonnades on the previous page, this building was part of the overall "town planning" of Bath directed by John Wood the Younger.*

Below: *Schinkel's design for the Altes Museum in Berlin, with colonnaded atrium along the entire breadth of the building, giving on to the Lustgarten.*
In the foreground is the river Spree's Kupfergraben canal. Today the Lustgarten is called Marx-Engels-Platz. The royal residence used to stand in front of the Museum, until it was demolished after the Second World War.

cepts are applied under northern skies. Leo von Klenze (1784–1864) built the west gate of the square (named the Propylaea after its model on the Acropolis) using Doric columns, and the museum on the south side (i.e. the Glyptothek) in a Hellenistic-Ionic style. The museum on the north side was designed by George Friedrich Ziebland (1800–73) with a raised portico, incorporating eight Corinthian columns. To the east lay the city, extending up to the square as the royal patron and his architect had envisaged. Thus the forum of this "Athens on the banks of the Isar" also included an urban element— although under Hitler this was spoilt by administrative buildings and so-called "temples of honour" (demolished in 1946).

Despite its promising beginnings, Neoclassicism declined in the Biedermeier period, to be replaced by historicism, which over almost half a century produced nothing but "sugar-icing castles." In retrospect one understands why the various short phases of Neoclassicism went by different names in different countries.

In England the style of Inigo Jones is known as English Classic, while Neoclassicism proper (i.e. the second period of Neoclassicism in Britain, *c.*1730–1850) was termed Classical Revival. In France the first phase is known as Directoire (1795–1805), referring to the Revolutionary government of the same name. The next phase is called Empire, after the Napoleonic empire (up to 1814). This style continued after the end of the Napoleonic era for some decades, but towards the middle of the century was replaced by historicism.

Above: *neo-Gothic house on the outskirts of London (1873).*
Below: *Munich's old central station, built by Bürklein in 1873.*
This attractive building was several times modified and
enlarged. After suffering considerable damage in
the Second World War, however, it was finally replaced by a new one.

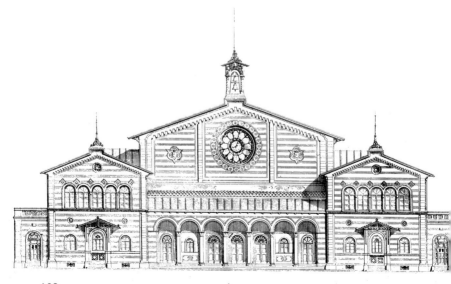

Neoclassicism underwent the same fate meanwhile in Germany. Historicism had indeed already been latent in Schinkel, who felt that to be able to build in any style one chose was an ideal state of affairs, offering the architect a freedom of choice such as had never before been available. Yet what was the result? A sort of technically irreproachable mud, with which any building could be rendered "grandiose"—churches, castles, town halls, stations and hotels.

The German name "Biedermeier" is applied to Neoclassicism when reduced to middle-class domestic proportions. In 1848, Viktor von Scheffel created two archetypal petty bourgeois characters called Biedermann and Bummelmaier for the satirical magazine *Fliegende Blätter*. These two names soon led to the portmanteau word "Biedermeier" for someone "proper," slightly fat and generally well pleased with life, seeing the world always through rose-tinted spectacles, whatever it might really be like.

Neoclassicism had now come to express reserve and modesty; yet in its modesty it was too noble for the brash entrepreneurs of the late nineteenth century and the *belle époque*, the founders of huge commercial and industrial businesses. It was as if critics had foreseen this development of ever greater concern for ostentation; and if artists ran out of new, original ideas, old ones should be revived, regardless of period— the more the merrier. Thus Egyptian, Byzantine, Romanesque, Gothic and so forth were all combined and fused. The age of historicism saw an uncompromising jumbling of everything that had ever been thought good and precious.

All great cities have examples of late nineteenth-century monuments—built, in a somewhat random way, on a characteristically huge scale. A long Doric colonnade, forming a public promenade, overshadowed by a vast statue of a woman called "*Bavaria*," crowns the grassy Theresienhöhe in Munich. Every October a farm market is held there, at the same time as the famous beer festival. This is just one example—by no means completely insignificant or tasteless—of architecture from the great period of "idea-lessness." There is worse: neo-Gothic country houses on hilltops; a so-called Crystal Palace in London; a neo-Baroque cathedral in Berlin decorated in a supremely competent way (at least from the point of view of technique) in some ten or so different styles; Pantheon-type domes on parallel-epipedal bases; and opera houses like wedding cakes, where the spectacle starts at the exterior façade, to develop with pompous solemnity into the foyer and corridors, until it reaches the royal box—only to become brusquely less theatrical as the tiers of seats rise to the gods. During this period theaters were known as temples of the Muses. Alas, poor Muses!

At a technical level this was all good and even quite acceptable. But technical expertise led to facile cheating: plaster corbels hung from stuccoed-over iron supports, pretending they could bear any weight in the world.

However, a new material, suitable for certain architectonic elements, had appeared on the scene: cast iron. Cast iron could do everything, and, what is more, on a mass scale—Corinthian capitals, Islamic-style window grilles, Gothic window tracery, and so on and so forth.

Paris, the city of lights, wanted a tower higher than any yet built. An engineer, Alexandre Eiffel, obliged—with an iron tower rising about 980 feet (299 m.) above the city. It is perhaps not exactly beautiful, as some would have us believe, but it is at least one of the few truly honest monuments—truly worthy of being called a monument—of the historicist age.

ART NOUVEAU

Towards the end of the nineteenth century, a new movement was making itself felt. The creators of this fresh spirit were painters, book illustrators and craftsmen. No exact birthplace for the movement can be pinpointed—perhaps it was Germany, perhaps England, perhaps France. Artists in various countries retreated to the country, away from the stucco and plush of the metropolises, which they found ennervating and stifling. Groups of artists here and there founded periodicals and reviews: in France the *Revue Blanche* (1891); in Britain *The Studio* (1893) and *The Yellow Book* (1894); in Germany *Die Jugend* (1895). No new style had yet been promulgated, but there was general condemnation of the current vogue of historicism, which threatened all that was new—and, as if of itself, the "new" emerged.

The painter Cuno Amiet (1868–1961), from Solothurn, visited the Breton artists' colony at Pont-Aven in 1893. "Everything was new," he wrote, "there were people, animals, trees, houses, and strange colours all with a luminosity I had never seen before, and lines linking bodies and surroundings in the most curious way."

The new style first appeared in painting and graphic art, in decorative border motifs and book printing, then spread to furniture, crockery, vases, staircases and finally, after a certain amount of hesitation, the façades of buildings. The basic characteristic feature of the style is the curve—rising upwards to the left, apparently trying to turn right, continuing for a moment in its leftward movement, then eventually succumbing to the impulse to swing back to the right.

This curve has something plant-like about it. It is slightly strange, full of tension and a sort of ecstatic sensuality—and, like any "ecstatic" experience, there is also something fleeting and ephemeral about it. Indeed, as a fashion in art it lasted less than twenty years, roughly from 1890 to 1905. In Germany it was called *Jugendstil* ("Youth Style") after the title of the Munich periodical; in England it was referred to as New Style; in France as *art nouveau* or *cloisonnisme* (a word invented at Pont-Aven: *cloison* means "partition," and the Pont-Aven artists felt they had partitioned themselves off from conventional artistic tradition); and in Italy as *Liberty*, after the shop in London, which imported goods manufactured in the new style.

The Austrian equivalent of the French *cloisonnisme*, indicating the same feeling of rupture with the past, was *Sezession* ("Secession"). This word was adopted in Vienna in 1897.

Art Nouveau featured mainly in painting, graphic art and quality craftsmanship, and was the product of many different developments. Partly a reaction against the stuffy, heavy-handed lavishness of contemporary decorative taste, it was also an exaltation of nature; imbued with a certain ingenuous sensuality, it was at times itself a trifle oppressive; and

Front of the Elvira Studio, Munich: a weird dragon-like composition designed by August Endell, realized in 1898 in reddish gold, glittering stucco on a green background. The building was demolished in 1936, under the Nazis, as it did not "fit in with the image of the street."

it also undeniably contained more than a pinch of ultra-sophisticated perversity— which is perhaps why the urban *grande bourgeoisie* had some reservations about accepting it in a context of general décor. Many artists, especially the most prominent among them, had highly dubious reputations.

It was not widely used in architecture, as there was hardly time for it to become established. Notable examples of the style include certain theater foyers, for instance the Münchner Schauspielhaus, stair wells, doors and doorways, and garden gates. There was indeed quite a

number of Art Nouveau façades, but the few that survive have on the whole been ruined by alterations and renovations. One of the most original, that of the Elvira Studio, a photographic studio in Munich (1897–98), was knocked down by Nazi town planners in 1936. The most remarkable examples of the style are to be found in Barcelona. Their architect, Antoni Gaudí (1852–1926), started his career as a convinced historicist, building in neo-Gothic style; but around the middle of his life he was brought, by purely functional considerations, to a style that in fact goes far beyond Art Nouveau, resembling in some respects aspects of present-day design.

At the age of thirty-one he designed a neo-Gothic church in one of the Barcelona suburbs. He was to work on this building until he died (absorbed in thought, he was tragically run down by a tram). Only part of the Templo Expiatorio de la Sagrada Familia had been com-

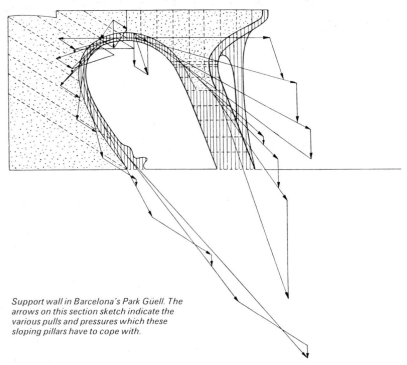

Support wall in Barcelona's Park Güell. The arrows on this section sketch indicate the various pulls and pressures which these sloping pillars have to cope with.

pleted at the time of this accident. However, from this single section—a main entrance with four spires, facing east, and a partial, soaring wall to the north—one gains some idea of the scale of the nave in Gaudí's own imagination. The basic inspiration and stylistic idiom are Gothic, but in the details historicism is abandoned in favour of totally original structural ideas, quite un-Gothic in feel. The pointed arch (the curve of which is essentially still only part of a circle) is replaced by hyperbolas and parabolas, curves stretching to infinity, dissolving into straight lines. These curves are at once more incisive, more free-flowing and more tense than straight lines formed out of the curve of a circle.

These new shapes of arch were based on new structural concepts, which Gaudí also incorporated on a smaller scale in buildings designed for Count Eusebio Güell. Like the Sagrada Familia, Park Güell (a planned garden city in the north of Barcelona) is only partially completed. It might be described as the brainchild of a mathematical dreamer. The static formula of an oblique pillar for a wall in Park Güell, developed from a drawing made in 1900, could equally well be a detail from Kennedy Airport in New York.

Gaudí's fervent, meditative spirit and religious piety appear in the inscriptions to the Virgin, in the austere language of Catalan, included on benches and parapets in Park Güell (although they are mostly hidden from view): "her delicate hands," "body of stars," *Si conocierais* ("would you but know her").

Opposite: the Sagrada Familia in Barcelona, seen at night. Antoni Gaudí worked on this neo-Gothic church until he died; it remains uncompleted to this day.

NEUE SACHLICHKEIT

Art Nouveau disappeared almost in its prime; in its latter stages, however, it was beginning to reflect a new awareness of the world, bringing up to the surface previously hidden aspects of the psyche and human consciousness. Art Nouveau feminists refused to wear corsets, and were generally anticonformist in dress—"secessionist" in their own way, indeed—and wished to appear open-minded, emancipated, unconstrained in their movements, and in all things absolutely natural. Men by contrast developed a certain "soft," otherworldly image, cultivating a dreamy—even sometimes somewhat droopy—look. At the same time, the style had become debased to the level of mere fashion, and its merits were neglected. It went out of vogue, just as historicism had before it.

Between the disappearance of Art Nouveau and the formation of the New Objectivity (*Neue Sachlichkeit*) movement, occurred the devastation of a world war. Art Nouveau lingered on in café architecture for a while, but in so negligible a way as to provoke no opposition. The one aspect of it worth attacking was a certain retrospective sentimentality; however, this was merely a last flickering of the flame, feeding on the past out of fear of a present inhuman bareness and a vulgar technology which had hitherto always been concealed behind terracotta, plaster or other veneers, but which had now emerged into the light of day. A building that revealed the private parts of its structure, or any of its functional elements, was felt to be naked. People were not used to such

Below: the Bauhaus in Dessau, built by Walter Gropius in 1925 (ateliers and workshops).

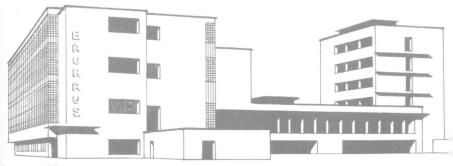

108

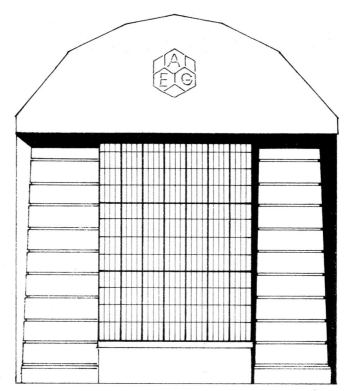

Right:
*façade of
the AEG
turbine factory
in Berlin,
by Peter
Behrens, 1909.*

sights. No one now spoke of decoration in the traditional sense: if a cornice was needed, it was made as inconspicuous as possible—a strip of tin sheet at most. No longer did one see columns, capitals, friezes, sculpted plinths or panels to fill up walls. A coat of paint was now the only form of decoration: superior houses were simply faced.

Historicism had given way to Art Nouveau, and Art Nouveau had in turn now become a thing of the past. A few ''-isms'' persisted, but only in painting, not in architecture. Otherwise there was nothing. The new patron of architects was industry. Of course, industrial buildings had appeared in the last decades of the nineteenth century, but neither those who commissioned them nor those who designed them had properly formal or artistic ambitions. Now and again work-

shops or boiler rooms were embellished with Romantic ornamental taste; there was certainly no lack of cast-iron architectonic motifs, stuck on for aesthetic effect. Yet in the final analysis these were the exception not the rule. Industrial buildings were on the whole squalid, monotonous, shapeless and uninviting. And by and large no one cared. Eventually certain more sensitive individuals began to imagine what the future would be like if things continued as they were, with ugliness spreading in the wake of lack of imagination. Very soon, they predicted, there would be a jungle of industrial structures.

An environment devoid of all beauty depresses the spirits, and this in turn destroys all those apparently insignificant things that in fact help make life more than merely a burden to be borne.

Ugliness infects everything with bitterness and joylessness, and most of those affected do not know why.

The horizon began to clear (at least in this field) already before the Great War. Isolated individuals started to become alarmed at the spreading jungle. The occasional head of a firm consulted a specialist—a proper architect—to build his factory: that is, not simply to shove up a structure of given dimensions, capable of housing a certain number of machines, with only purely practical considerations in mind, a limited budget to hand and a minimum of time in which to complete; but a building that would reflect the status of the company and the personal pride of its boss. It would have to be functional, but at the same time well proportioned, beautiful and prestigious.

The first factories built along these lines were the AEG turbine factory in Berlin (1909), designed by Peter Behrens, and the Fagus Werke at Alfeld (1910–11) by Walter Gropius and Adolf Meyer. They were hardly typical of "Wilhelmine" Germany, with its passion for hierarchy, its special brand of self-importance and its total refusal of all change.

After the war, however, these early buildings were copied, as representing the fruit of healthy architectural principles. The concepts that inspired them were simple, and in retrospect they appear so clear and illuminating that it is hard to understand why they were ever rejected. Starting again from first principles meant, above all, not forgetting the past—though this did not imply unquestioning admiration and imitation of everything from the past. It meant actually *building*, without cheating: selecting the most suitable materials, adapting form to materials and planning logically, not just according to the whim of the moment.

Two organizations made a decisive contribution to the evolution of this new attitude, the Werkbund and the Bauhaus. Among the founders of the Werkbund (an association of artists, industrialists and craftsmen formed in Munich in 1907) were Hermann Muthesius, Henry van de Velde, Theodor Fischer and Richard Riemerschmid. Theodor Heuss was appointed administrative director. The purpose of this association was to establish closer links between crafts, the arts and industry, designers, planners and workmen, on a basis of collaboration and mutual understanding, and to cultivate in the consumer (as he became known) a sensitivity to form and a disregard for sheer ostentation (on which, for the majority, good taste was based) as so much dead weight.

The Werkbund was not primarily concerned with architecture: its main sphere of interest was in the home—utensils, fittings and above all furniture.

Although it aimed to exert an influence on household life, setting itself educative goals and doing all it could to achieve them, it was bound by no rigid doctrine, was attached to no particular philosophy; its approach was liberal, and it avoided any imposition of artificial attitudes. In 1912 an Austrian Werkbund was formed along the lines of the German, and in 1913 Switzerland could boast a similar organization. Analogous trends already existed in Great Britain, one of these being a very loose association of artists and craftsmen known as the Arts and Crafts.

The German Werkbund was dissolved in 1933, to be refounded after the war in Munich and Düsseldorf. The Bauhaus was born in Weimar in 1919, when Walter Gropius (born in 1883), director of the Academy of Art and of the School of Applied Arts, decided to combine both institutions under the name "Bauhaus." His aim was to create real contact between two different areas of creative activity, to bring those who practised "pure art" closer to the artisan and thus to break down prejudices. The list of teachers at the Bauhaus gives a good idea of the level: Walter Gropius and Ludwig Mies van der Rohe (born 1886), the painters Lyonel Feininger

Opposite: *the Fagus Werke, Alfeld, built between 1910 and 1911 by Walter Gropius and Adolf Meyer.*

*Notre-Dame-du-Haut, Ronchamp
(Franche-Comté), designed and fitted out
by Le Corbusier, 1950–55.*

(1871–1956), Paul Klee (1879–1940), Wassily Kandinsky (1866–1944) and Oskar Schlemmer (1888–1943), and the sculptor Gerhard Marks (1889–1966).

In 1925 the Bauhaus moved to Dessau, into studios and workshops specially set up for it there by Gropius. Neither the school itself nor those who taught or studied there were appreciated by the Nazis, whose architecture tended to be on the one hand triumphal and tasteless and on the other lacking in true strength or dynamism. The new political party, just beginning to consolidate its forces, detected an "un-German" spirit in the school at Dessau—something dangerous, an incubation chamber of dissoluteness; and in 1933 the Bauhaus was closed down.

Most of the teachers and some of the pupils went abroad. It is rare for a new political regime to forbid a certain style of building. But this was an all-important decision for National Socialism, which had taken upon itself the task of vetting all forms of cultural expression. Anything that did not conform to its ideology was declared "degenerate."

The consequences in Germany were depressing, but the stylistic influence of the Bauhaus, despite the brevity of its existence, had spread throughout the world. A notion of "Bauhaus style" was already widespread before the Nazis closed the school. However, people very soon seemed to have forgotten all about it, and one cannot but suspect it of being "inaccessible"—as indeed was New Objectivity, which for all its clarity of design and its functionalism was never commonly appreciated.

Characteristic of Bauhaus were cubes, right angles, rationally articulated façades and a generally "pure" archi-tectonic idiom—all of which might well justify calling the style Cubist. Unfortunately, the term "Cubism," suitable as it would be, is applied exclusively to the figurative arts. Yet there is no point in desperately searching for a name, when people at the time were perfectly happy to call the style "modern" (although, of course, by the very meaning of the word, the passage of years renders it technically inappropriate).

Perhaps the expression "Bauhaus style" will return to favour; it is also perfectly possible that another name will emerge—a word or expression already familiar but not yet seen to be significant. Another problem is how long the name can survive, once created, and to what extent it is appropriate for the most recent architecture. The term "orthogonal," which is suitable for Bauhaus, is no longer applicable. For the right-angled cubic aspect of modern architecture is at the same time as it were tempered by a stylistic element that is already to be found, hidden timidly behind mosaic facings, in Park Güell in Barcelona: the hyperbola, and with it the parabola, closely related to it in the geometry of the conical section. These two curves, extending to infinity, became formative of a new style. Brasilia, New York's Kennedy Airport, Le Corbusier's chapel of Notre-Dame-du-Haut (1955) near Ronchamp, and the roofs of certain sports complexes translate them into the dimension of space with complete geometrical precision. And in a figurative sense they are well suited to an age that sends up satellites and lunar modules into space. Yet who can tell? In the future what we call "modern" may perhaps be called after one or other of these geometrical concepts.

THE PRESENT DAY

It is entertaining to try to guess what words the future may use to describe the period which we now think of as "the present." One could simply side-step the issue, as so many of us have and do, call our age (including New Objectivity, of course) "modern," and leave it at that. But this is a bit too easy—it does not exactly clarify very much. "Modern" and "present-day" always have to appear in inverted commas, since they can otherwise only refer to a constantly changing period of a few years, or at best a few decades.

Anyone with any respect for his own age will want to find some adjective either as precise as "Gothic" or as specifically restricted as "Baroque." The sceptic will be content with searching through textbooks and technical dictionaries for some appropriate "-ism," but any such word is liable to be at the very least inelegant. An "-ism" will not do. At this point the sceptic will lose interest, and maintain that one should occupy oneself in *making* the age in which one lives, or at least in following new developments and either approving or rejecting them. One need not worry about what to call one's own times. And indeed it can be argued that all great eras have acquired their labels posthumously. Thus, for instance, the architectural phenomenon of the twelfth century only became known as "Gothic" seven hundred years afterwards (incidentally giving a complete change of meaning to an already 400-year-old word). Those

periods which are given tags while still alive (Rococo, Empire, Art Nouveau and so on) are generally soon over and done with.

A tag can be, so to speak, a watchword of the times; but only later can it come to be indicative of, for instance, content and level of achievement, origins, attitudes, aims, methods and ideals.

Names of magazines illustrate this problem of nomenclature. Titles such as *Gartenlaube* ("Summerhouse") or *Ladies' Home Journal* are self-explanatory. *Vorwärts* ("Onward"), *L'Unitá* ("Unity") and *Salut les Copains* ("Hi, Mates!") give some idea of tone, but little of content or tendency. Finally, titles such as the *Manchester Guardian*, *Völkischer Beobachter* ("People's Observer") or *Bild* ("Picture") are completely uninformative: it is only through reading them and seeing for oneself what sort of "picture" of the world is presented in each case that one understands what each is concerned with.

The present age has been given various labels, some of which do have a certain descriptive interpretative value—"the Nuclear Age" or "Brutalism," for instance. Such terms are surely ephemeral. Nevertheless the latter, despite its somewhat partisan flavour, is worthy of closer examination, since it does, in its own disparaging way, express the spirit of architecture today. Clearly, though, it is most applicable to cement buildings unadorned with any plasterwork and to

Rome's main Termini station, built in 1950 by a number of architects under the direction of Leo Calini and Eugenio Montuori.

certain streets planned in a "rational" way, with avoidance of traffic congestion foremost in the designer's mind (certainly from this point of view they may often be considered highly successful), cutting brutally across the main, distinctive axes of a town. Opinion will always be divided over the problem of priorities here, and the only possible solution is a compromise. There is no possible way of satisfying everyone.

In fact almost every age has sacrificed the old to the new. The two great periods of the Renaissance and the Baroque were outstanding, not only for the amount that was built during them, but also for the amount of demolition that took place at the same time. Nineteenth-century historicism, which is so often criticized for being stuffy, dull and unimaginative, did at least inculcate a respect for architectural preservation by its very obsession with the styles of the past. Old buildings had never before been so carefully restored; and Cologne Cathedral, for instance, would probably never have been completed had it not been for that period's romantic nostalgia for the Middle Ages.

Who are the builders of the present? What are the distinctive elements of the style of our still anonymous era? Is it still in the process of development—i.e. is it still at a formative stage—or has it already produced buildings that will be admired in future ages?

The Bauhaus has not been forgotten, as was clearly demonstrated by a large exhibition on that period held in Stuttgart in 1968. Almost everything that was learnt, tried out and built during the few years between 1920 and 1933 remains valid and continues to inspire admiration, despite a certain lack of elegance in some cases. But the Bauhaus was only a beginning, and the main concerns of its exponents (standardization and production of architectural components on an industrial scale) were still in their infancy.

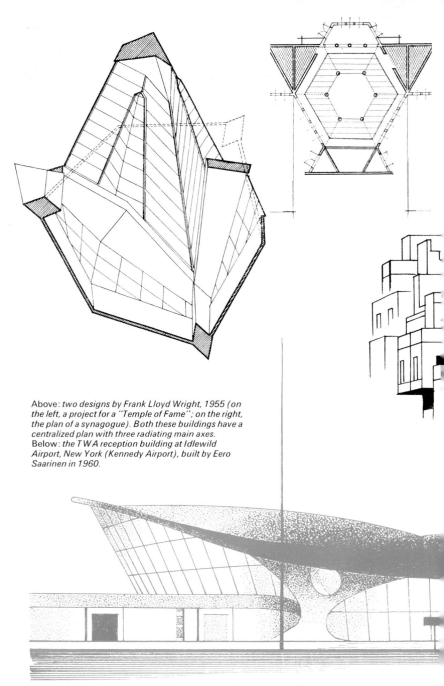

Above: *two designs by Frank Lloyd Wright, 1955 (on the left, a project for a "Temple of Fame"; on the right, the plan of a synagogue). Both these buildings have a centralized plan with three radiating main axes.*
Below: *the TWA reception building at Idlewild Airport, New York (Kennedy Airport), built by Eero Saarinen in 1960.*

Above: *design for a housing complex, using prefabricated units assembled into 158 different two- to six-room flats. Conceived by Moshe Safdie for the 1967 Montreal International Exhibition.*

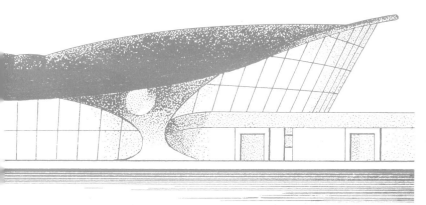

The Bauhaus is without doubt the point of departure for all present-day architectonic thinking. Cuboid units, right angles and the monotony of the typical grid-type modern façade all derive from it. (Curves then appeared, contrasting effectively with the "shoe-box" impression of plain cuboid designs, and lending this type of architecture an element of fantasy and geometric extravagance—which occasionally, it must be admitted, is not quite so functional as it would seem to want to be, yet which does relieve the uniformity of "logically" conceived walls.)

New technology then played its part, as it became necessary to put up tall buildings quickly and economically, using prefabricated components. Some apparently new techniques were in fact simply up-dated versions of old ones. Earlier on in this book mention was made of the origins of cement (cast concrete walls and vaults): now concrete was brought to a new standard of perfection, and the techniques by which it was made were vastly improved. The same went for building with frames. The principle was very old, and may be seen, for instance, in timber-framed buildings, in which—as in skyscrapers built around a steel skeleton—the actual walls have no supportive function. Nowadays wood has been replaced by specially designed iron girders that come prefabricated straight from the rolling mill; and for the wall "fillings" there is a huge variety of materials with different sound-proofing and insulating qualities. The idea of relieving walls of structural weight originated with Gothic architecture, and subsequent technical improvements have led to a high degree of sophistication. Technology is always the starting point, from which style evolves.   –

The style of the present day is not necessarily uniform, but it is always essentially a product of the same technology. The conception of outer walls as a shell or covering results from the technique of building around a structural "skeleton" made of reinforced concrete, or pre-stressed concrete with steel rods running through it, or of iron uprights and girders. The walls then "flesh out" this basic frame. Often there are no external walls at all, in the traditional sense—only fields of metal and glass.

Even when sixty or more stories high, this type of building conveys a sense of lightness and openness. The "spinal column" and all the other weight-bearing parts of the building can be concealed internally, and indeed the entire framework can be disguised behind glass and partition walls. This type of wall, developed in America, is known as a curtain wall. The prefabricated, ready-glazed sections of curtain wall (with iron or light-metal frame) are lifted by crane and hung on to the relevant concrete bars. When finished, the building is like a huge checkerboard mirror, reflecting the sky and clouds. In the evening it becomes a honeycomb of light; then, as people leave their offices, the squares of light go out one by one, producing a constant change of surface pattern. At night it rises block-like against the sky, reflecting the lights in the street at the bottom, and sporting neon advertisements (often nothing to do with the daytime business conducted therein) at the top: thus one may perhaps read a vivid exhortation to drink a certain sort of beer, or some brand name blazoned across the night.

Some people enthuse over the romance of the skyscraper and of big cities in general, without reservation. They appreciate the style of their own times and lose no sleep over what to call it— "modern" seems perfectly adequate. The large two-dimensional façades towering above the ant-like bustle of the streets are in a way reassuring by their very flatness, plain as they are: they are orderly, unambiguous and direct—considerably more ordered and unambiguous indeed than our age, for which they stand.

Some people, out of a too great respect for old buildings, find all this squalid, monotonous, mechanical and soulless. Nor do they limit their criticisms to the buildings themselves: they find it terrifying to see the same thing everywhere,

118

with only small variations due to climatic differences. The result of this "international" style, they maintain, is that a skyscraper designed and built in Stockholm would fit equally well into San Francisco, and that one modern church is very much like another. No one builds country houses any more, only bungalow-style "houses in the country," with too much of a southern look in northern countries and too many picture windows in hot countries.

On the face of it these criticisms may seem valid, and in certain cases they are; but one positive aspect of our times is that if an architect in one country finds the perfect solution to some specific architectural problem, it both becomes widely known about very quickly, through specialist journals, and serves as a stimulus to others, who take it up and modify it according to their own particular circumstances and environments. As architects acquire a reputation, so, nowadays, can they extend their influence almost as far as they please, as long as they are prepared to travel. Le Corbusier worked in France, India, Germany and the United States. In the Hansa quarter of Berlin there is a skyscraper designed by the Brazilian architect Oscar Soares Niemeyer, who also built a large building for a major publishing house in the Milan suburb of Segrate. One could cite innumerable other examples. Buildings by Gropius, Mies van der Rohe, Richard Neutra, Pier Luigi Nervi, Alvar Aalto and Eero Saarinen can be found in at least two continents.

This ease of exchange, across national borders and even over oceans, ought to be seen as a positive sign of the times, representing a world-wide language in which there is none the less still the opportunity for personal expression. New ideas come from all directions and spread in all directions. Japanese designs are taken up in California; Swedish concepts as it were migrate south. Even the Russians are looking about them, and probably no Soviet architects' collective now would dream of giving Moscow a cathedral-like university building.

This commonwealth of architectural ideas and ideals is highly encouraging— understandable as it is, given the fact that people's basic needs are the same anywhere in the world. Increasing traffic problems and population growth everywhere necessitate more careful planning and recourse to prefabrication.

The unconvinced, of course, see dangers everywhere, and are aghast at the thought that soon everything will be similar and equal. It was quite possibly somewhat the same vague feeling of horror that led first a few, then even more architects to rediscover curves and circles—the straight lines and right angles becoming in the end somewhat wearisome.

The claim that anything, or at least almost anything, could be "done" with reinforced concrete stimulated architects' imaginations; at the same time, however, it led to a certain stylistic extravagance, thus producing a kind of expressionism within Neue Sachlichkeit (although by now it was no longer exactly "new"). A work of architecture should be "expressive," have its own individuality, be unique and striking, so as to appear as little prefabricated as possible. There should be a minimum of right angles. This was the moment. After a period of extremely limited variety of shapes, such self-conscious restraint provoked a slightly too violent reaction. The familiar right angle was abandoned in favour of unusual curves—ovals and freely structured vaults and arches. A new Mannerist style seemed to be on the way: as a consequence straight lines were abolished, and no self-respecting roof would be seen to be flat. Slanting uprights, as used by Antoni Gaudí, became popular; walls became curved and roofs were like petrified waves. Opponents of the new trend described it as decadent. They were troubled at the thought of a future in which everything would be oddly slanted or crooked. As ever, opinions were divided, some bewailing the fate of architecture, others aspiring to a new Biedermeier.

Some critics actually considered the

new fashion totally ill-founded, claiming that it was not so much the result of new requirements as the product of too much "objectivity" (*Sachlichkeit*). Yet it was too soon to attempt to nip the new style in the bud. Frank Lloyd Wright's Guggenheim Museum in New York, where the visitor is obliged willy-nilly to see the paintings in a set order (displayed as they are in a spiral corridor), is perhaps one example of architecture that has in a sense gone astray. By contrast the little church designed by Le Corbusier on a hill outside Ronchamp remains "in the mainstream," despite the fact that it was an experiment. There will certainly be many other experiments, producing results very varied in quality, but it is precisely through experimentation that new, original developments occur. At the moment it is impossible to say whether or not we are steering towards a new architectural horizon.

However, the voice of the still-unconvinced continues to nag. One can no longer hope for a new—absolutely new—style. No new form of classicism will emerge now. This age is not destined to be "original," i.e. creative. Having burrowed into the bowels of the earth to dig up the heritage of all former ages, and having collated, arranged, exhibited, catalogued, interpreted and evaluated these finds, we are no longer capable of originality. We have created vast cultural treasure-houses for ourselves, becoming totally retrospective in the process. Enthralled and overawed by this heritage of treasures, the artist today is left no room for hope.

Whether such doubts are justified or not, it is certain that the present age is in a sense duty-bound to protect, restore and save, with all the technical means at its disposal, all of its past heritage that is now threatened with destruction. It was right to rebuild the Zwinger in Dresden, which was flattened by bombs in the Second World War, just as it was right to save Abu Simbel from being flooded by the Aswan Dam. Science and technology are able to cope with the problem, and financial considerations should not be allowed to take precedence. The amounts of money involved are indeed mind-boggling, but in justification of them let us make a comparison: the work at Abu Simbel cost forty million dollars; a single day of war would easily cost as much (if one can "cost" a war).

There can be no answer to the question: What will a future "present" make of our age? Will it admire or condemn us? And for what will they condemn or praise us? Trying to anticipate the answers to such questions may make one depressed or resigned, but the present author would encourage the reader to be less pessimistic. What basis has the sceptic for saying that technology and overconcern with the history of civilization and art are detrimental to creativity? And even if such is the case for a time, how can he claim that it will always be so?

Periods of great achievement alternate with periods of transition and uncertainty. But hope and questioning—a positive uncertainty, so to speak—especially of the validity of what the past has to offer, and of what is often unthinkingly accepted, can prove extremely fruitful.

NON-EUROPEAN CIVILIZATIONS

Africa

In 1897, in the lower Niger basin, a group of British explorers were attacked—by order of the Oba, the ruler of Benin—and killed, together with their African bearers. This massacre resulted in bloody reprisals. Admiral Rawson captured the city of Benin, with the royal residence, sacked the palace and the surrounding area, and sent back to London the sacred treasure of the Oba—bronze reliefs and votive heads, ivory and terracottas.

This confiscation (if so it may be termed) of the Oba's valuable possessions was meant as a humiliation of the native chief, since there was no question of real artistic appreciation of them. They were seen as artefacts from a corner of the world that could boast no history. However, even then there were specialists (and real eccentrics they must have been thought!) who considered that what are now known throughout the world as the Bronzes of Benin were indeed worthy of being exhibited in a museum. Their crude yet at the same time subtly delicate forms set them on a par with the reliefs on the church doors at Novgorod, Hildesheim and Verona (San Zeno).

On the whole the Benin treasures went unappreciated by conventional taste. It was typical of the mentality of the age to think of Black Africa—which was not

Matmata (southern Tunisia); Berber dwelling carved out of the rock. The rooms are on two levels for the most part, and receive light from a central courtyard resembling an enormous well.

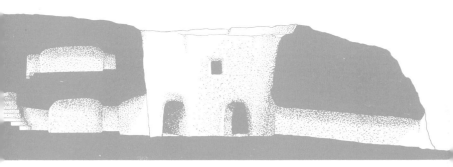

easily accessible, the other side of jungle or desert, and which was sparsely inhabited by people living an extremely simple life—as having no civilization, because it had no history. And this image was relatively friendly compared with those of savagery, cannibalism, primitivism and so forth that were also thought characteristic.

Africa was the Dark Continent, "illuminated" only along the Nile valley and the north coast by peoples who were at least partially Mediterranean. Historians for the most part concentrated exclusively on Phoenician, Greek, Roman, Early Christian and Islamic remains.

By the end of the nineteenth century the entire continent had been explored. Then, at the turn of the century, a certain change of spirit occurred. Africa, and other parts of the world that were remote from Europe both geographically and culturally, began to attract people's attention. The spirit of the age began to undergo a profound change. Aesthetes no longer believed solely in Winckelmann, with his rejection of anything nonclassical as barbaric. And the more perceptive of them began to detect a trace of artifice not only in historicism itself, but also in its very origins.

What is more, the new century was passionately fond of excavation and archaeological research, from which developed the need to interpret and understand. One vital truth emerged—not overnight, but slowly yet surely: words like archaic, barbaric, clumsy and crude may indeed be applicable to works of art and architecture at some levels, but not at that of artistic quality. Within a few decades archaeologists in Black Africa had, as in the Aegean, Egypt and Mesopotamia, managed to identify and trace back specific figurative forms of expression to early, puzzling fragments of rock paintings or arrangements of stones marking (perhaps) some ancient place of sacrifice. Some of those working in this field allowed themselves to be carried away with altogether over-ingenious interpretations. Of course not every little carving was an idol from which all kinds

A kasbah in the Draa valley, Morocco.

of conclusions could be deduced—they might simply be dolls, toys or mementoes. And when a building was bigger than and differed in shape from other buildings round about, it was not necessarily always a palace. Finally, the vast, gently sloping walls of a rock fortress in Rhodesia acquired the grandiose title "the Acropolis of Zimbabwe." Comparisons can be slightly exaggerated.

Those who discovered Zimbabwe were posed the same problems as most archaeologists when faced with a new find. The main question was who built this fortress? Many theories were advanced. The experts refused to believe that it may have been the black men living in the bush all around. All that is known for sure is that it existed before the

122

Portuguese arrived; nor was it the work of seafaring traders from Asia, since they too only appeared later on, and then confined their settlements to certain spots on the east coast. Equally puzzling for many years were the multistory dwellings in northern Africa known as kasbahs. Frequently ten or more stories high and built out of packed clay and air-dried bricks, kasbahs are common especially in the southern valleys of the Atlas mountains. These buildings gave effective protection from the heat of the sun, and could house either many separate families or one large patriarchal family; some of these "tower blocks" indeed give the impression of having been built progressively upwards in stages as the clan grew larger. The walls are extremely thick, with only a few small windows and doors, thus ensuring excellent thermal insulation. Only the more prestigious buildings have larger windows on the top floors. External decoration is either minimal or non-existent: what there is cannot really be said to constitute a style. Comparison with similar buildings in the Yemen might suggest Arab origins, except that the kasbah—developed from regular-shaped structures—already existed among the Berber tribes on the slopes and in the valleys of the Atlas mountains prior to the Arab invasion. What the Berbers *did* learn from the Arabs was how to build arches, tunnel vaults and domes—a considerable improvement on the old timber-beam roofs.

Over the centuries the kasbah has undergone various technical improve-

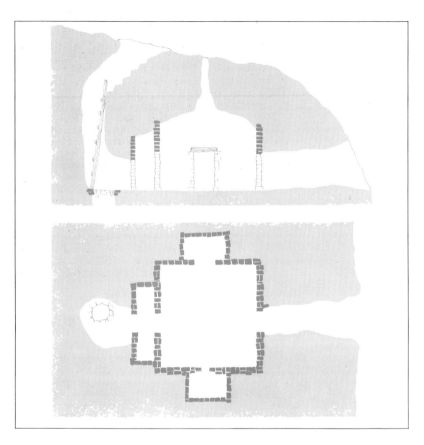

ments, especially in modern times. In its overall outline, though, it has remained as it was from the very beginning, suited to the climate, the defensive needs and the social customs of its inhabitants. Throughout the Atlas mountain range, houses continue to be built for vast clans made up of individual young family nuclei, following the same basic architectural principles that have been used for the last thousand years or more.

Not unrelated to this is the question of where in fact architecture as such first appeared. It has been hesitantly acknowledged that architecture did not begin with the Egyptian proto-Doric pillar, but much earlier, and at all events well before the first architectural drawings.

It was as in music: the earliest musical sounds had no written annotation, and later masterpieces were the culmination of centuries of steady evolution. And perhaps the most moving testimony to the spirit of our present age is the way in which bare and often uncertain simplicity produces the most profound effects both in music and in the visual arts. The elaborate and perfect now have less impact than the imperfect and perhaps unintended. This has nothing to do with romanticism or nostalgia, or disgust at the sight of tourist hotels in bucolic or historic surroundings: it is simply respect for the past. An over-keen desire for order and categorization resulted in the hasty coining and popularization of words that are neither particularly illuminating nor appropriate, such as "Hamitic" or "Ethiopian"—which were meant to be the opposite of each other, but which in practice merely mean anything not produced by the Blacks, the so-called "primitive" peoples.

From a stylistic point of view, these two words cannot properly speaking be used in opposition to each other and are worthless for any serious attempt at classification, as the actual geographic areas to which they refer are not the same. "Ethiopian" refers to a relatively small area, while "Hamitic" can apply (artistically) to anything North African

prior to the Arabs. "Berber" would be more apt than "Hamitic."

Expressions such as Black Africa and White Africa are useful for classification purposes, and are readily comprehensible, and there is no need for complicated or artificial terms to indicate regional variations within these sectors. On the whole the names of regions, large rivers and sometimes tribes suffice, together with such epithets as mountain, desert, plain, rain forest and so on. But here architecture stops. The jungle always overtakes buildings.

In Africa, just as anywhere, indigenous style is conditioned by the materials available on the spot and by the tools developed there gradually from very early on, right back in the Stone Age. Materials mean both materials for construction and colouring agents. Metals only played a secondary role in building, although metallurgical skills had already been mastered in some areas—as, for instance, in Nubia in the first century AD, in the mountains east of Lake Tanganyika and in Rhodesia slightly later, among the Berbers in the Sahara, probably from the sixth century on, and in northern Cameroon and along the course of the Niger. Metals were used almost solely for weapons, both for hunting and fighting, ornaments, and cult figures and statues.

Archaeologists are able to date their

Opposite: southern Sahara, dwelling adapted out of a cave in a hillside (of laterite), with more or less rectangular brick-lined rooms.
Below: "ghorfa" (barrel-vaulted storage chambers, built either in stone or in furnace- or sun-baked brick), Medenine, southern Tunisia. The individual chambers are disposed around a large circular courtyard which provides each with light. The entrance is now at ground level, though at one time, for defense purposes, access could only be gained by means of ladders.

finds fairly accurately. One certain fact is that the first Iron Age in Black Africa followed immediately on from the Stone Age. Oral traditions, however, throw up many problems. In most tribes, those who knew how to work metal, especially iron, belonged to a privileged caste which jealously kept the secrets of their skills within their own clan. Iron founders and smiths enjoyed a similar social position to that of the medicine man and the rainmaker. They were magicians, members of secret societies, imbued with animistic ideas and beliefs; in their hands inert matter and lifeless tools indeed became active servants, seeming to have a spirit of their own. There is some justification for assuming that the same applied to the art of building.

Black African ways of thinking were a mixture of science and soothsaying— logic and magic. The borders between disciplines were fluid. The craftsman was at once an artist, a man of science and a priest.

One of the most important building materials, other than roughly dressed stone, is mud (clayey earth or sand), especially where there was little or no wood. Clay is weathered feldspar which during the weathering process has acquired various other minerals. To become a load-bearing material, it is taken straight from the ground and made into bricks which are then left outside to bake in the sun. In the Sudan the clay is worked into adobe while still wet. It is mixed with chopped straw (reed stems), and thus stays damp longer, so that it can be shaped during the building process. Adobe buildings are not masonry structures, but are modelled; they are generally round, and often have a pointed dome.

Laterite is much used in the hottest part of Africa. This is also broken down by exposure to the elements, but is formed from eruptive schistose-crystalline rock such as gneiss or slate, usually containing iron or aluminum oxide. At the water-table level it is dry, soft and malleable, while in the open it slowly hardens.

Excellent bricks can be made out of laterite. But there was also another architectural option: not to build at all, but simply to carve out a light shaft in the solid rock, expanding outwards at the bottom into comfortable cool rooms. Such underground dwellings are still common on the northern edge of the Sahara. The colonial era affected this style of "building" very little. Problems, doubts and often lack of confidence in the traditions of the past arose whenever new—or indeed old—towns suddenly and rapidly expanded, leading people to develop false hopes of a better life; it was even worse when they were actually coerced one way or another into moving to wretched shanty suburbs. Around an old town center (aesthetically pleasing, if not always very hygienic) there would frequently emerge slums consisting of emergency housing, which in some cases was not even worthy of being called "housing." The word used for this kind of area on the outskirts of Casablanca (the commercial capital of Morocco), Rabat, Algiers and numerous other commercial centers on the coasts and uplands of Africa is *"bidonville."*

Colonial entrepreneurs were too greedy to bother about remedying the universal sprouting up of *bidonvilles*. The odd hospital or missionary settlement were far from being able to cope. Now the children and grandchildren of those who originally moved to these shanty slums no longer know how to build dwellings for themselves and their families. And even if they did, they would not be allowed to. They have to receive assistance from their new State, which came into being with the end of colonialism. Where new administrations have got over the birth pangs of recent independence, there may yet be hope. But the type of standardized hut one finds in the industrial areas of South Africa can hardly be said to solve anything. Crisscross bulldozed lanes and alleys may make for easier police rounds, but they are dehumanizing and alienating.

In Morocco, Algeria and Tunisia other systems have been adopted. European-style high-rise blocks of council flats did

Wadi Halfa, Sudan: wall of packed clay, with entrance to an inner courtyard. The ornamentation is usually white—very occasionally coloured—against a clay-brown background.

not meet with much enthusiasm from the Muslim populace, and in fact for many were still too expensive. So a number of French architects designed a cellular residential unit, varying between 230 and 290 square feet (21.4 and 26.9 sq. m.), complete with internal courtyard surrounded by walls on all sides. This corresponded well with the type of house the average small Muslim family might be used to, and could even be built on two floors. The results were excellent. But for how long will the same design remain viable? Will there again some time be a need for high-rise flats? All depends on population growth.

The economic and social changes of the first half of this century affected mountain areas particularly badly. Wherever low-cost workers' lodgings had to be erected in a short space of time, dreadful Nissen huts appeared, with tunnellike corrugated iron roofs, roasting hot during the day and streaming wet with condensation at night. But at the time no one came up with a better design. It was soon realized how unhealthy they were. Yet, of course, these fancy new sheds had come all the way from Europe—so they ought at least to be allowed time to rust.

Nevertheless, despite all foreign influence, the old building styles—adapted to the climate and the mentality of the local population—continued to be used, not necessarily even in very remote parts of the country. In some places they are actually making a comeback. Still, there is also the danger of returning to needlessly antiquated methods. At the same time elsewhere, in the vicinity of well-served airports, there is a danger of a sort of African Disneyland growing up to attract tourists.

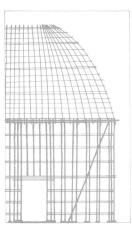

Left and below: *house of a tribal chief, Cameroon. Trelliswork of young palm trunks, about twelve feet (3.7 m.) high, with panels of woven leaves. Grass roof on a light basket frame rendered very stable by curved stretchers. Doorposts of old palm trunks worked with axes and wedges.*

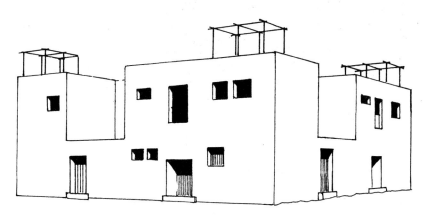

This page: *at Salé (Morocco), a solution to the problem of uncongenial modern living conditions, as conceived by the French architects Ecochard and Prost, and designed specifically for Muslim families unhappy with modern-style multistory residential blocks with no private interior courtyards. The amount of space given over to the upper-floor apartments (where the kitchen is) is restricted, though allowing easy access to the rooftop.*

Every quarter has its own hammam (bath) and souk (marketplace) in a pedestrian zone.

Opposite, below: *Lalibela (Ethiopia), cliff church dedicated to St George, patron saint of the Amhara, dating probably from the thirteenth century. The shaft in which the church sits is about forty feet (12 m.) deep, and access is via a gallery hewn out of the solid rock.*

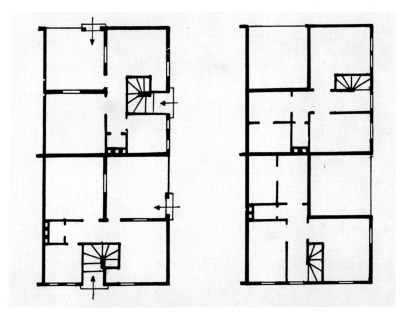

Musgu (central Sudan): courtyard surrounded by dome-shaped adobe structures (packed clay mixed with chopped straw). Separate huts for sleeping, for small livestock and for stores.

One very curious form of architecture would appear to have been abandoned, however. The cliff churches of Ethiopia cannot be said to be "built" in the normal sense: rather than one stone being laid on another, the solid rock was hewn, chipped and chiselled away, bit by bit, until finally there remained the house of God as envisaged in every detail—with cornices, pilaster strips, and window and doorframes—by the monk architects. Nothing had to be added later, not even the guttering. The "construction" process went roughly straight downwards into the bedrock of tufa, to a depth of forty to fifty feet (12–15 m.). Then, once the exterior had been delineated, the interior was carved out, through windows and doors.

But the builders did not create an interior consisting of a single large, empty space, as they well could have statically (at least up to a certain thickness of wall); they preferred to sculpt arches, domes, spandrels, lunettes and architecturally non-functional pillars, thicker at the base than at the top, giving a feeling of greater security. Once the

inside had been completed, the walls were painted with devotional pictures of the Almighty. These pictures, executed by torchlight, are intensely personal, despite certain precise conventions (for instance, saints and the elect are portrayed frontally, while the wicked appear in profile).

The oldest of these rock churches (numbering a hundred in all) probably dates from the sixth century. From their contacts with the Copts in Egypt, the Ethiopians were thoroughly familiar with early medieval ecclesiastical architecture. But they intentionally wished to be different—perhaps in emulation of Jeremiah, who, we are told, took a cave as his home, or perhaps to show that faith indeed could move mountains.

Jericho

Even the faithful may feel some doubt as to whether the walls of Jericho, the most ancient city on earth, did in fact collapse because of the divinely ordered trumpet blasts and shouts of the Children of Israel. The Book of Joshua, which contains this story, is neither revelation nor factual history, but national epic poetry, in which the complex events of three centuries are condensed, with poetic licence, into the account of the expedition led by Joshua (Moses' successor) against Canaan.

The Book of Joshua was written about five hundred years after Jericho had been reduced to ruins. Did Joshua indeed destroy the city or was an earthquake responsible? Doubts arise when the narrative describes how Joshua assigned to the twelve tribes cities that were not yet in existence at that time. It is hard to see why he should destroy everything just where he intended to settle, with his people, once the Canaanites had been driven out—in the land flowing with milk and honey promised him by God. Surprising, too, is the secondary episode (which strikes a moving note in the context of this "tale of sound and fury") in which "Joshua saved Rahab the harlot alive, and her father's household, and all that she had" in return for her having hidden his spies. It was not until the exile in Babylon (586–537 BC) that the Book of Joshua acquired its present form. At that point it was no longer possible to imagine how nomad warriors might have felt, driven by hunger across the Jordan and suddenly confronted by totally alien walls.

Archaeology can contribute to biblical exegesis, breaking up into long-term developments great events that are condensed in a few pages. Jericho shows better than sites in Mesopotamia (where the oldest ruins are buried deep in mud) that early cities were not built according to careful overall plans, but developed gradually around individual nuclei of, dwellings, becoming farming centers, then bit by bit, through social organization, centers of "civilization."

Cyclopean walls alone did not make a town or city, but they did make urban existence possible. When the first walls of Jericho were built, the area that was to become the city had already been settled for thousands of years. Radiocarbon archaeological dating systems put the

Jericho: reconstruction of a place of prayer, sixth millennium BC. Typical are the rounded corridor wall ends and the beaten floor (made of plaster baked at high temperature and then finely ground).

deepest layers of finds at around 10,000 BC (Mesolithic). A roughly rectangular patch of plaster floor with masonry around it presents something of a puzzle. It cannot have been a cistern, as the round, dish-shaped cavities in it would be pointless in a water tank. Charred wood and other traces of fire suggest that it was perhaps a place of sacrifice. Above this level of the ruins is a layer thirteen feet (4 m.) deep from a neolithic settlement. This reveals that dwellings on this site at that time were circular, with a masonry superstructure rising above a ditch, as at Khirokitia.

Only in the top quarter of the uppermost layer do the small finds start to date from the ceramic era. Not a single potsherd was discovered lower down, only thin-walled stone vessels, stones with holes bored through them, scrapers and pestles, and tools that point to a society of both hunters and primitive farmers.

The picture changes in the upper levels. Foundation walls of four-sided rooms become more common, often next to circular constructions. Graves were discovered beneath carefully flattened patches of earth. It would appear that the inhabitants of these dwellings buried their dead simply, under the floors of their houses, often in a crouched position (as in many other parts of the world).

From one layer to the next it is possible to follow—very approximately—the changing of artefacts, the changes of styles and way of life through the different cultures down the centuries. The base of an impressive defensive tower, twenty-six feet (7.9 m.) in diameter, twenty-three feet (7.0 m.) high in its present condition, and with an internal staircase, has also been unearthed.

Great building progress was made in the sixth millennium level. Typical of a certain stage of neolithic development (still in the pre-ceramic period) was a method of plastering walls and floors which, with the passage of time, produces an extremely smooth, fine-grained surface. In some instances, structures that have this form of plastering were clearly buildings of either social or religious significance. There were still no known forms of decoration, but it is worth remarking that the edges of corridor walls and doorways are carefully rounded, even in domestic dwellings. In a plastered niche in one room an upright carved cylinder of stone was discovered, the phallic shape of which leads to its frequently being interpreted as a fertility symbol. More than this, however, it can surely be taken to have been an object of special importance, from which strength, power and potency emanated, and which was approached with devotion and awe. It was probably a stone emblem—a sort of primitive stele.

The city walls—partly visible, partly hidden by banks and escarpments—enclosed an area of more than eight and a half acres (3.4 ha.), sufficient for thousands of families, at the time when the Israelites crossed over the Jordan (around 1200 BC). To judge from excavations so far, these eight and a half acres must have been very densely built up. There was little space between houses, and what space there was was too irregular to be called "street" in any proper sense.

The history of Jericho is archetypal of the emergence, flourishing and disappearance of a community over a period of many years. Its earliest days are not recorded in any form of pictographic or alphabetic writing, but the stones themselves tell of fires and floods, betray their own date of quarrying and building, and allow us to reconstruct their history of destruction or decay, restoration and new destruction—though who knows by what or at whose hands? At all events, life continued uninterrupted for ten thousand years in Jericho, the oldest city in the world. It never disappeared completely, but stubbornly lived on. At one stage merely an expanse of ruins, where odd flocks of goats grazed, it was a thriving city at the time of Herod; then it once again became a place of ruins, next door to a sleepy little town; then it became a health resort, and then finally a Palestinian camp. Today its inhabitants are unable to tell their children what State they will belong to when they grow up.

Thus the secondary, almost irrelevant story of Rahab and her household, which has come down to us in the framework of a nationalistic epic, may be seen as a sort of parable of the continuation of life even after major catastrophes.

Mesopotamia

"And Terah took Abram his son, and Lot the son of Haran his son's son, and Sarai his daughter-in-law, his son Abram's wife; and they went forth with them from Ur of the Chaldees, to go into the land of Canaan" (Genesis 11:31).

One should not begrudge archaeologists their feelings of triumph on once again striking lucky on a dig—even if they forget that it was largely thanks to guesswork that they started work in the right place. Where they feel they might find something, they proceed with extreme care, removing many feet of earth and rubble in tiny spoonfuls. The resultant piles of refuse and products of civilization—fireplace, bones, mollusc shells, potsherds, tools and utensils of every kind and description, and the odd fragments of works of art—are known as settlement rubble. What archaeologists dig up from the earth enables them to map out even cities that ceased to exist thousands of years ago, such as Ur in Mesopotamia.

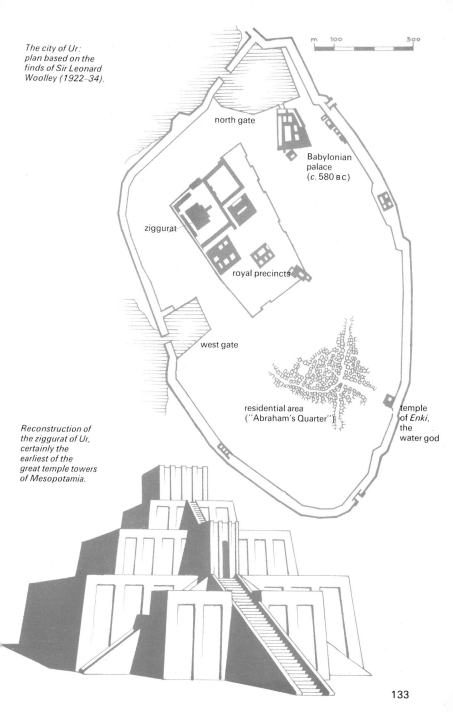

The city of Ur:
plan based on the
finds of Sir Leonard
Woolley (1922–34).

m   100   500

north gate

Babylonian
palace
(c. 580 BC)

ziggurat

royal precincts

west gate

residential area
("Abraham's Quarter")

temple
of Enki,
the
water god

Reconstruction of
the ziggurat of Ur,
certainly the
earliest of the
great temple towers
of Mesopotamia.

133

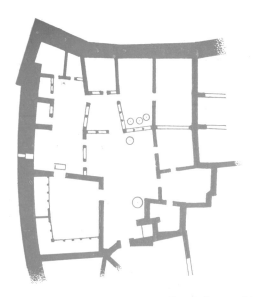

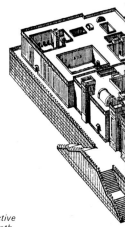

Above: *Hacilar, Anatolia; house in a village settlement, with thick protective walls. Early Bronze Age (c. 5000 BC). Spacious courtyard with rooms, both residential and for livestock and stores, around it.* Right: *Dur Sharrukin (Khorsabad) northern Mesopotamia, capital of the Assyrian king Sargon II (c. 720 BC). Reconstruction of the palace complex. Here for the first time the ziggurat, instead of having a straight staircase leading from one terrace to the next, has a continuous ramp snaking up the four sides of the structure to the sacred precincts at the top.*

Ur was discovered by the English archaeologist J. E. Taylor, who in 1854 was working in Mesopotamia for the British Museum. What first attracted his interest was a hill known in Arabic as Tell al-Muqayyar, the "Mount of Pitch."

Bitumen is asphalt formed naturally by oxidization of oil; this was what Noah used, on God's instructions, to make his ark watertight. For seventy years Taylor's successors worked on this site, with variable good fortune, the last being Sir Leonard Woolley (between 1922 and 1934). Walls of unusual thickness were discovered, enclosing two river ports and various residential areas built without any precise plan. Between the blocks of houses were well-segregated holy spots with lavish buildings, which have led some historians to deduce the existence of a highly astute priestly caste.

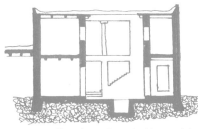

Plan of a medium-sized house of the Sumerian period, in "Abraham's Quarter" of Ur. The only external opening is the entrance.

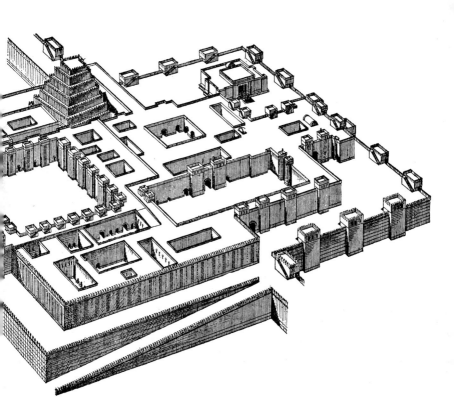

According to one theory (though who can be sure about any such theory?), the curious monuments known as ziggurats could only have been built in an extremely rigid society conceived according to the following assumptions: a divinity who (according to the priests) inhabited the clouds; a king receiving his power from this divinity; and a great army of brickmakers and porters to build a tower—panting endlessly up and down the innumerable steps, never knowing for certain whether in fact all their effort was bringing the lord who had commanded the building of this vast construction even a few inches nearer to the godhead. The slaves would never have felt that the divinity had the slightest interest in them; and those who had sweated to lay the foundations would all have been long dead by the time the tower was built.

However, the reality must have been rather different. It is perfectly reasonable to suppose that, to a certain extent at least, the work was seen as a quite natural form of tribute to the king, who communicated with the moon, not only for his own benefit, but also for that of his country and people as well, predicting eclipses and floods (though doubtless without complete accuracy).

At the time of Abraham, some four thousand years ago, the Euphrates still ran close by the magnificent city of Ur to debouch into the Gulf: and all the land round about, criss-crossed with a network of canals, was green and fertile. Ur was one of the many marvels of the Sumerian civilization. It had probably already been a royal residence for generations before King Ur-Nammu ordered the building of this ziggurat on the

*King David's palace at Jerusalem
(c. 1000 BC). Artist's impression of one of
the side elevations. Siting his capital on
the border between Judah and Israel,
David made Jerusalem the holy center of
both tribes.*

foundations of a ruined temple to the moon-god Nanna. The new structure was not exactly a tower in the modern sense of the word, but a sort of artificial hill, rising up in terraces.

"Temple Hill" might indeed be a good description of it. It is reminiscent of Egyptian step pyramids, although it is not a tomb but constitutes the outer shell of a temple, distancing the sacred precincts from the hurly-burly of life down below, and raising them closer to the god up in the clouds. It served both as place of sacrifice and as an observatory. It was smaller than the large pyramids of Egypt, and represented less of an engineering feat, since it was built of bricks rather than massive blocks of stone. These bricks in fact help us to date the building of the ziggurat.

Scholars have identified a frequently recurring pattern of symbols in the foundations as the seal of Ur-Nammu, while the bricks of the third terrace (the top one) bear that of his grandson. The height of the monument can only be guessed. The third terrace probably stood at about a hundred feet (30 m.) or more, and the actual temple itself is estimated to have been about twenty-six feet (8 m.) high. The ziggurat of Ur formed a model for later ages, which felt its extraordinary fascination. The various peoples who invaded Mesopotamia generally rebuilt what had been destroyed during the wars and also built more temple towers, fairly closely modelled on those at Ur, though some were more imposing, bolder and higher, with more than three terraces (thus departing from the "classic" Ur prototype).

Twenty-two former residences with ziggurats have come to light so far; in some there was even more than one ziggurat. Probably the largest was the vast ziggurat at Babylon, finished by Nebuchadnezzar II in around 600 BC, consisting of five terraces, with steeply sloping walls. The perimeter at the base measured 300 feet by 300 feet (91 × 91 m.), and the temple stood at a level of 230 feet (70 m.). (However, the pyramid of Cheops was more than twice as high as this.)

The basic building material was bricks baked in the sun. At regular intervals (roughly 5 ft. 6 in. – 5 ft. 9 in. or 168 – 175 cm.) the walls were covered with layers of reed matting, held in position by thick ropes of sedge running diagonally, vertically and horizontally. The purpose of these was to prevent the lower layers from slipping sideways as the building rose higher and the load on them increased. For the exterior, specially hard-baked bricks were used. This type of structure was extremely well designed, faultless from a statical point of view, and indestructible except by earthquake or systematic attack.

Unlike squared blocks of stone, bricks are easy to handle, and can be lifted without winch mechanisms or special inclined "tracks." Thus, building a ziggurat must have been rather less daunting a technical exercise than building a pyramid. Apart from the first-rate idea of the reed matting, there is little evidence of any great understanding of statics. Babylonian architects never calculated the weight resistance of a load-bearing wall. Walls were simply built thick, both for public, grand buildings and for ordinary houses. There was no shortage of mud, and no one seemed to worry about having small rooms.

During the excavations at Ur, archaeologists encountered one level that revealed the remains of a city destroyed by a fearsome natural disaster: a horrendous flood, that totally devastated this "Garden of Eden." This flood may possibly be the Old Testament Deluge. At all events, the city of Ur recovered. More recent levels were rich in finds, especially in ceramics, exquisite little sculptures and household objects, both from the palace and from ordinary homes. The same went for the other main Sumerian city-states, such as Eridu, Uruk, Lagash, and Kish, and for those cities whose original names have disappeared and which are now only known by Arab names (al Ubaid, Fara, Jemdet Nasr and so on).

The ziggurat of Ur was for Mesopotamia a symbolic monument of power, even long after Ur itself and the other ancient cities of the south had become abandoned and empty.

As the centuries passed, the Euphrates changed its course, turning ever farther south, until it finally joined the Tigris. Then everything changed. The irrigation canals dried up, and winds blew sand across a land where vegetation had now become sparse. Unable to grow enough food, the inhabitants of the area migrated. The south was now no longer worth the trouble of invading. Yet even in this semi-desert, with its occasional nomad shepherds, the old temple tower seemed to exercise a certain magic. In the sixth century AD, a Babylonian restored the decaying structure, rebuilding the top terrace and the temple, and replastering the walls.

The ziggurat should not be seen as the start of a new style, but as a citadel: high ground created artificially, with architectural elements that had evolved from the Stone Age, over two thousand years before. The area in which this process occurred stretched from Anatolia to the Persian Gulf, and within it there was constant cultural interchange between various different races. The essential features of this process of development were: an initially hesitant, but then ever more definite tendency towards rectangular shapes; symmetry in religious and other grand buildings; a certain monumental rigidity of architectonic mass; deliberately monotonous articulation of walls; broken "profile"; decorated surfaces; reliefs (hard, bare contours) on well-proportioned walls. Sumerian inlay work (little multicoloured bits of stone and bitumen) was delicate and attractive, and still showed the king feasting with friends and musicians; farmers and herdsmen also figure.

This was all long past in Assyria and

Babylon, however; there is indeed virtually no comparison with early representations of court life, and even less with the Egyptian tradition (the Pharaohs amongst their families, everyday scenes of life at court and on the building sites; scribes, craftsmen, farm labourers, servant girls and hairdressers). The Akkadian reliefs and cuneiform texts so far deciphered tell us much that is very surprising (and also much that is rather off-putting) about heroic deeds, regicides, schools, barracks and even hospitals. We also know about certain laws: the legalization of feuding and (rather a contrast, perhaps?) the protection of the weak against the powerful.

Hammurabi (1728–1686 BC) built his residence at Babylon—a four-sided palace, enclosed within walls, with the Euphrates running through it. Yet neither his own lifetime nor the might of his successors sufficed for the completion of the new ziggurat on a great heap of rubble. Babylon fell into ruin after the Hittite invasion.

The invaders came down from Assur, on the upper Tigris. They held power for many years, and rebuilt Babylon, though without altering the original ground plan. What they did introduce, however, was the fashion for decorating outer (brick) walls with coloured glazes, patterns and figurative reliefs, integrated as a continuous whole with the wall. The themes remained the same: processions, parades, bearded, well-groomed men, very occasionally a woman, no nudes, fabulous creatures—fish-men, lions with king's heads—lions with arrows sticking into them, vomiting blood, and files of dazed, impaled prisoners. No hint of *humanitas*.

The Assyrian king Sargon II (721–705 BC) founded a new residence north of Nineveh, where the city of Khorsabad stands today. Babylon was still important as a caravan crossroads, but it was not central enough for the administration of the empire. Khorsabad (anciently Dur Sharrukin, "Fort of Sargon") was essentially a copy of the royal cities of the south: crenellated

Decorative top of a column in Darius II's (c. 500 BC) audience chamber at Persepolis (northeast of Shiraz). The room was sixty-five feet (19.8 m.) high with, probably, a flat ceiling, of wooden beams supported by six stone columns on either side. The techniques of the old wooden post and beam forms of construction are here imitated in stone: a "double bull" carries the weight of the roof on its back. The distance between the bottom scroll and the beam is about twenty feet (6 m.).

towers rising from smooth walls, with behind them suites of rooms around square courtyards. One remarkable new feature was the heavy-relief stone monsters guarding entrances—winged bull-men, sculpted in such a way that sideways-on they looked like reliefs, while from the front appearing to be free-standing sculptures. (Seen from the side, these bulls somehow acquire a fifth leg.)

The temple tower of Khorsabad features one interesting innovation: instead of having flights of steps leading from one terrace to the next, there is a ramp six feet (2 m.) wide spiralling gently upwards around the outside of the tower. Totally new and surprising within the general traditional context are the columns with their "proto-Ionic" capitals, consisting of two scrolls—like slivers off a flower stem, curling up as they dry out. This most attractive decorative motif, originating in Anatolia, came to full maturity with the Greek Ionic capital.

On the 28 May 585 B C there was a total eclipse of the sun. In that year a furious war was being waged. The Median king Cyaxares had taken the Assyrian citadels of Dur Sharrukin, Nineveh and Babylon. As the light began to fade suddenly at midday, he instigated a truce, and the two sides came to a peaceful compromise which held good for several decades.

Nebuchadnezzar II completely rebuilt Babylon, with its city walls, its palaces, its temple tower and the legendary Hanging Gardens, created by a former king on a rising complex of terraces for his bride, a princess from the mountains.

Then came the Persians, who, however, did not settle in Mesopotamia. The Achaemenid Darius had his court in the uplands of southern Iran, not far from Pasargadae, where Cyrus II's capital was. Rather than a city, though, this was more like a highly fortified citadel, with palaces, treasure-houses, storehouses and army barracks.

Iran

Persepolis stood on a high, levelled plateau. Stylistically it in a way recalled Khorsabad, with its heavy-relief figures guarding the gates and its colonnaded halls, with scroll capitals—although above these scrolls were bulls or rams, as it were growing out from each other like a head of Janus, and bearing the burden of the heavy roof beams above on their one nape. Everything was on a vast scale, as can still be seen from the ruins. In fact Persepolis was never finished. After the war against Greece, which went against Persia, Susa became the center of an empire that stretched from the Nile to the Indus.

Apart from their irrigation and canal

Ctesiphon (Taq-i-Kisra), on the Tigris, southeast of Baghdad. Palace of the Sassanian kings, built in the second century A D. The height up to the keystone of the barrel vaults is a hundred feet (30 m.); the width, seventy-five feet (23 m.). This palace, with its impressive open hall, is a good example of how Hellenistic architectural principles were changed about. The blind arcading, with its irregular axes, bears no relation to the different floor levels. It is a typically Parthian building— Sassanian architecture took over that of the Parthians. The drawing below shows the building as it was before the 1888 earthquake, which brought down the right-hand wing of this elevation.

systems and their roads, architecture in Persia was pure conquerors' architecture. There was nothing Persian about it. Everything was in traditional Mesopotamian style. From the technical point of view they were superb achievements, but architecturally—that is, from a more aesthetic angle—they were heavy and monotonous: the decorative figures seem frozen in mid step; every detail, even down to folds of clothing, is sculpted and polished smooth with meticulous precision.

The few works of "lesser" art that have come down to us create a more favourable impression. Religious objects

Above: a commercial quarter of Isfahan, with clay-brick domed and barrel-vault roofs. The street and courtyard elevations are a more modest version of grander edifices.

Below: grass and reed nocturnal shelter, Iraq. This style of structure has been used since time immemorial by shepherds and fishermen in marshland areas, where reeds grow to a height of twenty feet (6 m.). The reed bundles, which thin towards the top, are planted about three feet (1 m.) deep in the ground, and then curved to form extremely stable semielliptic arches. The walls and roof covering are a mixture of grass and reeds.

and vessels in precious metals are elegant in shape and have delicate filigree work; they convey a greater sense of serenity than the reliefs, and already display something of the magic of medieval Oriental fairy tales.

Pasargadae crumbled into ruins and Persepolis was destroyed, for no reason, by Alexander (nobody had tried to defend it, so it was hardly necessary to destroy it: perhaps because the Persians had destroyed the Acropolis, everything that could be burnt at Persepolis was reduced to ashes).

None of Alexander's successors was able to hold the vast new Perso-Macedonian empire together. Architecture seemed to be the only element of continuity, wherever it was still possible to build in the East. And this was not so much due to a determined defense of tradition as to an acceptance—albeit cautious and restrained—of numerous different influences. Hellenistic, Parthian, Roman and Byzantine motifs were all taken up and reworked, with remarkable results. The Orientals learnt much from the street lined with "Corinthian" columns near the great temple to Baal in Palmyra, as also from the sanctuary at Baalbek dedicated to the Heliopolitan triad, Jupiter, Mercury and Venus. Among other things they realized that better arches could be achieved with carefully cut stones than with bricks— and furthermore that with stones no mortar was needed. Very soon arcades and domes had become integral features of Eastern architecture. The old-style well-like courtyards, by which inner rooms were given light, went out of fashion. The Parthians were the first to build the spacious, arcaded courtyards that later provided models for the caravanserai. These courtyards were both attractive for visitors and functional for traders. No longer was it necessary to stay cooped up in ill-lit rooms. Two sides of the courtyard were always in the shade.

The liking for cuboid architectonic shapes persisted, but not in the old Babylonian style. Within the basic frame-

Examples of Persian Islamic styles.
Above: *garden elevation of the Ali Qapu palace, Isfahan (c. 1600). This graceful building appears to be of stone, though in fact all the load-bearing elements are of wood.*
Below: *façade of a small mosque. The minarets and the dome are covered with glazed ceramic tiles.*

work of the traditional ideas, anonymous architects now created a new stylistic concept: the larger the building, the lighter and airier it should look. The Parthians initiated this change. The Sassanians, building according to a predetermined design, established the essential character of Islamic architecture, which spread throughout the East as rapidly as the new faith itself.

There would appear to be no Hellenistic elements in the Islamic heritage, and apart from the totally exceptional Hagia Sophia, with its dome, very few Byzantine. Islamic architecture represents the final maturity, after seven centuries, of a certain stylistic idiom and aesthetic sensibility. The *iwān*, a hall open on one side, with an extremely high ceiling, was also inherited from the Parthians. The *iwān* (modelled on the audience chamber at Ctesiphon) now features as an inviting entrance to almost all religious and civic buildings in the Middle East and North Africa, and to Islamic buildings in India. However, certain other elements were added later: the pointed arch, and the development of the round arch into horseshoe, trefoil or multifoil arches, the obligatory minaret, and the characteristic intricate (occasionally even excessive) decoration of all surfaces.

It is as though a sort of *horror vacui*, a fear of empty spaces, had made Arab architects cover all walls, floors and domes with decoration, both inside and out—using paint, coloured stucco, and multicoloured enamels and mosaics. This Middle Eastern passion for sumptuous, intricate decoration springs out of a characteristic taste for filigree and calligraphy. Beauty as delineated in Arabic and Persian literature is subtle and delicate, always perfumed, and fragile as a crystal bowl. The arabesque typifies and at the same time provides the consummate embodiment of this sense of the beautiful. The word has passed into numerous other languages, thus indicating the impact of Islamic style. Yet other factors also demonstrate that this style still lives on as a major stylistic tradition, and the recent oil wealth of the Arab states will surely lead to a further evolution. It should be stated, however, that departures from the strict tradition tend to be distinctly less colourful and elegant.

India

The Rig-Veda, the most ancient Indian work of literature (a collection of 1028 texts, including hymns and magic formulas), makes frequent reference to the hero-god Indra, also known as Puramdara, "Destroyer of Fortresses." Indra is partial to the intoxicating drink soma; he is fierce and strong as a bull, and can "rend walls as if they were old garments." Originally from the mountains in the north, according to tradition, he is a typical hero of the age of myths—at once fatherly and to be feared. Later on,

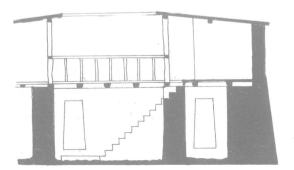

Section of a house at Mohenjo-daro. All the buildings in the (roughly square) residential areas had two floors, and the rooms were arranged around internal courtyards of varying dimensions. As an entrance, each house had at most a simple opening; there were no windows giving on to the outside.

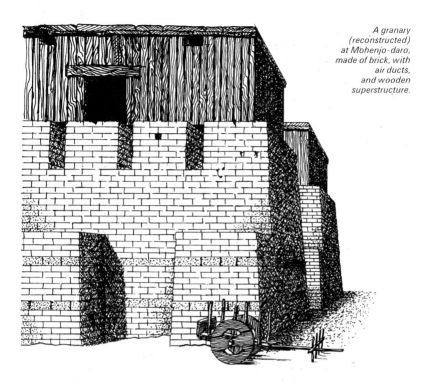

however, he lost much of his power in the face of the Brahma-Vishnu-Siva triad. These divinities also (in their visual representations) came from the mountains in the north, as did the *rishi*, the holy seers, and the *tirthankara*, the twenty-three predecessors of Mahavira and Siddharta-Gautama, the first Buddha. The lord and destroyer Siva came from the Himalayas, and from his snow-covered head issued his daughter Ganga, in the form of a river (the Ganges).

Even in the very beginnings of Indian mythology, with the despotic figure of Indra, one can see how the various myths and legends are poetic treatments of events that either fostered or threatened life. This theory was backed up by the discovery in 1921, on the right bank of the Indus, near a ruined Buddhist monastery, of a vast expanse of remains now known as Mohenjo-daro, after a modern place-name in the Pakistan district of Larkana. An early Bronze Age site, it was once an important city, built in the shelter of a hill on which there must have stood a fortified citadel.

Excavations reveal that this city was built around 2500 BC according to a precise plan, and that it experienced several disastrous floods. The final disaster in around 1500, however, was not a natural one, but was caused by outside aggression. Floods do not leave streets and houses littered with bodies—of men, women and children—with their skulls smashed. Mohenjo-daro was not captured, it was destroyed, in the same way as Harappa, about 370 miles (592 km.) up-river to the north, and probably other cities as well, now rendered inaccessible to archaeologists by a rise in the water table.

The invaders were traditionally known as Aryans. Their chief god was Indra. A

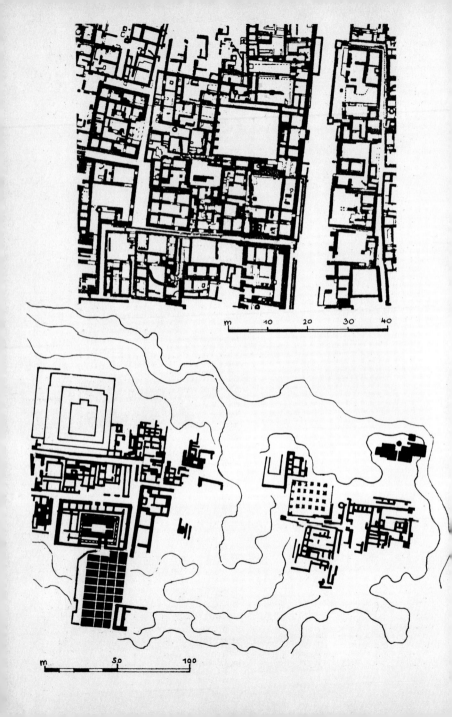

m   10   20   30   40

m   50   100

warlike people from the north, they apparently had no idea what cities were. The members of this race, or the group of tribes that constituted it, can hardly be said to have been bearers of civilization. They made up a horde of hunter-warriors, expert horsemen, who had no very clear idea of where they were going, and who brought no real civilization with them when they did finally settle in the vast territories of the south. All they had to offer was the irrepressible energy of a young people. Yet this vitality brought new life to the dark-skinned Dravidians who inhabited this rich farming country.

Two more dissimilar types whould be hard to imagine. Men of action used to wide open spaces had burst in on the bamboo huts of jungle peasant farmers like a dry, invigorating wind; however, they were unable to destroy the complex mythology of innumerable demons and divinities evolved by this race of dreamers, neither were they able to extinguish the defenseless yet highly developed agrarian culture of the Indus valley. The invaders felt they had become entangled in a labyrinth which fascinated

them and which perhaps also was a sort of intoxicant for them. Two totally alien worlds had met, and despite the violence of the impact they were to become inseparably fused.

The result was ancient India—neither a people nor a nation, but a society from which later emerged the complex hierarchical caste system. This society formed a sort of seedbed for a curious civilization which, though not acutally introduced by the Aryans, could never have come about without them. Surviving right through to the present day, it has proved impervious to the religious and political upheavals of history.

The early centuries of the integration of the two peoples saw the appearance of the Vedas—mythic poems which in translation tend to seem inflated and banal. And it was through the Upanishads ("Esoteric Doctrine"), Sanskrit philosophical and religious texts requiring close acquaintance and deep study, that the doctrine of the transmigration of souls (metempsychosis) evolved. Sciences were also developed at the same time, but being imbued with theology were reserved for the upper castes, the brahmins and Kshatriya (warriors). Those born below this social level had to content themselves with imagining the long path leading from magical formulas to rules—the magic of numbers and lines to mathematics.

The province of theology was to perceive the order of the cosmos and discover its meaning. As a symbol of this order the brahmins took the square, which, as opposed to the circle (symbolizing movement), is motionless and so to speak at rest within itself. However, describing it in these terms is only possible in retrospect. According to the legends, the square represents the magical figure (mandala) within which Brahma has imprisoned the indefinable demon who aspired to destroy both heaven and earth. To give this demon a name, Brahma had to give it a form: thus Purusha came to be, in human form. Brahma confined him in the smallest possible space, in a square, and pressed

Opposite, above: *plan of part of the inhabited center of Mohenjo-daro.*
Below: *plan of the "citadel" of Mohenjo-daro. The theory that the hill used to serve as a fortress was soon abandoned, since no remains of fortifications came to light. This was most probably the highly sophisticated economic center of the great city before the flood; the residential areas spread southeast, along the river. Covering a total of some 5000 square feet (465 sq. m.), the complex on the left is a granary; the baths (right) were made watertight with bitumen.*
The concentric squares on the far right represent the ground plan of a ruined Buddhist monastery, founded long after all urban life had ceased in the Indus valley.

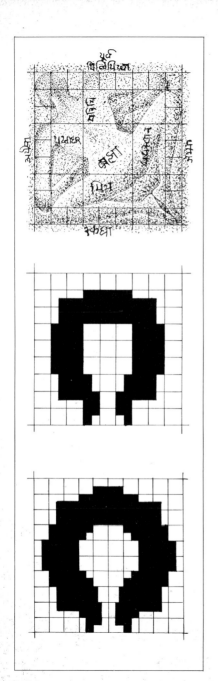

Top: *the magic diagram of Brahma, the* vāstu-purusha-mandala. *The myth of the victory of Brahma over the demon, recorded in narrative or in floor decorations, might tempt one to imagine the practice of human sacrifices in prehistoric times; however, the myth itself contradicts any such practice, since Purusha was not a man but the personification of all that threatened the good order and smooth running of the world, including, therefore, the art of building. The actual victory of Brahma disappeared as a model, leaving behind it geometry, proportion and a certain way of dividing up a surface area according to a ritual in which the sacred dung and urine of the cow and the act of ploughing a furrow assume profound significance.* Center, and bottom: *examples of basic layout designs for north Indian shrines, on surface areas of 81 × 100* pada. *The grid is abandoned for the sculptural decoration of the outside walls.*

Opposite: *the temple of Lingarāja, Bhuvaneshvara (Orissa). This complex dates from the early eleventh century.*

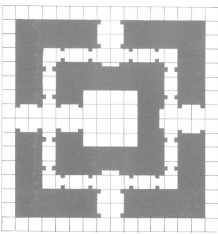

Above, right: *mandala square for a shrine with two ambulatories, one internal, the other external. Ritual processions would pass by sculptures that—from the inside working outwards—symbolized the worlds of the demons, of men, and finally of the gods.*

Opposite, above left: *system of determining the proportions of a shrine by means of significant superimposed geometrical figures, rather than the mandala. These "noble" geometric figures consisted of a circle divided into twenty-four parts of fifteen degrees each, symbolizing time, a square within the circle, and then four equilateral triangles.*

Opposite, above right: *plan of the princely quarter of Jaipur, in northern India. This town, planned in the eighteenth century, obeyed the ancient rules of the vāstu-purusha-mandala. The east–west axis, forming the main street, for ceremonies and elephants, is not very precisely constructed, but on the other hand the squares adjacent to it are perfectly accurate and regular in size. The palace itself is also well integrated with the overall scheme (see the southern and eastern sides). Variety was permitted, and indeed even prescribed,*

within the strict framework of this grid. The peculiarities of the terrain had to be borne in mind—for instance the ground falls sharply to the north-west. Right-angle crossroads were obligatory only in those areas where members of the higher castes lived. The perfect rectangle format was deemed unsuitable for the Vaisya (merchants), and totally inappropriate for the outcast Sudras. Here different rules applied. There were special streets for masons, carpenters, basket makers and so forth, and even special quarters for bicycle sellers, grocers and teachers of writing. These dictates from above did not survive long, since as always excessive legislation soon led to endless abuse.

Opposite, below: *plan of the temple city of Srirangam, in southern India.*
This complex was designed around the shrine at its center, which was enclosed within five rectangular brick walls.
The longitudinal axis is slightly irregular, orientated in the direction of the shadow cast by the midday sun. As occurs in many other temple complexes, the highest towers are those on the gates of the outermost wall. The buildings become smaller the closer they are to the sanctuary.

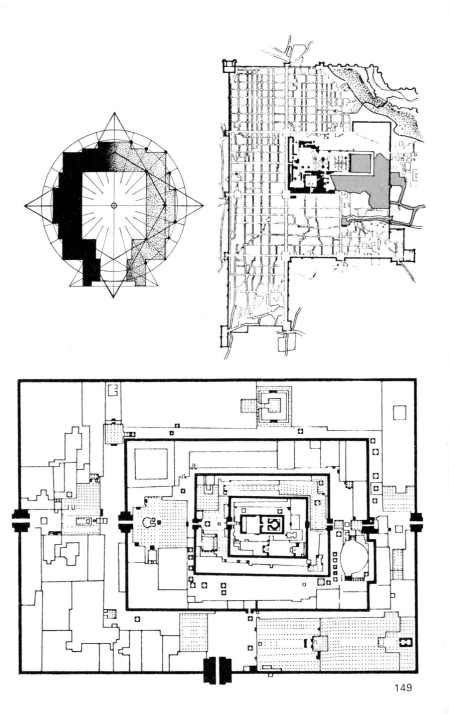

149

him to the ground, face down, his arms akimbo, and his legs drawn up so that the soles of his feet lie flat against each other. So it was that the mandala of the square came about. Perfectly containing the demon, it is in turn subdivided into smaller squares (*pada*) containing divine figures. There where threats lurked serene peace now reigns, as the demon has been identified, given a name and overcome.

Numerous folk traditions contain reference to the taboo against pronouncing names—either one's own or that of the Devil. The German fairy tale of Rumpelstiltskin, for instance, tells how the eponymous child-snatching imp declares his own name in a fit of pride, is overheard and thus reduced to impotence, able only to stamp with rage till the earth holds him fast.

This short excursus into the world of mythology is necessary for an understanding of Hindu architecture, consisting as it does of a well-defined system based on the magic diagram of Brahma, the *vāstu-purusha-mandala*. (The word *vastu* can mean either the remainder of a division with an infinite quotient, or a place on which to build.)

Hindu architecture only underwent slight changes of style over the centuries, until it came to an end in the eighteenth century. Individual changes occurred as a result of engineering progress, personal artistic talent, or the aesthetic sensitivity of patrons during happy periods of general well-being.

The design of religious buildings and the planning of towns (both allocation of surface space and construction of dwellings) were the exclusive privilege of the brahmins. The Sanskrit word *sthapati*, meaning architect, is often translated "priestly architect." However, that is not strictly what it means: a *sthapati* was not necessarily a priest (many brahmins in fact were not priests, but philosophers, historians, astrologers, mathematicians, land surveyors or poets).

The Hindu theory of architecture, the Vastu-Vidya, was kept a closely guarded secret, passed down from father to son, in ancient times. Nevertheless, from the Middle Ages on, there were works for teaching the various rules of architecture and ritual, although they were only drawings on strips of palm leaf, with scant explanations referring to a complex theory of proportions in which, in the divisions, the remainder was often more important than the result. For modern scholars and even for Indian scientists they raise more questions than they answer, especially when dealing with details of temple architecture. The main purpose of the *sthapati* was to give information about rituals, including those to be observed during the building process. But everything written on these palm-leaf manuscripts presupposes a knowledge of information passed down by word of mouth: and this oral tradition died out in the eighteenth century.

Blame for this loss of a cultural heritage can be laid at the brahmins' door, because of their esoteric attitude. Much of great value had certainly been lost. When, in the nineteenth century, philanthropically-minded colonials suggested that it might be a good thing to teach members of lower castes (such as the Sudras, or servants) to read and write, the normal answer, from brahmins and Sudras alike, would be "Why?" Nothing could bridge the gap between the two castes, at least not in this life.

Despite our only partial knowledge of the old tradition, what we do know does at least give us some notion of the basic inspiration of Hindu architecture. Up to a point, at any rate, the drawings do reveal the versatility of the *vāstu-purusha-mandala* idea: they do allow us to appreciate its inherent potential. Above all it is important to realize that the *pada* does not always have to be the same size; it could be the size of a monk's cell, a dance floor, or a whole market place. Nor does the partitioning of the mandala into *pada* necessarily produce square rooms.

Opposite: *the central courtyard of the temple of Kailasa at Ellora, Maharashtra; second half of the eighth century* A.D.

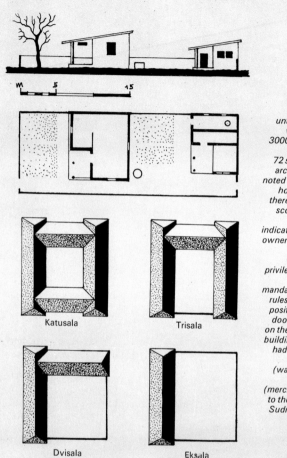

Katusala

Trisala

Dvisala

Eksala

Rectangles also occur, consisting of, for instance, 1×2 *pada*, 2×3, and so forth. The dimensions of the mandala in terms of *pada* vary considerably: thus 2×2 *pada*, 3×3, 4×4 (i.e. 4, 9, 16 *pada*), and so on. In sacred architecture the mandala is divided into at least 25 *pada*— preferably 49, 64, 81 or 100; occasionally, in large holy places, much bigger mandalas occur.

The drawings indicate that this system of squares is in fact to all intents and purposes very like the squared paper that architects and designers elsewhere find so useful, and which can of course also consist of triangles or hexagons. In Western architecture, however, the system originated in a different way: here it was more a case of the geometry being the product of the designer's mind, while the *vāstu-purusha-mandala* was pre-ordained by Brahma.

Those who went about the country preaching after the death of Siddharta-Gautama did not talk about houses or temples or the correct way of building a town, nor did they exercise their minds on whether or not sunbaked clay bricks were a worthy building material for a shrine. They had quite enough to do and preach about simply with their message of basic virtues—which surely all but complete drunkards, thieves, power-hungry warlords or for that matter brahmins find eminently acceptable.

Prince Siddharta's life was not transformed only by the three figures of human misery whom he met in his park (a decrepit old man = old age; a sick man = disease; a rotting corpse = death), although it was these that made him set off down the Ganges valley in beggar's clothing and sit under a fig tree in one of the villages beside the river meditating on human wretchedness. After seven years of reflection on the world and on those quarrelsome ascetics who wished to ennoble earthly existence by suppressing all human desires and passions, he—the Bodhisattva (i.e. "the one predestined for illumination")—"set in motion the wheel of the teaching" which, though frequently modified, was to spread irresistibly from mouth to mouth across the whole of eastern Asia. Siddharta-Gautama's original point of departure was the teaching of Brahminism, which in its degeneracy had become extraordinarily cruel, ensnaring the people in a tangle of hopes and fears about the afterlife, forcing Sudras to throw their meager food into the gutter if even the shadow of an untouchable had fallen on their fireplace.

Buddhist doctrine as preached by the first monks was extremely simple, and although it did not provide for faith in redemption of the world (in the way that Christianity affords a glimpse of the New Jerusalem), it nevertheless always showed the way to personal salvation. There was no justification for the caste system into which everyone was born: anyone, whether a king or a beggar, could convert to Buddhism. Around 480 BC, the Enlightened One at the age of eighty passed from this world to nirvana. His body was cremated according to brahmin ritual. Above the remains of the first Bodhisattva (burnt bones and teeth in white wood ash), a high, rounded tumulus was erected, as over the grave of a hero. As Buddhism spread in the course of the centuries, similar monuments were raised above the graves of innumerable Bodhisattvas, so that this type of barrow (stupa) became the symbol of Buddhism.

The shape of the stupa changed considerably and it was known by different names. The Dravidians called it *anda* ("egg"); in Sri Lanka it was known as a *dagoba*; Tibet and Nepal knew it as a *chorten*, and Japan as a *gorinto*. Finally, the most dissimilar architectural form to derive from the stupa was the pagoda, in which the original dome-shaped mound has become a circular or polygonal base-structure supporting a tower that becomes ever more slender as it rises floor by floor, yet continues to resemble the pointed peak of the stupa, which, like the shield of honour on the tombs of ancient Indian heroes, identifies the status of the dead person. The word "pagoda" was originally Malay. The Chinese for the same tower-shaped mausoleum was the monosyllabic *t'a* or *t'ing*.

From very early on, the converts to Buddhism included princes, who, as well as money to help spread the faith, also donated large areas of land, with specially erected buildings, to which the monks could retire and be sure of finding a dry bed during the rainy season if they were unable to take shelter in the natural caves left abandoned by the ascetics. Thus appeared the first Buddhist monasteries, which then quickly multiplied throughout northern and central India.

As yet there were still no set rules of community life. These were to develop from the ideal concept of a settlement of monks: sixteen to forty cells arranged in a

square, accessible from a covered ambulatory around an interior courtyard. This type of layout resembled that of a Carthusian monastery, although in fact it was not a monastery, since it was also open to members of the laity who wished to hear the preachers. The monastic life was for a long time similar to that of the Hindu ascetic, and was determined by the requirements of each individual in his pattern of meditation. Only superficially does the ground plan of the monastery relate to the brahmin system of squares. The *vāstu-purusha-mandala* had now fallen into desuetude.

Towards the end of the fourth century BC, northern India saw considerable political change. Eudemos, the Greek governor appointed by Alexander the Great, was defeated by Chandragupta, the military leader of Gandhara (in the northwest), who had succeeded in winning great prestige and authority for himself. This hero from the north was the founder of the Maurya dynasty. During his career as a conqueror he was responsible for much bloodshed; but then, when his son determined to relieve him of his power, he secretly left his own residence and set off for the Himalayas as a mendicant ascetic.

A similar inner transformation took place also in Chandragupta's grandson, Ashoka. By means of wars and treaties—broken as well as signed—he succeeded in conquering almost the whole of India. Then, after one victorious battle, he relinquished his power and retired to a monastery for two years. On leaving the monastic life, he declared Buddhism to be the State religion; at the same time, however, he avoided offending the brahmins, who were on the whole well-

From top to bottom, and left to right: *transitional stages from the stupa (barrow) and the* chorten *to the Oriental pagoda. A small stupa generally indicated a place of worship rather than itself actually being a reliquary.*

Opposite: *stupa 3 at Sanchi. The center structure dates from the first century AD, but the gateway (torana) is more recent.*

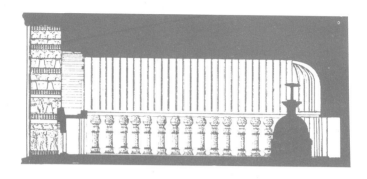

M   5   10   15

disposed towards him. The emperor-monk went about his entire realm personally preaching the new faith, had religious edicts carved on cliff walls and border pillars, promoted the building of stupas and instituted communities of ascetics, adapting natural caves as places of retreat and prayer.

Yet the faith prescribed by decree evoked little popular sympathy, even though there was a sort of police force to ensure that it was observed. As Ashoka interpreted it, it was too severe, uncompromising and austere for simple folk, whose imagination has to be stirred. After Ashoka's death (232 BC) the Mauryan empire rapidly collapsed. This was advantageous for the itinerant monks, who were now free to conduct their missionary work in the way they wanted to.

As a result of their efforts, the teachings of Buddhism became the *Mahayana*—the "Great Vehicle." Where the old doctrine, *Hinayana* ("Little Vehicle"), had been restrained and formal, the gaiety and exuberance of popular feeling now also found an outlet. Ritual processions became lively, colourful affairs. Monasteries were adorned with paintings and sculpture, and acquired their first portraits of the Bodhisattva—a male figure, cross-legged, with hands either together in his lap or raised in a significant gesture, and his face suffused with the smile of one already in bliss. His long ear lobes are a reminder of the heavy earrings that

Siddharta-Gautama wore when still invested with the riches of this world. Countless numbers of these statuette "Buddhas," as they are known in the West, were made for popular devotion.

The years following the collapse of the Mauryan empire were extremely troubled. A certain degree of stability was gained in the Gupta period (AD 320–499), but even then it was only political. Religious unity was no longer possible. Despite everything, however, architecture (mainly the great shrines of both religions) was only temporarily affected. Slowly, but unremittingly, the monks and their helpers carved out places of prayer in the cliff faces of the Waghora valley (AD 450–640). Meanwhile Hindu centers and temples began to spread around the Gulf of Bengal and at Madura (southern India). These buildings, decorated almost to excess with carvings, testify to the wealth of the upper castes, which still remained very powerful.

The Buddhist influence was on the decline during the "golden" Gupta age. This was not so much due to the sporadic persecutions as to the lack of doctrinal cohesion within the faith itself, and perhaps also to the irresistible fascination of Raja Krishna (the Black), who had commissioned the vast temple to Siva sculpted out of Mount Kailasa. (Krishna believed himself to be the earthly incarnation of Vishnu, and had no qualms about passing on his belief to his people.) Another powerful influence on the popular consciousness was the great military leader Vimala, who originated from the west coast of India. Vimala once asked a Jain monk how he might expiate his guilt for the rivers of blood he had shed. The monk told him to found a great shrine. And thus it was that the temple city on Mount Abu was built.

The Jains, who are opposed to the brahmins, draw their beliefs from Mahavira, a contemporary of Siddharta. Their tradition is rich in legends, and they have produced poetry of great beauty. Many Jain monks practise extreme asceticism, even sometimes (once they feel they

Opposite: *drawings of a prayer-hall, carved from the rock at Karli, south of Bombay; first century BC. Imitative of early Buddhist places of worship built of clay bricks, wood and bamboo. The ground plan is reminiscent of a three-aisle basilica, with the apse enlarged so as to form an ambulatory around the stupa. Very striking are the teak ribs set into the barrel vault, echoing the long-obsolete wooden roofs of ancient times. The great window over the entrance also seems to evoke the former wooden structures.*

have attained total liberation from desire) going so far as to remove their white mendicant habits, throw away their drinking cups and stretch out in the shade to "celebrate" a fast that takes them out of this life.

The holy place founded by Vimala, and almost finished by his successors, consists of three temples all roughly the same size, each essentially made up of a forest of pillars enclosed by a square wall, with a sanctuary in an inner courtyard, and a ritual dance pavilion. From an architectonic point of view, these structures are occasionally awkward and overmassive; yet the extraordinarily rich figurative carvings (mostly dancers) and ornamental motifs, which are filed rather than sculpted, make one forget the heaviness of the columns and architraves. As in many other Indian religious buildings, there is a striking contrast here between a faith which aspires to nirvana, or to rebirth at a higher social level, and the sumptuously ornate decorative style, with its mystically, often even crudely sexual carvings. This riot of beauty was doubtless intended to give human beings, while still on this earth, some intimation of the far greater beauty of the supernatural world.

There are virtually no stylistic differences between Buddhist and Hindu religious buildings. The architectonic grouping and the basic layout of the holy places reflect different attitudes towards ritual, but the fundamental inspiration in both cases is the same, and the building techniques are similar. Even from an aesthetic point of view the decisive factor of differentiation was the difference between the traditional legends in each case, rather than any purely formal artistic manner.

Hindu carvings bring out—indeed even exaggerate—a certain temperament ascribed to the various divinities and goddesses. To profane eyes these scuptures may appear obscene; however, the faithful do not see them in the same spirit: for them they merely mirror their apprehension of the most intense pleasures of a higher existence. Often these figures are caught perfectly balanced in some dance movement. Ecstasy (including erotic ecstasy) is the great theme of these carvings—not the bloodthirsty rapture of slaughter.

Compared with Hindu carving, the holy figure of the Bodhisattva is always a symbol of intimate serenity, meditation and withdrawal from the world, it instils in the viewer a desire to emulate that experience as far as possible.

Long before the disappearance of the Indian architectural and artistic traditions at the end of the eighteenth century, Buddhism had practically died out in India. This was not even a result of the great religious and cultural transformations initiated by Islam around the year 1000; it was, rather, a slow process of decline, caused neither by violence and persecution during politically turbulent periods nor by the fierce persistence of Brahminism.

Due to the vast number of exegeses of the simple, ancient teaching of Siddharta-Gautama, so many contradictory interpretations were produced that it became fragmented and ceased to have any influence other than sporadically here and there. The original revelation and impulse of faith, which could potentially have shaken up the social framework of India, out of its tendency towards paralyzing fatalism, in the event disintegrated into religious sects with increasingly little to say to each other. Isolated voices speaking up from the few monasteries still surviving evoked no response in the country at large. The *theravadin*—preachers of the old teachings—had emigrated to Southeast Asia, China and Tibet in their desire to spread their faith throughout the world. The Chinese Buddhists subsequently carried their religion to the empire of the Rising Sun and to the islands scattered about the serene wastes of the great ocean.

The internal tensions within the Indian subcontinent in the centuries immediately following the fall of the Gupta empire undoubtedly contributed to paving the way for the Arab, Iranian and Afghan invasions. These invaders plundered the

Astronomical instruments in the guise of buildings: two drawings of the Jaipur Observatory built in the reign of Sawar Jai Singh II (1699–1743). Passionately fond of astrology, the prince had had European works on mathematics and astronomy translated into Sanskrit. At his invitation, two Jesuits went to Jaipur in 1740 to reform the Islamic and Hindu calendar. A relatively small structure, some sixteen feet (5 m.) high, it serves as an enormous sundial.

country wherever they went, encountering serious resistance only rarely, generally from the Rajputs ("Sons of Princes"), who belonged to the second highest caste, that of the Kshatriya. The fortunes of war were as variable as the different temperaments and outlooks of the invaders, who saw themselves not only as conquerors for their own ends but as founders of a new Islamic state.

More buildings were destroyed than built during this troubled period; things changed, however, after the newcomers started to defeat the valiant but out-manned armies of the Rajputs. A desire for ostentation, luxury and splendour began to grow. The Afghan Muhammad Ghori (or Gord, "Hero") succeeded in breaking up the alliance of the Sons of Princes, and installed as governor his Turkish slave, Aibak, who became the first sultan of Delhi and founder of the dynasty of the "slave kings."

The columns and architraves from a

demolished Jain temple were used for the first Delhi mosque (begun in 1193); when this mosque needed to be enlarged—which was soon the case— the Muslims felt no scruples about pulling down a Hindu shrine. The same happened elsewhere, at least in the early days of the sultanates. There was no shortage of good craftsmen. The sculptors and engravers of stone, who from time immemorial had been relegated to the lower castes and associated in a sort of guild, found themselves busier than ever. They received excellent salaries and enjoyed privileges which, under the brahmins, they would never have dreamt of being allowed; they completed the work requested of them with consummate mastery, and the delicate, detailed style of decoration that had been developed by generation upon generation of artist-craftsmen was perfectly suited to the Arab taste for filigree.

Indian bands of vine tendrils and flowers made an exquisite complement to Arabic-Persian calligraphic ornamentation, with its Islamic blessings and endless repetitions of the Prophet's monogram. The general outline of Islamic architecture had already been set. The buildings erected by the "slave kings" to the glory of Allah and their own persons in the fourteenth century were characterized by *iwāns* (arcaded courtyards with pointed arches), minarets and, on civic buildings, symmetrical façades that presented a direct contrast to brahmin concepts of architecture. Mosques, palaces, citadels and even streets, canals and border fortifications all reflected the same style.

At the political level, the Turkish sultans and the Afghan leaders were more rivals than collaborators. The land they wished to rule was too huge and intractable. They were stern despots (some, of course, more so than others), with little of the missionary zeal enjoined upon them in principle by their faith. They had almost nothing with which to counter the spiritual strength of Brahminism. Thus, in isolated districts, far away form the sphere of action of the

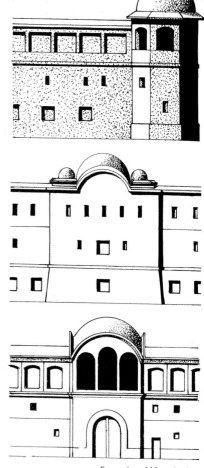

Examples of Mogul urban architectural styles.

occupiers, the Hindu temple complexes and simpler, lower-caste shrines (which in fact were barely, if at all, affected) continued to flourish.

The founder of the Mogul empire—the first great Indian state since the Mauryan period—was Babur. Originally from Samarkand, he was a descendant of Timur (Tamerlane), who in 1399 had driven the Turkish sultan out of Delhi (though then soon continuing on his path of conquest). During his brief rule (1526–30), Babur was able to consolidate only the central part of the state he had envisaged, the area around Delhi, which he left to his mutually belligerent children. Its heyday began only under Akbar the Great (1556–1605), Babur's grandson. The buildings put up during his reign and under his successors—who ruled with various political ups and downs—display remarkable clarity of line and stylistic cohesion, notwithstanding their lavish decoration, and reflect a

Ventilation shafts in a residential quarter of Hyderabad. Between April and June temperatures often rise to 122°F (50°C) at noon, then fall to between 85°F and 95°F (30°–35°C) in the evening due to a wind which always blows in the same direction. This "air-conditioning" system, as effective as it is simple, was devised some six hundred years ago by an unknown architect.

serenity such as India has only rarely known.

The fusion of Indian and Islamic-Persian styles resulted in an exquisite unity that is more than simply a mixture of styles. The style of the Mogul era reflects the perfect harmony achieved between two very different ways of seeing the world. And this harmony might have been indicative of that in which two great religions, with quite different concepts of the supernatural and the afterlife, coexisted. Yet such a harmony was in fact never attained. A certain degree of intermixing was possible in the higher reaches of society, where there was more openness to religious tolerance. Peaceful coexistence was encouraged by marriages between sultans and Rajput princesses, as well as by the moderation and serenity (however esoteric) of the brahmins, who either "retreated into their shells" or with astounding "progressive thinking" acknowledged a new caste as being the only way round the problem.

The chasm between rich and poor prevented this altogether desirable and

praiseworthy desire for harmonious coexistence from being even partially realized among the lower castes. There was too much religious fanaticism. No mere example, law or police presence could quieten those who felt strongly on the subject. Even with the different power structure of the colonial era, little progress in this direction was made: indeed the Christian missionaries actually aggravated the situation—the Dominicans believed they were fulfilling the will of God through the Inquisition.

Yet none of all this detracts from the pleasure of looking at Mogul buildings, exquisitely built as they are, in beautiful materials and sumptuous colours. Multi-coloured, enamelled ceramic work, reflecting the initial Persian influence on the Mogul style, gradually disappeared. The "classic" style was characterized by filigree surface work and the natural colours of the materials (red or yellow sandstone, white or black marble, with the enhancing effect of the seasonal colours, according to region—from the snows of Kashmir to the greyish-yellow of dry, hot areas before the rains and the transformation of everything to deep green).

In reality the long "intermezzo" of Islamic style in the artistic tradition of India constituted a sort of epilogue for that tradition. The British colonial authorities, who allowed the Mogul empire to continue, at least nominally, until 1857, could think of art only in "Victorian" terms.

Southeast Asia

One of the rulers of Java, after his death in c. 950, was posthumously known as Sivabuddha. According to the legends about him he was a powerful prince committed to the cause of peace, who for many centuries watched over his island kingdom from the other world, granting the prayers of the people when they begged for strong sons, beautiful daughters, good harvests, gentle winds and dormant volcanoes. This saint's name indicates that the local religion was compounded equally of Brahminism and Buddhism. This was true not only in Java but throughout Southeast Asia. Siva's very character makes him a specially important god (depending on how he is made to look and the attributes with which he is invoked, he can be either benevolent or savage). To indicate the

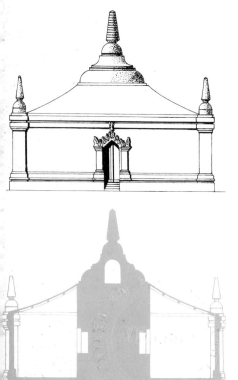

Left: a cetiya, the Burmese equivalent of the stupa. This particular shape is the result of hiding the square stupa proper under a cladding of brick.

Opposite: partial view of the Schwedagon Pagoda, Rangoon. In its present form the complex dates from the fifteenth and eighteenth centuries.

many different aspects of his being he is frequently represented (in India as well) with many arms. Siva, the "benign lord," has endless offspring, has legendary erotic fascination, is the bearer of health, and is full of compassion; when he wishes, however, he can provoke volcanic eruptions and cause earthquakes by his dancing.

Southeast Asia saw no Islamic invasions such as India was torn by; and the spread of the teachings of Muhammad, starting in the fourteenth century, was gradual, very rarely violent, and not on the whole socially or politically disruptive. The effects on the mainland were not lasting. Hindu states (though mostly now without strictly defined borders) had already had autonomy for some time, and in the last two decades of the thirteenth century the Mongol invasions had come as devastating whirlwinds, but without causing any profound political changes. In the islands (modern Malaysia and Indonesia) Islam has remained predominant up until our own day, though without greatly affecting the cultural characters of the various populations.

The basic architectural concepts in this area stem from India. However, surviving buildings reveal that probably around the year 1000 a certain distaste began to be felt for excessive breaking up of exterior surface and solid ornamentation of all internal walls with carvings. The religious buildings of Burma especially testify to this rejection of the old traditions. Thus, for instance, the temples in the old capital Pagan openly flout the rules of brahmin architecture, having smooth white surfaces, articulated by plain projections. Decoration is limited to the door and window frames, and the elegantly contoured corner "turrets." A typical feature of the design is the symmetrical balance of the building on two axes. The tent-roof rises step by step, to finish in a pointed (and often gilded) stupa. The primary architectural type, found throughout Southeast Asia, consists of a cuboid base structure—which appears peculiarly high in the flat landscape of the area—with

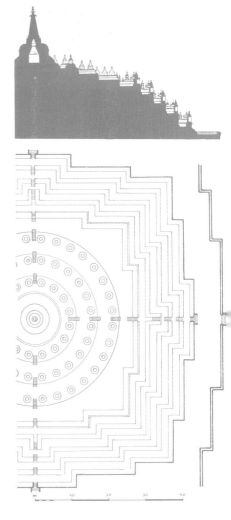

Borobudur (Java), the most important Buddhist building in Southeast Asia, built around 850. Five terraces rise up as a sort of support structure for the complex ambulatory by which the pilgrim approaches the triple ring of seventy-two small stupas, each of which houses a Buddha. The ultimate focus of prayer and meditation, however, is the great enclosed stupa at the very center.

Detail of the Ananda
temple complex at Pagan, in
the Irrawaddy plain, Burma
(twelfth to thirteenth century).

stupa on top, rising up in a graceful pear shape, decorated with innumerable delicate, longitudinal, cornice-like mouldings.

The shape of these temples was probably determined by the way in which religious festivals used to be celebrated. To begin with, only the middle, the stupa (known in this region as the *cetiya*, the "reminder") was sacred. Around the *cetiya* there then appeared a square enclosure, at first fenced off with bamboo, but later properly walled about, with gates on all four sides. Stalls were soon set up along the inside of this wall, where devotional objects and sweets were sold. To keep off sun and rain, mats were subsequently stretched between the top of the base of the *cetiya* and the wall. There thus emerged a literal tent-roof, which in time became a permanent, solid feature of temples, though still retaining its original graceful curve.

China

At the end of his career in AD 1100, Li Ming-chung, an official in the Chinese province of Honan, presented to the emperor a detailed manual on architecture, in which the most ancient techniques and traditions were recorded and collated. Its thirty-four chapters cover both brick and stone building techniques, carpentry, roof construction, advice on proportions, and rules of work for labourers, foremen and architects. The strictures on the role of the architect help explain the astonishing continuity (that is, compared with European equivalents) of the basic stylistic concepts of Chinese architecture. The architect's job was not to design something new, but simply to resolve organizational and technical problems, and he had a wealth of documentation—a sort of builder's library—at his disposal. Li Ming-chung's manual was published in 1103. This first (woodcut) edition has been lost, apart from three pages discovered in 1918 in the National Library in Peking; the original documents themselves vanished in 1126, when K'ai-feng, the old capital of the (northern) Sung dynasty, was sacked during political upheavals.

A new edition of the manual was produced in Su-chou near Peking in 1145. But this has likewise failed to survive the centuries. Nevertheless, it is said to have served as a model for later works on architecture, the most recent of which appeared in 1734. And although this modern work doubtless differed in many details from the original, it does faithfully duplicate the original concepts concerning the role of the architect.

The Chinese architect was an official. In other words, it was not deemed necessary that he should belong to any kind of guild or profession; what was required was aesthetic sensitivity, wide education, and a certain knack in finding genuine artists and experienced craftsmen—sculptors, engravers, painters, potters, founders and blacksmiths—who could turn a plain construction into a veritable work of art.

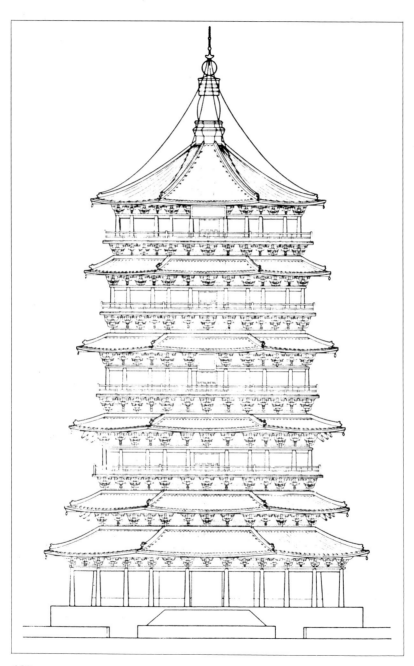

166

It is up to Chinese archaeologists to ascertain whether the architectural tradition of China followed a similar, long and steady course of development to that of the other arts. Surviving buildings testify to continuity, to cautious stylistic change within the same traditional basic context (this is the case even in religious buildings, the fundamental shapes of which were barely affected even by Buddhism). However, no absolutely certain information can be gleaned from the most ancient ruins, despite all attempts at imaginative reconstruction, since all the original wood—the one essential material determining style—has rotted away.

Stone, pottery and bronze can lie in the earth undamaged for thousands of years, though, and finds in these materials tell us much about both practical life and artistic achievement. Stone or bronze "foundation bases" indicate where wooden stakes or pillars once stood, but one can only speculate on the shape of these pillars and the structures they supported.

Although, of course, few and far between, enough sites of wooden buildings have been discovered to show that, even in the earliest times, wooden architecture was considered by no means inferior to stone, and indeed that, during the transitional period between the sixth and seventh centuries A D, wood was held to be a distinctly higher-grade material than stone. Chinese wooden architecture was famous even beyond the remotest frontiers of the vast Chinese empire during the T'ang period (AD 618–907). The "Hall of Gold" in the Japanese capital of Nara, which was copiously imitated for hundreds of years afterwards, was the work of Chinese architects and artists.

The burial place discovered near Anyang in Honan in 1927 was an extremely lucky find for archaeologists. Yin-hsu ("remains of Yin") is the name by which this site is traditionally known. Yin is an aristocratic name from the Shang dynasty, which ruled over China from the seventeenth to the eleventh century BC, and which lost power in the so-called Warring States period (starting around 1030 BC). Magnificent bronzes three thousand years old were found on this site. Unfortunately, however, many disappeared during the war years after 1937, when people used to rummage around the old burial ground in search of oracular bones (the shoulder blades of sheep or pigs covered with now undecipherable marks from ancient divination rites: these bones would be sold to chemists to be ground into powder as an elixir of health).

Excavation work was resumed in 1950 at Chengteh, north of Peking, and in the mountainous province of Shaanxi. Two-thousand-year-old tombs of Han dynasty princes were discovered in a suburb of Canton. Great interest was aroused by these, not only because of the funerary trappings (weapons and tools, vases, and clay models of ships and houses), but also because of the masonry—technically almost faultless—of the burial chambers: tunnel vaults built of smooth, wedge-shaped bricks.

Only blackened traces in the loess remain of ancient wooden constructions. Archaeologists have nothing else to go on. However, they can hunt for clues in literature, which as a "tradition" goes back farther than architecture. The origins of Chinese literature are mythical, and are traced back to the legendary king Fushi, who inspired (though he did not write) the *I Ching*, or "Book of Changes," which is seen as the basis of all Chinese thought from antiquity up until our own times, and Mao Tse-tung. In one of his writings, *On Contradiction* (1937), Mao reflects on the "transformation of opposites into each other," as in the *I Ching*.

The *I Ching* is a book of wisdom, and at the same time (and probably to begin with) was used for divination. Although architecture is not discussed in it, it does deal with wood; and the symbolic

The pagoda of the Fo-kuang-tzu temple in Shaanxi, c. 1050.

167

significance of wood highlights the feelings—almost of love—then felt for this noble, "natural" material. Together with fire, earth, metal and water, wood was one of the five elements. In the richly metaphorical language of the *I Ching* it is "that which gently penetrates," and its ideogram, one of the eight oracular signs, in the same way stands for "wind" (the gentle breeze that blows away the clouds and leaves the sky clear and empty). "It is thus that the noble man gives his orders, thus that he performs his duties."

This sense of some being indwelling in wood fits in well with a section from an old myth about the transformation of human ways of life: "When the age of the great hunter was over the heavenly farmer came and fashioned a piece of wood into a plowshare, and bent a piece of wood to make the handle of the plow, and taught the whole world the benefits of opening up the earth with this plow." The wood penetrates gently into the ground; it is a peaceful act, the earth does not suffer. Enough said on this subject now, however: such qualities in wood are as obvious as the wetness of water.

Wood was so highly considered that it was placed on a level with porcelain and other forms of glazed pottery (marble was no longer on the same level). It is such a noble building material that man has used it since the very dawn of time. Attractive to the eye, it also favoured inventive handling. The result was the Chinese roof. On first seeing a Chinese roof, one is both struck by its lightness and elegance, and at the same time made to feel that its architect was being driven by a perverse urge to make it as complicated as he possibly could. In grand buildings at any rate it certainly was complicated. The more it cost, the better (its elaborate structure was, as it were, the ceremonious homage of the owner to wood—a material that should command the very greatest of respect), and it had to be both stable and sophisticated, practical and decorative.

Of course mere stability could be achieved with no difficulty, in the same way as the overhanging roofs typical of,

say, Bavarian farmhouses: elongated rafters supported by two or three bracket beams one on top of the other. However, such a solution would have rendered a concave roof an impossibility—and a concave roof was a stylistic necessity. It had to look as if it were hovering, independent of all support; furthermore it should give no indication of the enormous weight of the curved roof tiles (fluted, and arranged in rows alternately convex and concave) which it had to bear.

To create the effect of a continuous curve the rafters did not consist of single beams, but were made up of two or three sections, according to the desired curvature, anchored to purlins (the horizontal beams supporting them from below) running parallel with the ridgepiece. The lowest purlin, bearing the eaves, rests by means of small wooden brackets on the lower ends of twin slanting arms, the upper ends of which are held down simply by the weight of the roof-covering. Hence the roof is only fully secure when complete in every detail, since it is the roof tiles themselves that make it stable. One could say that the same sense of lightness and the same degree of stability could be equally well achieved more simply. Yet any other technique would be alien to the spirit and intentions of the ancient master, Li Ming-chung.

The tradition of building in wood now survives only in the fields of conservation and restoration. Serious work, supervised by scientists and executed by skilled craftsmen and artists, started late—in many cases too late. Wood is a highly perishable substance, and when it is not replaced in time it is lost for ever.

Only in 1950 did the People's Republic begin to promote archaeology and history of art. And once again, as in the age of Li Ming-chung, the job of ensuring precision engineering and craftsmanship was given to bureaucrats. Yet the better they did this job, the clearer it became that the new master builders, their heads full of Russian and European ideas, had little to show in place of the ancient

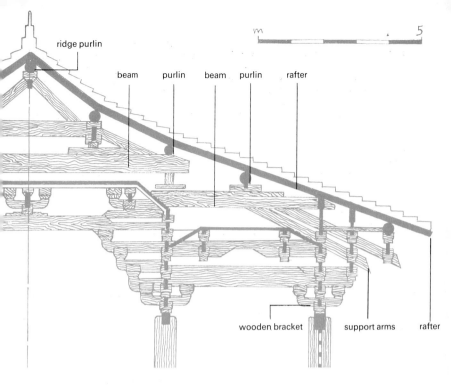

ridge purlin

beam   purlin   beam   purlin   rafter

wooden bracket   support arms   rafter

traditions now rejected by recent history: their work including among other things, for instance, a gateway restructured for political parades, and a palace of culture about which the critics complained "too little wood, unnecessarily austere design, too much marble."

Central-perspective building as developed in Europe from the fifteenth century on, based on geometric laws, was never used in ancient China. Indeed, the technique of building in this way was virtually unknown. Those architects and planners who reflected on European architectonic principles had concluded that this essentially two-dimensional use of space was quite foreign to the Chinese character. According to this system, they argued, objects, houses, rooms, surfaces and figures were portrayed only as seen from a certain viewpoint, not necessarily as they really were. It also presupposed a certain way of looking at things, with

Section of the roof of the Fo-kuang-zi temple (see p. 166). The wooden brackets were important both structurally and as forms of decoration. The more important the building, the greater the number of these brackets.

which they were not able to come to terms.

Europeans who admire Chinese painting, in which, despite the lack of perspective, space is suggested in an extremely subtle way, may find this attitude of Chinese artists somewhat arrogant. The illustration on p. 171 can be used to highlight the validity of both points of view. The European will find that, after all, perspective was not wholly absent in the Far East, and that resort had to be made to the simple trick of "collapsing" the composition; the Chinese artist will demonstrate that he can do without European-style representative geometry, and in the process depict both ground plan and a realistic image on a single plane.

This illustration reproduces a "first impression" drawn off an engraved and coloured stone slab. A form of lithography known ever since the earliest days of printing in China, this technique is not dissimilar to that of the woodcut, except that it gives a "negative" picture. Here we see Huashan Temple on China's sacred Western Mountain, in the province of Shaanxi—a vast building enclosed within walls, built in the ninth century AD, during the Tang dynasty.

Walls which on a normal ground-plan drawing would be shown as just two single lines are here depicted frontally or at an angle. By "collapsing" the picture upwards or sideways the temple elevations and doorways can be included. None of the distant details are hidden away. There is no meeting and crossing over, as is unavoidable with central perspective. The rectangular grouping perfectly embraces the whole complex, and, while not diagrammatically strictly accurate, it will do. In any case, without this rectangular compositional solution it would have been hard to achieve so simple and concise a treatment of the subject.

The plan of Peking (p. 172) shows the ideal propounded in the ancient texts: clearly structured main axes, the resultant areas precisely demarcated (imperial residence, market, popular residential sector), well-guarded administrative area and securely protected residential quarters.

The earliest writings on town planning go back probably over two thousand years, and include ideas inherited from the Shang period (seventeenth to eleventh centuries BC), the first extensive period in Chinese history that can be more or less accurately dated. Archaeologists in Henan have unearthed the ruins of two Shang palaces, the layout of which is in places still not very clear, unlike later sites. However, the main outlines are clear enough. The idea of a

north–south axis had always existed. An approximation to a perfect square, or at least a rectangle, dating from some two thousand years ago, was found at an urban site in modern-day Xi'an; nearby, ruins dating from five hundred years later were overlaid by a small palace built under the farmer dynasty of the Ming.

The first town to appear on the site of Peking was Chi, built during the Warring States period (1030–221 BC). Its center was where the western wall of the outer city was later erected. Chi experienced several changes of ruler and was often abandoned for long stretches of time. From 905 to 1125, it was the seat of the Liao dynasty. Then came the Jin emperors, who reinforced the packed-clay ramparts thrown up by the Liao and renamed the city Chung-du. In 1215 the Mongols appeared, and the city was ablaze for thirty days. Within the same four walls Kublai Khan then established the first imperial residence of the Mongul Yuan dynasty.

However, it soon proved too small. Kublai (the grandson of Genghis Khan) therefore had an area of approximately sixteen square miles (41 sq. km.) to the north enclosed by a vast square wall, along traditional Chinese lines: this area comprised the new capital, Tatu or Khanbalik ("Residence of the Khan"). This was the city of which Marco Polo gave Europe such enthusiastic descriptions. The first European ever to have seen such sights, he was accused of exaggerating.

Nevertheless, Peking (including the residential areas outside the walls) could already boast at that period some two million inhabitants. It became the last call on the trade routes from the south and the southwest, and its fame spread throughout the world. A vast metropolis, it was the home of Arabs, Tibetans and Nepalese, who all had contact with the Khan's court. A number of Christian missionaries also lived freely there and elsewhere in the country: one of these, Brother Andrea from Perugia, wrote that he would rather say nothing about China, so unbelievable would his experiences

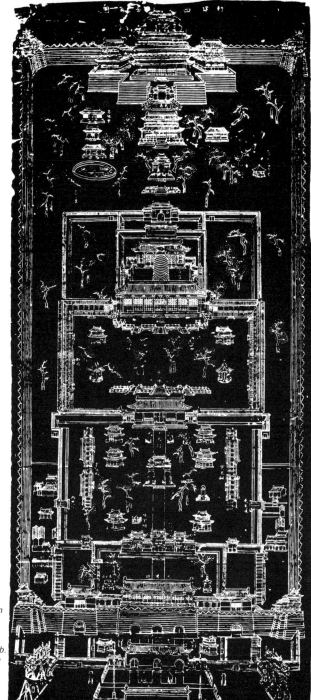

A "first impression" of Huashan Temple on China's sacred Western Mountain, in the province of Shaanxi, drawn off an engraved and coloured stone slab. For a fuller explanation see pp. 169–170.

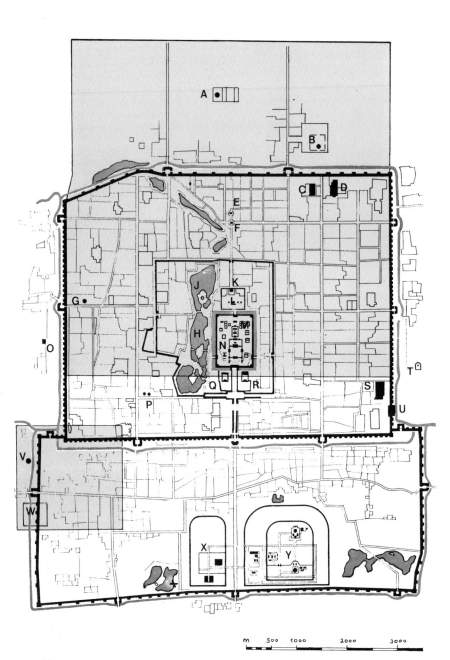

m   500   1000   2000   3000

have seemed.

At the end of the Yuan period (1367) it became the capital of the Ming dynasty. The new emperors came from a farming background, and so their desire for display and ostentation struck many contemporary observers as totally out of place. The Ming rulers wished particularly to emphasize their own power. Under them were erected the imperial city and palace, which together with their various annexes later became the Forbidden City. Khanbalik became Peking ("Northern Capital") in 1420. It was extended to the south, and then fortified—no effort or expense being spared on the walls and gates. The imperial city and court sector were similarly enclosed by walls.

The magnificence of the palaces and the harmonious alternation of open areas, bridges, pavilions and walks are so beautiful as to need no justification. The imperial palace was restored several times, but never up to the original artistic standard; the overall impression is still unimpaired, however.

Plan of Peking, with
the Ming and Qing
dynasty walls (1368–1911).
A   Yellow Temple
B   Temple of Earth
C   Temple of Confucius
D   Temple of the Lama
E   Bell tower
F   Drum tower
G   Pagoda
H   Western lake
J   Pagoda
K   Temple of Ancestors
L   Hill of coal
M   Imperial palace
N   Forbidden City
O   Temple of the Moon
P   Pagodas
Q   Temple of the Tutelary Gods
R   Temple of Ancestors
S   Civil Service examination room
T   Altar of the Sun
U   Astrophysical observatory
V   Pagoda
W   Palace of the Liao
X   Temple of Agriculture
Y   Altar and Temple of Heaven

Today the Forbidden City is by far and away the world's largest museum. The government lavishes money and care on it. Historic parks and palaces elsewhere are also protected and well looked after. The most splendid example of Ming architecture is the Temple of Heaven complex, including the Qi nian dian, the most important building in the yearly imperial ritual for good harvests. A circular construction standing on a triple-stepped white marble terrace, it forms an exquisite unity both inside and out. The three-tiered roof has blue-glazed tiles which recall the blue of the heavens even when the days are overcast.

One notable exception from the norm of the rectangular ground plan for imperial capitals is Hangzhou, seat of the (southern) Song dynasty (AD 1127–1279). This town grew up without any strict plan because the Song, who dreamt of reconquering the north, only ever thought of it as a temporary home. Despite this, however, records from its most flourishing days bear eloquent witness to its great beauty. Hangzhou is located about a hundred and twenty-five miles (200 km.) southwest of Shanghai, not far from the sea, on hilly ground between a lake and a navigable river. Marco Polo, who visited the city during the last stage of its period of splendour, admired the houses and gardens of the rich merchants and praised the "ladies of pleasure," who lived in luxury, with retinues of servants. The city survived as a trade center until the end of the Song period. It was several times destroyed by fire and rebuilt, but without any great insistence on architectural quality. Only the Pagoda of the Six Harmonies remains to reflect its past glories.

The modern Chinese city retains the ancient layout in its basic essentials: rectangular axes and an agreeably flexible use of space within the square outline. Planners in the old days steered clear of street patterns radiating from a single center, and so too do their modern counterparts. Recent years have seen a revival of interest (albeit somewhat hesitant) in old buildings which have long

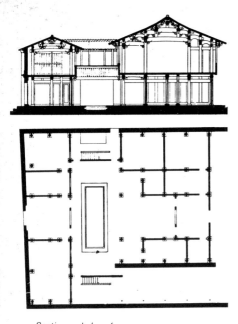

*Section and plan of a
two-story seventeenth-century house.
The total surface area is rather
over 1000 square feet (93 sq. m.).*

thus emerged with equal sides, between eleven and a half and thirteen feet (3.5–4 m.) in length: this square could then of course be duplicated or repeated *ad infinitum*. Houses therefore developed essentially as squares, elongated rectangles, L- or U-shaped forms, or finally again squares.

The ideal shape (at least for the town dweller, not for the farmer) was a nine-fold square, the central area being without a roof, to form a courtyard, garden, atrium or whatever else one wishes to call it. The Chinese name is pretty: *tien ching* ("pool of heaven"). If there was enough space, a walled garden would be built at the back of the house; and if a stream happened to run through this garden a miniature palace could be created, with little bridges (even if the stream were no more than a couple of feet wide), a stone lantern shaped like a pagoda among the shrubs, and dwarf trees. Odd-shaped rocks were also very popular. Above all it was necessary to have a surrounding wall or thick hedge.

A Chinese family's home has traditionally been its castle for centuries; hence the outer walls have only one opening—the entrance. Windows occasionally feature high up in narrow alleys—but then the wall opposite has to be window-less. Today the rapid increase in the numbers of people living in cities has forced the Chinese to build multistory housing blocks, in which of course the traditional privacy can no longer be maintained. However, as far as one can gather, the new generation of city dwellers do not seem too unhappy about the new conditions. Mao was able to persuade them that that too was a viable living style.

In all previous ages there had been innumerable rules to follow when building the traditional-style house (which is now becoming ever rarer). In buildings with modillion roofs, twin or triple

been neglected, yet which well deserve to be properly cared for. At the same time, the open spaces which once so to speak formed the stage for the ceremonials of the ruling classes are now used for political parades. From time immemorial red had been the colour of splendour and solemnity. Sacred doors used to be painted with red lacquer; now red is the colour of flags, ribbons and bunting, and air balloons.

In China, as in most highly civilized countries, the decision whether to build round or square dwellings seems to have been taken very early on. Vestiges of circular constructions have been found here and there in Shang period burial grounds, but they were mostly for storage. The advantage of four-sided constructions are obvious even at the planning stage. It is the length of the available beams alone that dictates the spacing of the uprights. A basic model

Opposite: *a corner of the imperial Summer Palace, a few miles northwest of Peking.*

The Great Wall of China, the most remarkable work of military architecture in the world, was begun around 200 B.C. One of the Qin dynasty emperors began by strengthening the earthworks thrown up in the northern provinces during the Warring States period, with blocks of stone. The same emperor also erected the first watchtowers. Work on the first wall (in the north) continued for almost a thousand years. Common criminals were put to work on it. By the sixth century these totalled about 150,000. Over a distance of two and a half thousand miles (4000 km.) the wall afforded protection for the northern provinces against the Mongol raiders—until Genghis Khan finally stormed it in 1210. Under the Mongol Yuan dynasty, the Great Wall lost all importance. With the rise of the Ming dynasty in 1368, a second wall was begun, much farther south, and eventually brought to completion around 1500. This wall had a far stronger parapet, with crenellations the height of a man, and with 20,000 watchtowers. The top of the wall, measuring eighteen feet (5.5 m.) across, is properly surfaced over its whole length, and wherever there are steep gradients there are steps.
Its average height is about twenty-six feet (8 m.).

brackets were exclusively for the nobility or senior civil servants. "Officials below the third rank may not have reception rooms with more than five bays between pillars." Or: "Eleven bays between pillars, in a square, are permissible for an eminent philosopher." For ordinary people three was the limit; yet there would still always be the "pool of heaven," with eight rooms around it, covering a total surface area of 290–430 square feet (27–40 sq. m.)—plenty room enough for a whole family, who were quite happy to live all together. According to the traditional building pattern, the poorer the owners were the less wood was used. The outer walls—and indeed usually also the interior partition walls—would then be of brick (either baked or dried out in the open). The only wooden elements would be the framework, the pillars of the internal courtyard, and the roof structure. Such a building would not be very comfortable. Yet the inhabitants would be happy enough simply to be safe inside four walls, away from the all too often agitated outside world. The vital things were a good stove, one corner dedicated to the ancestors, and a bed for every member of the family. A touch of luxury might be a grasshopper in a little bamboo cage to announce dusk and time for bed.

Japan

China's architectural tradition was scrupulously copied by the Japanese. It persisted longest in temple buildings, although certain simplifications had very soon been introduced. The slanting arms supporting the wide eaves of the roof were replaced by long beams running parallel to the rafters. The wooden brackets (of which in China quantity meant solemnity) were restricted to one or at most two. The line of the roof was no longer continuously concave, but was merely raised at the ends. Many Shinto shrines dating from before the immigration of Chinese Buddhist monks and their followers, and many times restored, still survive. From these can be deduced at least the structural principles, if not the actual proportions, of early Japanese domestic architecture.

These ancient shrines are mostly to be found in the least populated areas, in the quiet provinces in the southwestern tip of the island of Hondo (the largest in the whole island group). The earliest shrines date back two thousand years. They have a square or rectangular ground plan, with a veranda running round all four sides. The floor rests on beams fixed into the ground. The saddleback roof is steeply graded (about forty degrees), and is thatched or shingled, and the pediment has a curious scissor-shaped form of decoration. None of the posts, rafters or floorboards of these little shrines are old: even if they were lucky enough to survive fires and earthquakes, they were in any case replaced every twenty or thirty years.

In the mountainous western part of Hondo, however, there do still survive a few extremely old farmhouses. They bear a very slight resemblance to the type of building one sees in the Black Forest, but are on the whole less well looked after. Their thatched roofs slope at up to sixty degrees and cover three or four floors, depending on the size of the ground floor. In one of these houses the *hinoki* beams (a type of cedar, now very rare and expensive) are a thousand years old.

Around the year AD 1000, Japanese temples still had a distinctly Chinese look about them. One famous example is the so-called Phoenix Hall, built *c.* 1050. In vernacular architecture, however, an indigenous style was beginning to emerge. The pupils were overtaking their teachers. The style that evolved for grand vernacular buildings was called the Shinden style. The *shinden* was the main central room, around which the whole symmetrical rectangular layout extended. Only in the garden did the overall rigorous symmetry become deliberately—but nevertheless carefully—disrupted.

The Shinden style paved the way for all the subsequent major developments of Japanese domestic architecture: structural airy lightness and well thought-out use of materials—wood, bamboo, paper, and reeds woven into wickerwork or matting. The partition walls between rooms were generally of plaster or adobe, within a framework, and were papered over. The old saddleback roof made way for the hipped roof style. However, the slope of the roof stopped short of the ridge, thus forming a small pediment, an opening through which air could pass into the attic. In connection with this the outer walls had shuttered openings at their upper level (which constituted a fifth of the total height of the building), to let out "bad air and evil spirits."

Around AD 1200, the warrior class, the *samurai,* developed their own stylistic variants to suit their way of life, doing away with the sumptuous decoration for which the wealthy of the day had an almost excessive fondness. "Spartan" would have been the ideal epithet for the *samurai,* had they known the word. The insistence on symmetry was rejected. The result was the Buke style, one partly inspired by that adopted by priests for their own houses: corridor separated off from the *shinden* by walls, and the *shoin*—a reading room with desk and transparent paper window, for which an alcove or niche with a short wall across was built out on to the veranda.

With the advent of new ideas in terms of basic design and interior layout, there gradually evolved the Shoin style, which

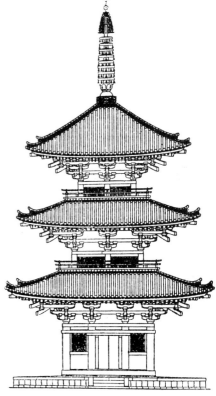

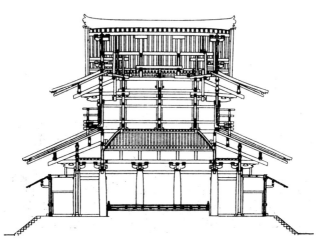

by the end of the sixteenth century had established a structural and aesthetic norm that continues in use to this day. This type of design, known as *kiwariho*, uses predetermined units of measurement to arrive at the correct proportions both of the structure as a whole and of the individual sections. The basic measurement is the *ken*, roughly equivalent (although with slight regional variations) to 5 ft. 11 in. (180 cm.), or in other words the gap between two support posts. It is permissible to use a unit half as long again, so that the length of a wall may be one *ken*, one and a half, two, two and a half, and so on. Measurements for the floor mats (*tatami*) can also be arrived at by the distance between the posts. About four inches (10 cm.) thick, the *tatami* cover those parts of the floor on which one should not walk with one's outdoor shoes on. The width is always half the length, i.e. the space required for a man to stretch out in comfortably. When one hears that the Japanese have no beds but sleep on the floor, one has to bear in mind that the floor is already quite pleasantly springy and is always clean. At night a linen-covered straw mattress the same size as the mat is put out to sleep on. Sheets and sausage-shaped pillows are also used. All this bedding, including the mattress, is stored in a wall cupboard

Below: *in about 760 the Chinese monk Xian-chen came to Japan, with 180 disciples, many of them craftsmen, and built, near the capital of Nara, the Kondo ("Hall of Gold") of the Toshodaiji temple. Tradition has it that this was commissioned by the Empress Koken. It was dedicated to the memory of the Emperor Shomu, who had died in 756. Typically Chinese in every way, it was to inspire the architects of numerous other temples.*
Opposite, above: *three-story pagoda in the Taemaiji temple complex, Nara, one of the oldest Chinese-style towers. Built in the eighth century, it has several times been restored.*
Opposite, below: *structure of the roof (longitudinal section) of the main hall of the Horyui temple, Nara. This building dates from c. 760, and was built on the site of a temple erected a hundred years before which had burnt down.*

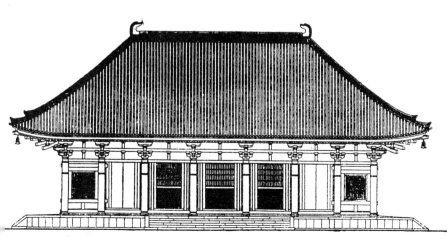

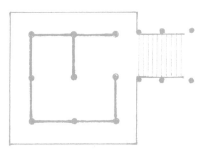

during the day. The standard size of the mats determines the size of the room. A small three-mat room measures barely seventeen and a half square feet (1.62 sq m.); four mats will make for about forty-six and a half square feet (4.31 sq. m.). A reception or living-room room, even of reasonably modest standing, will measure from six to eight mats.

Even the smallest houses have a corridor, the floor of which is half stone, and which is lower than the actual rooms. Visitors sit on a wide wooden threshold to remove their shoes. Woven straw sandals are then given them to wear.

Except in the smallest homes there are

Opposite, above: *example of the* Shinden *style, favoured by the Japanese aristocracy around the year 1000. This is a prince's palace, and, as may be seen, the reception rooms, the private apartments and the offices are disposed with rigorous symmetry, and all connected by corridors.*

Opposite, below: *layout of a* shinden, *the main reception room from which the name* Shinden *style derives. The dominant features are the light, airy economy of design overall, and the open veranda running all the way round the room.*

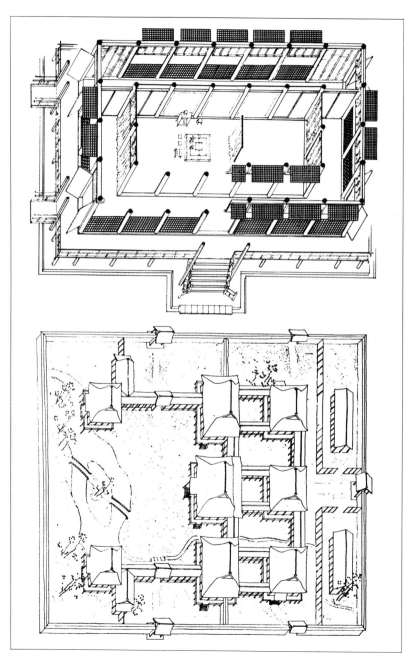

181

Left, above and below: *the partitioning* (kiwariho) *of rooms with structural components of dimensions dictated by the* Shoin *style.*

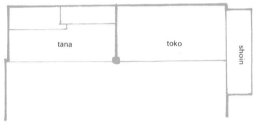

| tana | toko | shoin |

Below, right: *section of a single-story* Shoin-*style house. The* shoin *itself is strictly speaking a small reading room, as used to be found in the houses of priests and scholars.*

traditionally two features which reveal the family's religious attitudes and its good taste: the *tokonoma* (shortened to *toko*), which might be freely translated as "picture alcove," and the *tana*—an alcove adjacent to the *toko* with shelves and little wall cupboards fitted with either sliding doors or drawers. The *toko* is in effect a shrine where the family performs Buddhist rituals. Its floor is about a foot (30 cm.) higher than those of the other rooms; on it stands either an incense bowl, a small statue or a vase of flowers. Hanging from the wall at the back is the *kakemono*, a scroll painting with a figure and some holy text, which frequently needs to be changed as it always refers to either a specific religious festival or day of observance, or some domestic event.

At the end of the narrow dividing wall between the *tokonoma* and the *tana* there is always a kind of small wooden

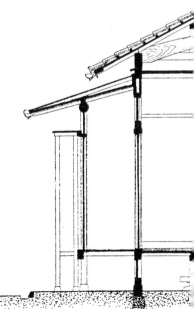

182

pillar: this has no structural function, but is a symbolic specimen of the wood chosen after much thought for the house by the owner—a particularly beautifully grained piece, an aged *hinoki* post from some old farmhouse or just a slender trunk, either straight or curved, with lacquered bark or highly polished with the bark removed, with either a few or several stumps of branches. One comes across an infinite variety; it is up to the householder to find exactly what he wants. The style and layout of the typical Japanese house were conceived ideally for rich townsmen, eminent scholars or princes.

The most outstanding example of the Shoin style is the Katsura Palace in Kyoto, built in the early seventeenth century by Kobori Enshu, a disciple of the famous master of the tea ceremony, Rikyu. This well-proportioned, symmetrical architectural complex no longer bears any resemblance to the original Chinese models; its expresses a certain idea of power and splendour unique in its way—without any lavish or ingenious decorative devices, without a trace of marble or gold, but yet with an overall serene dignity, created with simple, noble materials and by harmonious proportions. It must be placed in a class of its own.

The disciples of the Chinese have surpassed their mentors, attaining a rare degree of perfection and successfully integrating new materials (glass, cement and plastics) with their own particular aesthetic. As for technology, the erstwhile patient students have become

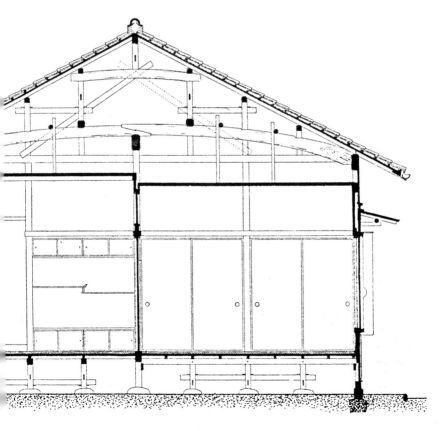

The Shokintei tea pavilion in the garden of the Katsura Imperial Palace in Kyoto, built around 1620, and several times restored and renovated.

sorcerer's apprentices. The same society that can, with such unique love and philosophical depth, make even the tiniest garden into a hymn of praise of landscape, nevertheless allows rivers to spew industrial pollution out into the sea—so that very soon no fish will be able to survive in the bays and inlets of its islands. It does nothing to halt this ecological scandal, intent as it is on flooding the world with its goods, seeing such economic growth as the only way of ensuring future prosperity. Bird-song can only be heard on tape or on the radio in big cities like Tokyo and Yokohama. Legislation is insufficient to protect the environment; and the new generation would appear not to have learnt the lesson of Hiroshima and Nagasaki—for which, though, they were of course hardly responsible. Those in charge of Japanese industry have long forgotten such horrors. They go their way, expanding urban centers even out into the sea.

Mesa Verde

Mesa Verde (literally, "Green Table") is a plateau in the state of Colorado, cut into by the deep, narrow, rocky valley of the Colorado river. Around 1800, this vast area still belonged wholly to the Indians, despite its Spanish name. The *conquistadores* who had ventured up north in the sixteenth century had on their return home relayed much false or misguided information about it. They were not able to say exactly where the natural borders of the Mesa Verde ran, and those Indians who were unwise enough to allow themselves to be captured failed to satisfy the adventurers' thirst for booty, gold and other such riches.

Franciscan missionaries, among them Fathers Marcos da Niza (*c.*1544) and Vélez del Escalante (*c.*1780), managed to become better acquainted with the Indians, thanks to their medical skills; and they told their compatriots of houses built entirely of gold, with silver roofs, on the mountain sides. Father Marcos claimed to have seen—though from a distance—a whole "city of gold." Perhaps this "city" indeed shone in the sunset—but it was not of gold. It was of stone and mud. Escalante and his three travelling companions had passed fairly close by the Mesa Verde, but had skirted round the steep, rocky slopes. They were not aiming to explore north, across the mountains, but to find a passage to the sea. What they found in the end was the Salt Lake in Utah.

In the autumn of 1874, the American W. H. Jackson was sent by the Government to take photographs of the Mesa Verde for a report. His photographs were later to earn him the nickname "the Pioneer Photographer." Beneath an outcrop of rock in Mancos Canyon he discovered the ruins of a masonry-built house, consisting of two rooms, one on top of the other. Workers from a nearby copper mine told him that there were

The Indians of the west coast transformed the old-style ditch dwelling into a wooden cabin, integrating into it at the same time the traditional totem pole. On this building (intended for community festivities, for which the Kwakiutl and other coastal tribes had a vigorous appetite), the jaws of the head at the bottom of the totem pole serve as an entrance. There are no partition walls inside. Around the central fireplace the floor level is lower, so as to form a comfortable bench.

many more round and about. One of his finds was a large building with sixteen windows. His photographs of these ruins aroused surprise and interest, but the discovery was not considered particularly important. Not until forty years later did the scientific world, to its amazement, hear from two cowboys about a cliff terrace over a hundred yards long, with traces of walls on it, under a huge overhang of rock, where they had found square constructions of one to three stories, with towers between them, the masonry reaching up to the rock ceiling, and, in front, within the terrace (extended by means of support walls), circular rooms somewhat higher than a man.

This find was called "Cliff Palace." The appellation was rather too hasty, however. Neither the interlocking houses nor the towers really justified such a description. The purpose of the circular "cellars" was soon discovered. They were *kivas*—the ceremonial and assembly rooms used by those farming tribes known collectively as the Pueblo Indians (Hopi, Zuñi, Acoma, Pima, Papago), who live, as they have lived since time immemorial, in village communities in Arizona and New Mexico.

Among the Hopi, the *kiva* was originally square, and only became round, as among the other tribes, later on. It is always three-quarters underground, and access to it is via a ladder through an opening in the flat roof. The floor is packed down hard (the result of much dancing), and in it is dug a hole for a fire, the smoke of which is accompanied up to

Above: "Cliff Palace," the Pueblo settlement on the Mesa Verde, Colorado, which was abandoned in 1300.

Right: *irregular masonry joints, a typical feature of the buildings of the Mesa Verde.*

through natural causes. Unburied skeletons bear witness to human slaughter. This massacre seems to have occurred, however, at a time when many families were in any case having to leave the area because of a prolonged drought (*c.*1250—it has been shown to have lasted several decades). By 1300, Cliff Palace had been abandoned after some three hundred years of habitation.

The Mesa Verde ruins (also found in large numbers in Mancos Canyon and in the various side valleys) are the oldest examples of Indian architecture in North America. The word "architecture" is perfectly appropriate: many buildings, in better condition than Cliff Palace, reveal the remarkably high level of Stone Age building techniques. Finds such as tools and earthenware vases also show the aesthetic sensitivity of the craftsmen of the time—still to be seen in the shapes and decorative patterning of the pottery and woven goods produced today on Navaho reservations. The only essential difference is that Navaho potters now work with wheels. The inhabitants of Mesa Verde did not know about the wheel, and so fashioned their fine bellied clay vases (intended for storing maize) by hand. All the tools they had were standard Stone Age utensils; and these, together with the ancient inherited knowledge that soft stone can be shaped with harder stone, and that a mixture of mud, straw, water and pebbles makes first-rate mortar, sufficed for the inhabitants of the Mesa Verde to build astonishingly accurate masonry work.

These cliff dwellings, as they are known, are all of hewn sandstone. The stones cannot quite be described as squared, however, since only the long vertical faces are relatively smooth. Little time was apparently spent on making the stones fit neatly together. It was easier simply to fill in the gaps with mortar and press splinters of stone into it while it was still wet to bind both stone and mortar solidly together. (The interiors of tiled stoves are still built in a similar way today.)

The cliff dwellers set great store by neat

the sky by prayers for the clouds to drop their precious rain over that spot rather than elsewhere. The Mesa Verde farmers were always desperate for rain. The high plateau land they worked was not as verdent as the Spanish name implies. The soil is poor and the summer short, while winter can be freezing, with heavy snow.

Cliff Palace did not fall into ruins just

The entrance to
a kiva or cellar,
ceremonial room of the
Pueblo Indians.

corners and window and door openings (these are generally slightly trapezoidal). Many doorways become narrower two thirds of the way down—projecting in about a hand's breadth on either side. This made a handy support for negotiating the high threshold (see illustration on pp. 186–7). Domes were unknown, and roofs were usually made of roughly hewn tree trunks, wattle and daub.

There were still no suitable tools available for doing solid carpentry, but, despite this, hurdles such as the descent hole of the *kiva* were overcome by simply making a kind of grille of wooden beams (shown on p. 188). Thus only eight beams had to correspond in length to the full internal diameter of the *kiva*.

The architecture of the cliff dwellings is logical, well proportioned and quite admirable, given the limitations of equipment, land and materials.

Very little is known about the Indians of the Mesa Verde: they had rounded skulls and short limbs, and were probably peaceful, sedentary hunters and farmers. By about 1300 they had disappeared.

The walls of many rooms bear two mysterious painted symbols, which can safely be assumed to be more than mere decoration. One is a rectangle on its side, with up-and-down zig-zag lines in it. The other consists of a long horizontal line with, every so often, groups of three triangles; between each group are twelve short vertical marks, as on a ruler. According to one somewhat bold suggestion, this could be a sort of calendar, a device for counting the days, and the three triangles may be a simple representation of the divine trinity sent from heaven to provide sustenance for human beings, of which later Pueblo myths speak: deer, maize and the peyote cactus. The peyote cactus was the source of mescaline, which induced wonderful, vividly coloured dreams, and raised the mind beyond all desires, granting absolutely serene acceptance of fate.

Opposite: *the Pueblo settlement of Taos, Santa Fe (New Mexico), whose inhabitants are of Tiwa stock.*

Reconstruction of a Mexican temple pyramid. In the foreground, the ball court. On the left, a stone pillar from the gate of a temple at Chichén Itzá in the form of a plumed rattlesnake.

Mexico

Although at first sight the buildings and carvings of the ancient Meso-American civilizations may appear "brutal," such an impression is misleading. Strength and energy are certainly expressed in this architecture, but it is no mere brute strength; and what to us may appear to be bloodthirsty cruelty is in fact a kind of art that cannot be judged according to aesthetic standards, and that was intended to be neither formally perfect nor even beautiful. What to the Spaniards in the sixteenth century seemed totally pagan and eminently worthy of being destroyed, must be understood in terms of the religious feelings that permeated every aspect of Pre-Columbian Indian life. The *conquistadores* as a gesture brought back a few Indian converts to present to the Pope, but otherwise felt themselves fully justified in trampling down a rich culture with traditions dating back two thousand years, and ruthlessly and thoughtlessly exploiting people whose religious observances had already been outlawed (and of course for Europeans it was hard to comprehend the

peculiar fatalism with which these sufferings were born).

One of the finest examples of pre-Columbian architecture is Teotihuacán, in a valley area north of Mexico City (once a lake basin, now almost completely dry: the whole area was named after the valley when the name Nueva España went out of use). By the time of the Aztec warrior kings the temples and artisans' houses all around had long been ruins; however, they were still used as places of prayer and sacrifice. Towering above all the other structures was the Pyramid of the Sun, the stepped structure of which is reminiscent of the pyramid of Saqqara. About 260 feet (79 m.) high, it is a veritable hill of stone, containing nothing—no tomb or treasure chamber—but merely forming a base for the temple proper and a fine stage for the enactment of bloody rites. The original tales related by the first Spaniards are quite truthful, however horrendous they sound. Research has shown that they are exaggerated only where linguistic problems created misunderstandings. Under Montezuma, the last Aztec king before the Spaniards arrived, sacrifices were celebrated in which the hearts of ten to twelve thousand prisoners of war were immolated to give strength to "the lord of our flesh," and thus to ensure a continued smooth course for the sun.

This faith, in which blood sacrifices were considered to put men in the divinity's favour, was extremely ancient and was widespread throughout Central America, although the excesses of the Aztecs were rather exceptional. One Spanish bishop wrote of a shrine to the water god—wells near Chichén Itzá in Yucatán. The sactifices offered here by the Mayans to the god during his annual festival included flowers, gold, precious stones and virgins. Investigations of this sacred spot have confirmed that the bishop's report was no mere fabrication.

In striking contrast to such blood-curdling death rites, other records refer to the gentleness and courtesy of the Aztecs, and to their love of flowers, perfumes, brightly coloured feathers, and a special ritual ball game, for which extremely intensive training was required. The object of this game was to pass a rubber ball through a small stone ring jutting out from a wall: however, only the forehead or the shoulders could be used to "throw" the ball. Almost all places of religious worship had walled and paved ball courts.

A society that was able to develop its own numerical system and introduce "corrective" days into its calendar, to adjust it to the progress of the stars, must also have been skilled in the science of measurement and, specifically, geometry. This ability is manifest in the well-proportioned, solidly composed and richly inventive ornamentation with which walls of every description were graced. Yet this geometrical expertise was somehow never applied to the fields of mechanics and statics.

Thus Aztec architecture tends to be cuboid, massive and heavy-looking, and wasteful of materials, as though the architects never realized that the same spatial effects could be achieved with fewer stones. The realization would have been useful—all the more since the peoples of Pre-Columbian Mexico had not invented the wheel, and so had no form of winch mechanism. All loads had to be dragged or lifted. Probably the only tool used was the wooden lever.

Arches and domes were also unknown, as was too the "false" dome of the *trullo*. Mountains of stone and enormously thick walls are the hallmarks of ancient Mexican architecture. There is

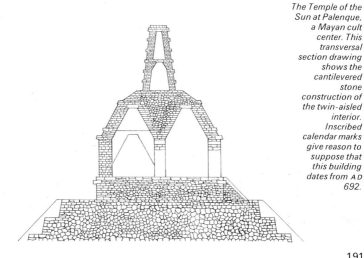

The Temple of the Sun at Palenque, a Mayan cult center. This transversal section drawing shows the cantilevered stone construction of the twin-aisled interior. Inscribed calendar marks give reason to suppose that this building dates from AD 692.

no lightness anywhere, but everywhere endless vast columns: atlantes and supports in the shape of animals which look as though they were rammed into the ground by giants—a stony riot of wild imaginings.

Many of these figurative carvings are surprisingly humorous; yet the humour they convey is similarly wild. A curious fondness for cripples and acrobats appears. Here as elsewhere, hunchbacks were thought to bring luck.

Both in ornamental friezes and in space-filling decoration rounded forms are strangely rare. Even snakes—still just recognizable despite the stylization—coil themselves up in right angles.

The exact symbolism of certain decorative motifs that commonly crop up is unknown, but in most cases it is highly unlikely that they were merely the whimsical products of individual, creative stonemasons and sculptors. Aztec figurative manuscripts reveal symbolically simplified versions of a good many objects and ideas: fire, water (both waves and rain), flint, flower, house, eye, wind, movement and animals (as emblems of months—deer, alligator, dog, monkey, jaguar, iguana and others). The animals also feature in extremely compact form as numerical symbols on calendars; again, however, they often occur as carvings on buildings, either engraved into the stone or as bas-relief. The Aztecs had at their disposition materials of varying degrees of hardness, from anthractite (which is easily worked) to sandstone and obsidian (which is as hard as glass).

Little is known about the day-to-day life of the people—who were doubtless employed in huge numbers on building projects. Near Teotihuacán and other centers (Monte Albán, Chichén Itzá, Tikal) there grew up whole settlements of craftsmen, forming small and medium-sized towns, which must have been supported by the local farmers.

In the so-called *Codex Mendoza*, craftsmen are portrayed as being neither slaves nor even poor men. They wear the typical citizen's cape, knotted at the shoulder, rather than the farmer's poncho. They were highly respected and probably earned considerable reputations during their lives, depending on their craft status and their expertise. However, no names have come down to us.

Peru

Civilization evolved uninterruptedly for over two thousand years in Pre-Columbian Peru, until finally being halted by the Cajamarca disaster in 1532. It was in the mountains through which the Marañón winds its way (then to turn east and, with the Ucayali, become the Amazon) that Francisco Pizarro, with a hundred and sixty-eight men, sixty-two horses, and two low-caliber cannon, closed with the now exhausted army of the Inca Atahualpa. After their victory, the Spaniards discovered that the Inca was at war with his half brother. For the first time in the history of the Inca kingdom that vast empire had become split. The Spaniards thanked Providence for giving them such an easy victory.

Less than a year later the capital Cuzco was in Spanish hands. The Inca, who had ordered his brother's death, was sentenced to death by Pizarro: justice had to be done, even though he had paid the *conquistador* a whole room full of gold and silver for his release.

Only gradually did the Spaniards realize how far the Inca empire stretched southwards; and it took them a long time to acquire a clear idea of the (now destroyed) Inca state structure, instituted a hundred years before by Pachacuti (or Pachacontec). Pachacuti it was who created the north–south road system, covering about two and a half thousand miles (4000 km.), substituted the solar calendar for the old lunar version (thus paying homage to the sun god whom he worshipped), and established the yearly round of sowing, harvesting, llama-rearing, religious festivals and sacrificial rites according to the progress of the sun.

The Inca state was organized down to the last detail, and was governed by the Inca himself together with his "civil

servants" —military leaders, priests, astronomers and agricultural advisors. A bureaucratic hierarchy controlled every level of public life and state activity: supervisors, administrators, statisticians, village mayors and so forth. The ordinary people (farmers, shepherds, foresters, labourers and masons employed in road building and the construction of terrace gardens) had no responsibilities. Their job was to ensure the efficient functioning of the services. All salaries, taxes to the Inca, local government organizations, road-construction materials and equipment—everything was strictly regulated, and a certain austerity reigned, even after bumper harvests.

There was peace for over a century in this "super-collective" state, protected and directed as it was by the Inca, aided by accurately gathered statistics and an efficient information service. Fighting occurred only on the borders, and hostilities ceased as soon as the defeated tribes were incorporated into the imperial system. There were neither prisoners of war nor slaves. A degree of phlegmatism was no doubt needed to make such a life

Detail of the façade of the "Governor's Palace" at Uxmal, Yucatán. The ornamentation on either side of the tall niche, executed with stone "plug" blocks, is not entirely successful. Probably the builders did not quite get the right outline for the square-cornered serpentine motif as they erected the wall. The drawing top right shows it as it should have been according to the original plan. Below that are two examples of consummate decorative genius—each so composed that the dark and light patterns in each case are mirror images of each other.

193

Above: *the "Gate of the Sun" on the Bolivian plateau, built around 800 (i.e. considerably earlier than the Inca period). Its height is almost ten feet (3 m.); its width, twelve and a half feet (3.8 m.). Carved from a single block of stone, the Gate of the Sun is the best-preserved vestige of a sacred spot that has otherwise been virtually completely destroyed.* Above, right: *detail from a frieze; the significance of this figure is uncertain.*

Below: *the* Intihuatana, *Machu Picchu. This structure definitely served some astronomical purpose. For instance, from one corner of the pillar on the table-like stone base, taking one's sights from the edge of the house on the right, it is possible to locate the point at which the sun rises at the summer solstice. The* Intihuatana *is also aligned for lunar observations.*

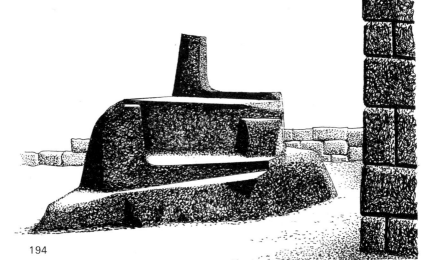

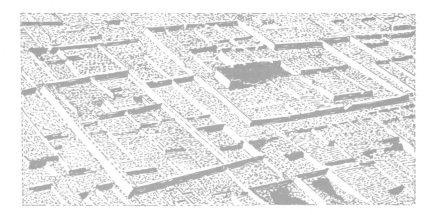

bearable. It was not a joyless existence, but all adventurousness and creativity must have been stifled. Thus perhaps there is no such thing, strictly, as an Inca style. All the works of applied art that we now admire (carvings, pottery, woven materials and jewelry) date back before the Incas: they belong to a much older tradition, and contrast strikingly with Inca architecture, which, for all its dramatic, tense aggressiveness of form, is distinctly monotonous. Inca buildings do not bear comparison with earlier structures such as the Gate of the Sun at Tiahuanaco or the temple complex of Chanchán (on the north coast of Peru: later destroyed by treasure hunters). The Inca kings and their circle of dignitaries, all from élite families, did not bring any culture with them. Civilization was, so to speak, there waiting for them—the fruit of a thousand years of relatively peaceful evolution. What the Incas constructed in the course of their two hundred years of domination was a political and administrative system which, for all its authoritarian character, certainly raised standards of living.

Perhaps the Incas were not great artists: but in their eyes this was no defect. The various tribes who were gradually absorbed into the Inca state were rather more artistically imaginative, and their aesthetic and technical traditions were incorporated into Inca build-

Drawing of the city of Chanchán, now in ruins, in the coastal region of northern Peru (based on an aerial photograph). This town was destroyed by the Incas in 1450, and was subsequently often looted by treasure hunters.

ing designs. It is impossible to say whether this process was natural or forced. Writing did not exist in Pre-Columbian Peru; and the *quipu* (a length of knotted string) was not a preliminary technique of writing, as certain sixteenth- and seventeenth-century Spanish writers believed. Conceived according to the decimal system, and of no use except to those who knew what it was, it was in fact a mathematical aid, for stocktaking, long marches or astronomical data.

Both in ornamentation and in sculpture, there was an unbroken stylistic evolution of more than two thousand years. All stylistic dividing lines somehow break down—intermediate forms being found to fill the gaps between chronologically or formally distinct types. Pottery motifs recall the woven reed baskets of pre-ceramic days. Scratched or engraved decorations on mud walls were probably inspired by weaving or crotchet patterns.

Three-dimensional objects—pots or sculptures—often express the character, imagination and creative ebullience of the craftsman or artist. The many vessels with handles (fourth to sixth centuries AD) that have been discovered are rarely very functional in shape. Mostly they represent something—a gourd, a man squatting or an animal. Popular forms were fat shepherds with pipes, heads with vividly delineated features, and sometimes also slightly banal, realistic faces, with bold yet worried expressions. Little remains in Inca architecture of this highly inventive Peruvian creativity.

Machu Picchu, in the high mountains north of Cuzco, is an outstanding example of how mute and uninformative stones can sometimes be. This mountain town, or whatever it was, was only discovered in 1911, although it had never actually been entirely forgotten. Despite the difficulty of getting there, it was frequently visited by mountain Indians searching for useful objects. None of the roofs are left, but otherwise it would seem that everything has been spared human destruction.

The most important buildings date back to about 1450, i.e. around the time Pachacuti, the ninth Inca, founded his capital at Cuzco, which made a suitable center for his "empire of the four regions of the world." To look at, Machu Picchu has the air of a mountain fortress. But this is perhaps deceptive. The mountain on which it stands was not a strategically important point; and what enemy would have been able to climb up from that sea of tropical jungle below, splendidly visible from above? Perhaps the Inca used to retire to Machu Picchu to converse with the godhead; or perhaps again it was simply a sacred observatory. Yet the sheer amount of building materials used contradicts this theory.

The Spanish chroniclers make no mention of Machu Picchu. They only noted down what they learnt from oral traditions. Their *Ensayos* and *Comentarios Reales* are extremely interesting from certain points of view, but they are not very accurate. However, the authors of these works can hardly be blamed for such inexactitude, since in the Peruvian oral tradition the Inca monarch was a god. Their lack of interest in architecture is also frustrating. Spanish records only mention the buildings of Cuzco and elsewhere when describing their destruction or their transformation into Christian churches (as happened in the case of the "great Illa Tecce Viracocha," rebuilt and consecrated as a cathedral to the Virgin).

Inca architecture is too monotonous to merit close description. Yet the remarkable achievements of their stonemasons should be mentioned. Their work is exceptional not only in Pre-Columbian America: compared with it the Great Wall of China is primitive. In terms of the engineering involved it must be classed alongside the works of the Egyptian stonemasons. However, the remarkable precision of Peruvian masonry work was not developed under the Incas, but was the product of an ancient tradition which was strong also in other areas.

Machu Picchu is built in grey-pink granite. The blocks of stone (often enormously heavy) are not for the most part strictly parallelepipedal: their edges slant, probably so as to obtain the maximum possible volume each time, within the structural limitations of course; they all fit smoothly together and do not even require mortar.

The visible surfaces are curved slightly outwards. This was both aesthetically pleasing and practical. Those stones that did not lie absolutely flush with the others could be chipped away at *in situ* until they were perfect. The rejection of right-angled corners, which are normally so convenient in stonemasonry, meant that each stone had to be individually adapted to those already in position.

In some places walls have been distort-

Opposite, above: *the* Choquequilla *("Golden Moon") of Cuzco—a "false gate" sculpted in the rock face. The spherical vault that originally topped this splendid sculpture was dynamited by treasure hunters.*
Opposite, below: *Machu Picchu, an illustration of the remarkable precision achieved by Peruvian stonemasons during the Inca period.*

ed by earthquakes, but for the most part they have been immune to the ravages of time. Although Machu Picchu has been researched and mapped out down to the tiniest detail, it still remains as much of a mystery as when it was first discovered. No records tell us why or for whom it was built. The stones themselves are silent. One can only conjecture on the meaning and purpose of such a massive complex of stone buildings up in the mountains, cut off from everywhere. There will never be an answer. Perhaps it was just some ruler's desperate form of self-aggrandizement; perhaps it was simply the product of immense religious fervour.

THE MAIN FEATURES THAT DISTINGUISH STYLES

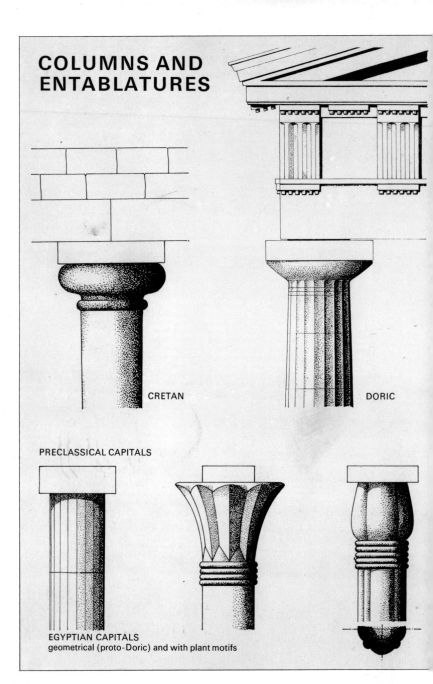

COLUMNS AND ENTABLATURES

CRETAN

DORIC

PRECLASSICAL CAPITALS

EGYPTIAN CAPITALS
geometrical (proto-Doric) and with plant motifs

The three classical orders of columns, according to Vitruvius

IONIC

CORINTHIAN

cube capital (Iberian)
Jaén, southern Spain

scroll capital from an
Etruscan tomb, Caere (Cerveteri)

scroll capital
Megiddo, Syria

CAPITALS

The austerity of the ancient orders of columns gave way in late Roman times to a greater freedom, albeit void of imagination, and was then lost altogether for centuries. During the early Christian era, capitals from old ruined palaces were used for churches. The Middle Ages then saw a remarkable creative flowering of the art of the capital, which began to lapse only with the advent of the Gothic style.

ROMAN
composite capital

ROMAN
from the Capitoline temple

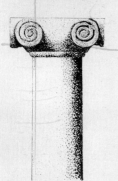

FRANKISH
Fulda, c. 820

PROTO-ROMANESQUE
cushion capital

ROMANESQUE
Wimpfen, c. 1200

GOTHIC: foliate capitals, with acanthus foliage (center)

TUSCAN
temple column, Vulci

BYZANTINE
from Hagia Sophia

BYZANTINE
from Ravenna

ROMANESQUE
Quedlinburg

ROMANESQUE
Eschau, near Strasbourg

MOORISH
Alhambra, Granada

RENAISSANCE

BAROQUE: capitals based on Hellenistic styles

PILLARS AND PILASTERS

ROMAN

ROMANESQUE

GOTHIC

RENAISSANCE

BAROQUE

NEOCLASSICAL

DOORWAYS

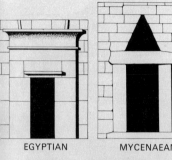

EGYPTIAN

MYCENAEAN

GREEK

ROMAN

CAROLINGIAN

ROMANESQUE

MOORISH

GOTHIC

RENAISSANCE

BAROQUE

ROCOCO

NEOCLASSICAL

WINDOWS

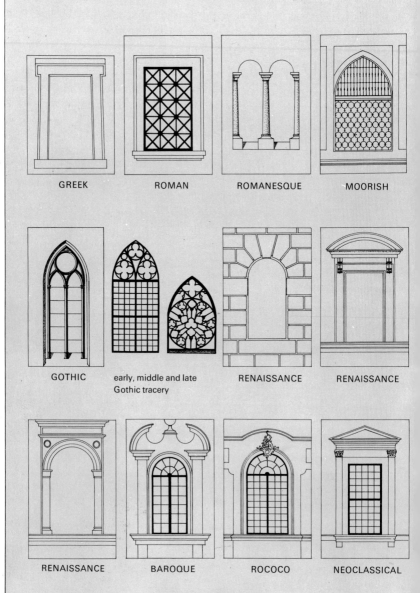

GREEK

ROMAN

ROMANESQUE

MOORISH

GOTHIC

early, middle and late
Gothic tracery

RENAISSANCE

RENAISSANCE

RENAISSANCE

BAROQUE

ROCOCO

NEOCLASSICAL

PEDIMENTS AND GABLES

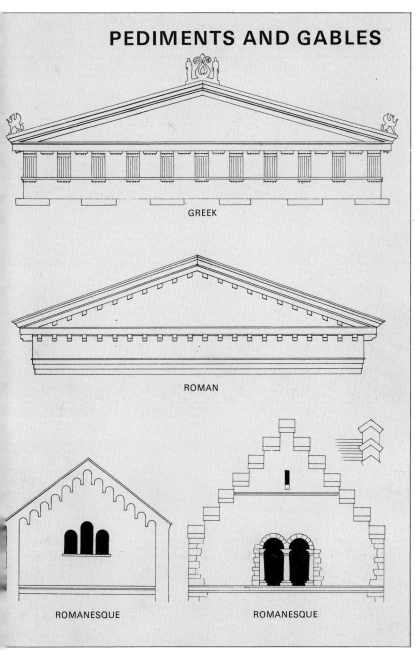

GREEK

ROMAN

ROMANESQUE

ROMANESQUE

GABLES AND FAÇADES

ROMAN
reconstruction of a house at Ostia

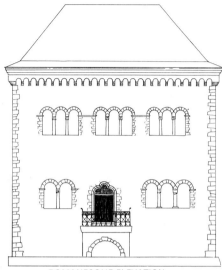

ROMANESQUE ELEVATION
Gelnhausen, the old town hall

GOTHIC

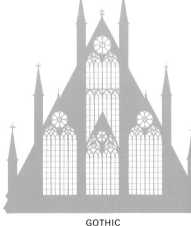

GOTHIC

GOTHIC
Greifswald, Town hall

GOTHIC
Nuremberg, Nassauer Haus

FAÇADES

RENAISSANCE
Right: Palazzo de'
Porti, Vicenza,
designed by Andrea
Palladio and begun in
1552
Below, left: Leyden
Town Hall, 1599
Below, right: house in
Brussels, 1680.

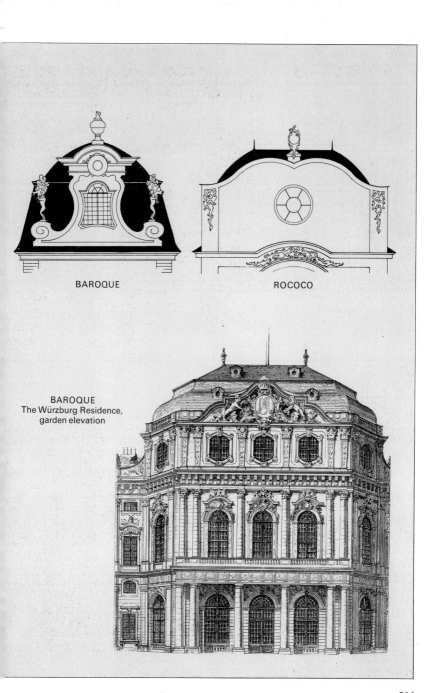

BAROQUE

ROCOCO

BAROQUE
The Würzburg Residence,
garden elevation

211

TOWERS

GREEK
evolved from
the circular temple

ROMAN
original
form

ROMAN
watchtower
with wooden
superstructure

FRANKISH
the Frankish
tower at Treviri,
c. 500

SAXON
Earl's Barton,
England,
c. 1000

GOTHIC
Teyn church
Prague

GOTHIC
unfinished

GOTHIC
Esslingen

RENAISSANCE

RENAISSANCE
bell tower

section of
battlement

hole for
pouring
down
boiling water
or oil onto
attackers

ROMANESQUE
small
bell tower

tower over a crossing
(abbey church of Maria Laach)

ISLAMIC
tower at
Jerusalem

minaret

GOTHIC
battlemented
defensive tower

RENAISSANCE

BAROQUE

BAROQUE

NEOCLASSICAL

THEATERS

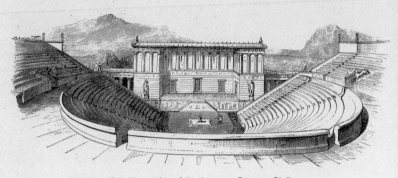

artist's impression of the theater at Segesta, Sicily

plan of a Greek theater

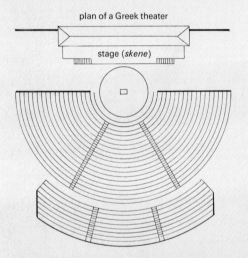

stage (*skene*)

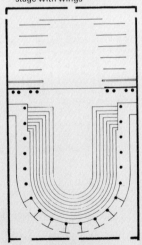

plan of a Renaissance theater: stage with wings

For the Greeks a theater was a sacred place of recreation and culture. Their dramas originated from the rowdy festive processions of musicians, dancers and singers in honour of Dionysus. To begin with, the stage was simply a podium attached to the main dance platform, with a tent (Greek: *skene*) on it. This tent soon became a low, three-door hut. In the sixth century, three centuries before Aeschylus, the first of the great Greek tragedians, the theater finally acquired its definitive form of a stepped semicircle.

stage of the old
Kurfürstliches Opernhaus
(Opera House) in
Munich, *c.* 1690

the Swan Theatre, London,
in Shakespeare's day;
"apron stage" in front
of the "study," with
audience galleries
all the way round

plan of
a modern
theater with
revolving stage
(with curved
horizon)

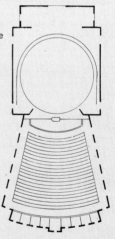

section of the Berlin
Philharmonic Konzerthaus
(designed by Hans
Scharoun, 1963)

GROUND PLANS OF CHURCHES

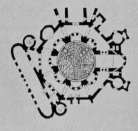

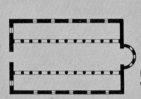

Plan of an early Christian basilica with three aisles and an apse.

ROMANESQUE
Church with triple apse: Sankt Maria im Kapitol, Cologne. Consecrated in 1067, the vaulting was finished around 1200.

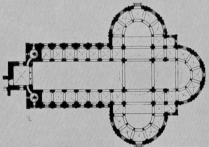

ROMANESQUE
Three aisles and two choirs, four circular towers, and one octagonal tower over the crossing: Worms Cathedral. Started in the eleventh century; east chancel consecrated in 1181; center nave finished c. 1220.

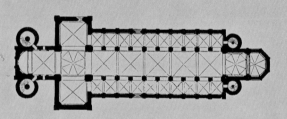

GOTHIC
Five aisles—nave and four side aisles—with a tower above the west crossing: Ulm Cathedral. Architects: members of the Parler family, 1377; then Ulrich von Ensingen, 1392; and Matthäus Böblinger in the fifteenth century. The tower (530 ft., 161.5 m.) was not completed until 1890.

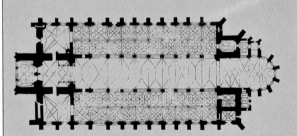

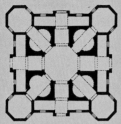

RENAISSANCE
Plan of the church designed by
Antonio Filarete *c.* 1460 for the
ideal city of Zagalia: octagonal
centralized plan, symmetrical
entrances, side chapels.

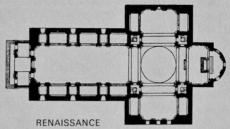

RENAISSANCE
San Andrea, Mantua, designed by
Leon Battista Alberti around 1470:
main nave with side chapels,
and domed crossing.

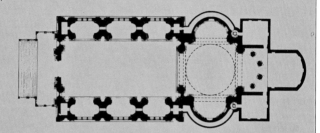

RENAISSANCE
Il Redentore
(Church of the
Redeemer) in
Venice, designed
by Andrea
Palladio, 1577.

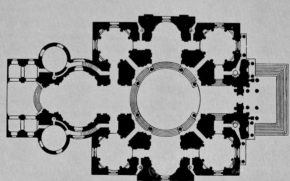

BAROQUE
Saint-Louis-des-
Invalides, Paris,
built in 1706 by
Jules Hardouin-
Mansart: plan
based on St
Peter's, Rome.

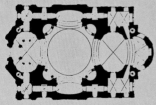

Sankt Laurenz, Gabel (Bohemia),
built by Lukas von Hildebrandt, 1710.

GROUND PLANS OF HOUSES

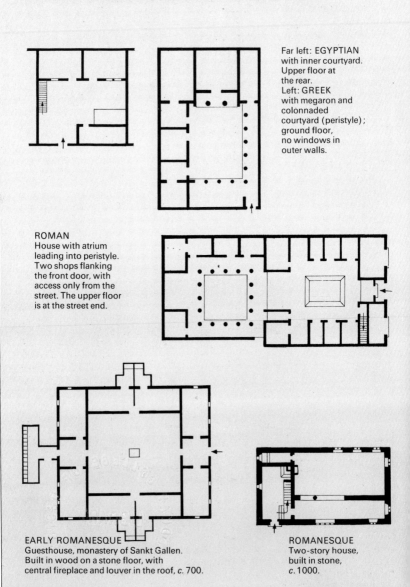

Far left: EGYPTIAN
with inner courtyard.
Upper floor at
the rear.
Left: GREEK
with megaron and
colonnaded
courtyard (peristyle);
ground floor,
no windows in
outer walls.

ROMAN
House with atrium
leading into peristyle.
Two shops flanking
the front door, with
access only from the
street. The upper floor
is at the street end.

EARLY ROMANESQUE
Guesthouse, monastery of Sankt Gallen.
Built in wood on a stone floor, with
central fireplace and louver in the roof, c. 700.

ROMANESQUE
Two-story house,
built in stone,
c. 1000.

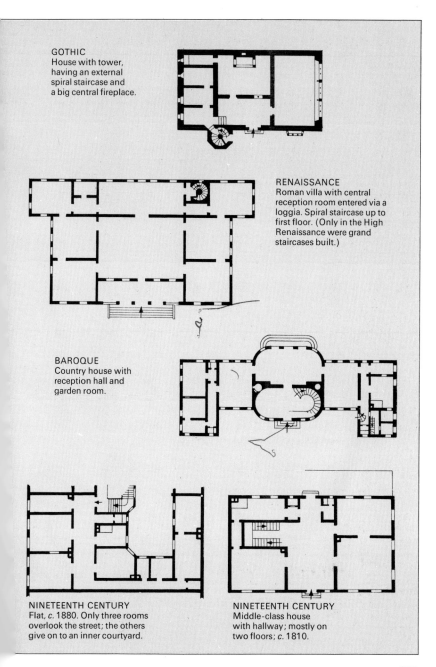

GOTHIC
House with tower,
having an external
spiral staircase and
a big central fireplace.

RENAISSANCE
Roman villa with central
reception room entered via a
loggia. Spiral staircase up to
first floor. (Only in the High
Renaissance were grand
staircases built.)

BAROQUE
Country house with
reception hall and
garden room.

NINETEENTH CENTURY
Flat, c. 1880. Only three rooms
overlook the street; the others
give on to an inner courtyard.

NINETEENTH CENTURY
Middle-class house
with hallway; mostly on
two floors; c. 1810.

GLOSSARY

This glossary includes both a number of architectural terms and biographical details about certain major architects.

Abacus
The top of a capital (generally square) on which the architrave directly rests.

Acanthus leaf
Naturalistic decorative motif of the Corinthian capital.

Adam, Robert (1728–92)
Scottish neoclassical architect, whose main works are private houses in and around London (e.g. Syon House, Middlesex, 1762).

Adobe
Crude form of brick baked in the sun, found particularly in Mexico and the Southwest.

Aedicola ("small house")
Architectural ensemble often abutting on a larger edifice, and usually intended as a niche for a statue (illustrated on p. 230). As decoration it frequently incorporates two columns and a pediment.

Aesculapius
Temple or shrine of Asclepius (Lat. *Aesculapius*), the Greek god of medicine. His temples generally stood near a spring or well, and had lodgings for pilgrims, as well as a portico and facilities for purificatory ablutions.

Aisle
In a church, the area parallel to the center nave, from which it is separated by a row of pillars.

Alberti, Leon Battista (1404–72)
Man of letters, art theorist, and one of the greatest early Renaissance architects. Main works: S. Francesco, Rimini (Tempio Mala-testiano, 1447, unfinished); renovation of the Palazzo Rucellai, Florence (1447–51); S. Maria Novella, Florence (façade, 1456); S. Andrea, Mantua (1470). Author of treatises on architecture, painting, perspective, and sculpture.

Altana
Covered loggia on a roof.

Alternation of pillars
Constructional formula often found in medieval churches, whereby pillars are inserted every so often into a row of columns (e.g. P–CC–P–CC–P etc., or P–CCC–P–CCC). Illustrated below.

Ambon
A raised desk resting on either a solid base or on pillars, and with a parapet. Intended in early Christian churches for the "Liturgy of the Word," the ambon later became part of the *schola cantorum*.

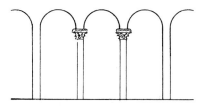

Alternation of pillars

Amphiprostyle
Used to describe temples having a colonnade both at the front and the back.

Anta
Pillar-shaped end feature of a colonnade or section of wall.

Antefix
Ornamental block hiding the ends of temple roof tiles.

Apse
In churches, the semicircular end of the choir. Carolingian churches often had apses at both ends of the main nave. During the Romanesque period they increased in number, sometimes also featuring at either end of the transept (originally a Roman design).

Aqueduct
Invented by the Romans, a structure for "transporting" water usually carried by a string of piers and arches.

Arabesque
Decorative motif consisting of interweaving lines or curved geometrical figures endlessly repeated (as in Islamic art). In late Roman and Renaissance architecture, an intricate curvilinear design incorporating vegetable and animal forms.

Arcade
A regular series of arches supported on pillars or columns.

Archaic
Used in art history to denote the early phase of a style.

Arch, shapes of
A round or Roman arch; **B** ogive or lancet arch; **C** flattened arch; **D** horseshoe arch; **E** ogee (common in Islamic and late Gothic buildings); **F** depressed or longitudinal arch; **G** trefoil arch; **H** curtain arch; **J** Tudor arch. Illustrated below.

Architrave
The lowest of the three main parts of a classical entablature.

Archivolt
Moulding following the line of the intrados of an arch. A purely decorative feature, it none-theless accentuates the spatial quality of the arch.

Art Nouveau
Style that influenced various art forms in Europe from about 1890 to the early years of the twentieth century.

Asam, Cosmas Damian (1686–1739)
Painter and architect, southern German Baroque. Main works: monastic church of Weltenburg; Rohr Augustinian chapter house; and St John Nepomuk, Munich, with his own house next door.

Asam, Egid Quirin (1692–1750)
Sculptor; collaborated with his brother Cosmas Damian.

Atlas/Atlantes *see* **Telamon**

Atrium
Central room in a Roman house, receiving light from a square opening in the roof known as the *compluvium*, which also allowed rain water to fall into the *impluvium* – a pool set into the floor.

Attic
Low wall above the cornice intended to hide the roof (illustrated below). In Baroque archi-tecture a balustrade was often used instead.

Auricular style
Style of decoration widespread in Germany and Holland in the sixteenth and seventeenth centuries, executed in stucco and inlay (G. *Ohrmuschelstil*).

Avantcorps
Any part of a building that projects beyond the line of the façade. Of major importance in the arrangement and balance of architectural volume. Already a feature of medieval archi-tecture, the avantcorps may project either from the center or from the sides of an elevation. In modern buildings it tends not to be sym-metrical, its shape generally varying according to functional requirements.

Azulejo
(Spanish, from the Arabic *azzulleíg*) a ter-racotta strip with interlacing geometrical design.

Bahr, Georg (1666–1738)
Master carpenter and architect, designer of the Dresden Frauenkirche.

Baldacchino
Less commonly, baldachin. Ornate flat or tentlike cloth roof suspended above a throne, pulpit, altar, or bed. By derivation, in archi-tecture, a similar structure in any material.

Baluster
Small variously shaped column (illustrated below). A line of balusters connected by a

Balusters

common base strip and a rail on the top is a balustrade.

Baptistery
Building specifically designed for baptism. Starting as a simple covered *piscina*, it devel-oped into a small church – octagonal, round, or square – separate from that built for worship.

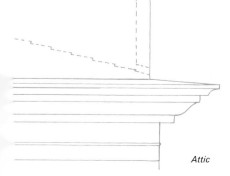

Attic

Baroque
See the **Baroque and Rococo** chapter for the origins of this word. Denotes the period roughly between 1600 and 1750 in both the arts and social history.

Base
The part of a column or pillar between the shaft and the supporting substructure. In the Greek Doric order there was no base.

Basilica
(From the Greek *basilikstó*, "royal portico.") In Roman architecture, a rectangular building with central nave and two side aisles separated off by means of columns or pillars, and with the entrance usually in one of the short elevations. Christian basilicas were churches with several naves or aisles (three to five), having a double pitched roof over the center nave and single pitched roofs over the side aisles.

Baths
In the Roman world, a building equipped with steam baths, generally consisting of one large main room and numerous smaller rooms. The most sophisticated baths (the imperial baths) incorporated a *frigidarium*, a *tepidarium*, and a *caldarium* in succession along a central axis, together with various secondary rooms such as changing rooms, massage rooms, and even gymnasiums and libraries.

Behrens, Peter (1868–1940)
German architect and architectural theorist. Worked in Düsseldorf, Vienna, and Berlin. Both industrial and residential buildings. In 1936 placed in charge of the *Meisterklasse für Baukunst* (architectural masterclass) at the Preussische Akademie der Künste in Berlin.

Bema
(From the Greek *béma*, "a step.") The presbytery or sanctuary and apse in a Byzantine church, always semicircular, with a vaulted roof.

Bernini, Gianlorenzo (1598–1680)
Architect and sculptor, the greatest Italian Baroque master. Main works: the colonnade of St Peter's basilica; the Fontana dei Quattro Fiumi in Piazza Navona; and the angels on the Ponte di Castel Sant'Angelo (all in Rome).

Bibiena
Family of Italian architects, stage designers, and painters. Real name, Galli, but called Bibiena after their place of origin (presently Bibbiena, near Florence). Active in the seventeenth and eighteenth centuries. Main works include: the Teatro di Corte, Mantua (1731), probably designed by Antonio; the Jesuit church at Mannheim (1740), designed by Alessandro; the Markgräfliches Opernhaus at Bayreuth (1748), by Giuseppe; and the Teatro Comunale, Bologna (1763), by Antonio.

Biedermeier
Style that emerged in Germany towards the end of neoclassicism, just before the Revolutions of 1848. See **Neoclassicism** chapter for the origins and connotations of the word.

Borromini, Francesco (1599–1667)
Italian Baroque architect, and first exponent of the Rococo in Italy. Main works, in Rome: S. Ivo alla Sapienza (1642–1660); S. Agnese, Piazza Navona (1653–1661); S. Carlino alle Quattro Fontane (1634–41).

Boulle, André-Charles (1642–1732)
French Baroque cabinet maker and decorator. Made furniture for Louis XIV. His masterpiece is considered to be the *cabinet* of the Dauphin.

Bracket
Corbel at the top of a tower supporting balconies and battlements.

Bramante, Donato di Pascuccio d'Antonio (1444–1514)
Architect and painter of the Italian Renaissance, active above all in Milan and Rome. Main works: S. Maria presso S. Satiro, Milan (?1480–86); work on the new Fabbrica di S. Pietro and the Vatican (1506–13); the "Tempietto" of S. Pietro in Montorio (1502).

Breuer, Marcel (1902–)
Hungarian architect, studied at the Bauhaus, where he then taught alongside Gropius. Active in Berlin till 1931, then in London, and after 1937 in the U.S.A., where he later found himself once again teaching and working together with Gropius. Gropius and Breuer continued to be associated for many years. His main works include: a house in Wiesbaden (1932); a house in Zurich (1935); Breuer House in Cambridge, Massachusetts (1938); the New Kensington Center, Pennsylvania, in collaboration with Gropius.

Brunelleschi, Filippo (1377–1446)
Architect and sculptor; together with

Donatello and Masaccio, one of the first geniuses of the Tuscan Renaissance. He evolved new methods of architecture, accentuating certain architectonic features to achieve perspective effects. Main works include: the dome of S. Maria del Fiore (1421–36); the Ospedale delgi Innocenti; the Capella de' Pazzi; S. Lorenzo; S. Spirito; the Pitti palace (central block) and the Villa Pitti (all in Florence).

Bucranium (bucrane)
(From the Greek *boukránion*, a compound of *boús*, "ox," and *kránion*, "skull.") Ornamental motif in the shape of an ox skull, evoking animal sacrifices. Variously adorned with swags and garlands of foliage.

Buttress
The most striking characteristic of Gothic architecture. A means of distributing the weight of a building evenly away from the external walls. Flying buttresses in particular thus serve both to support the building as a whole and, so to speak, to deflect the pressure of the vaulting from the walls, thereby enabling them to be at once thinner and yet able to accommodate vast windows.

Byzantine art
Grew up and evolved in Byzantium (Constantinople). The term is generally used to include all Eastern Christian art between the fourth and fourteenth century, in which late Roman and Oriental elements are fused.

Canon
(From the Greek *kanón*, literally "stick," then "rule" or "norm.") In architecture, the set norms determining the proportions and symmetry and the relationships between individual features of a building. The whole

Spherical (spheroidal) dome

question of the classical canon was explored in depth in the Renaissance.

Capital
The top section of a column, often quite elaborate, and always a striking stylistic feature. It is the shape of the capital that

principally determines architectural order (Doric, Ionic, etc.). **Cube capital** (illustrated below): **Romanesque capital** in the shape of a die, rounded where it is joined to the column. **Composite capital**: Hellenistic style, combining the Corinthian acanthus leaf with the Ionic scroll. **Sculpted capital**: a common

Capital

feature of French Romanesque – the capital carved with figurative decoration. In a row of arches the capitals may thus recount stories from the Bible.

Carolingian art
That flowering of art under the Franks during the so-called Carolingian Renaissance, influenced by pre-Romanesque Italian models. It was in this period that houses north of the Alps began to be built in stone.

Cartouche
Ornamental motif shaped like a shield or paper scroll in the middle, or a simple framed rectangular panel. Set above a window or door, it usually contains some heraldic device or inscription. Mostly either of plaster or wood, it may also merely be painted onto the wall.

Caryatid
Statue of a woman serving as a pillar. Rare in antiquity. The only remaining example is the Erechtheion, part of the Athens acropolis. Caryatids were introduced in Romanesque art as decoration on pulpits and episcopal cathedras.

Catacomb
(From nonclassical Greek *katá kúmbas*, "caves." Subterranean burial place in the early centuries of the Christian era, consisting of low, narrow galleries (*cryptae*), in the walls of which the actual "graves" (*loculi*) were cut, in varying arrangements. The oldest catacomb is probably that of St Sebastian in Rome, on the Via Appia.

Scrollwork

Cathedral
A church housing a bishop's *cathedra* (throne). In the early days of Christianity the bishop's throne was in the middle of the apse; later it was placed on one side of the choir.

Cavalier
Tower (small, often a bell tower) on the ridge of a double pitched roof.

Cella
In ancient temples, the inner room (Gr. *naós*), mostly without windows, where the statue of the god or goddess was. In private Roman houses, any four-sided storeroom or box room.

Cement
Building material composed of sand, gravel, and water mixed in an agglomerate with other hardening substances. Method of production: limestone and clay are mixed and heated until they fuse; the resultant clinker is then broken up and mixed with gypsum, and finally ground to powder. Produced on an industrial scale for the first time in England in about 1825. Germany nowadays is Europe's biggest producer of cement, with Italy second.

Cenotaph
(From the Greek *kenós*, "empty," and *táphos*, "tomb.") Funerary monument erected in memory of a famous person; often similar in shape to a barrow or a large urn.

Centralized plan
Ground plan of a building conceived around a central point of intersection of axes of equal length, the ideal shape being a circle; squares and regular polygons are also possible shapes for such buildings.

Chinoiserie
Style of decoration based on Chinese models, though highly idiosyncratic and individual in inventiveness. Especially common in the Rococo.

Chippendale, Thomas (1718?–79)
English cabinet maker who has lent his name to a certain style of furniture, in which Baroque, Gothic, and Chinese elements are all combined. Author of *The Gentleman and Cabinet Maker's Director* (1754).

Choir
In early Christian basilicas, that part of the building reserved for the singers. Situated in front of the altar, it was separated from the area behind by high stalls. Enlarged in Romanesque

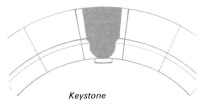

Keystone

and Gothic cathedrals to accommodate the bishop and chapter.

Churriguera, José Benito de
(1665–1723/25)
Spanish architect and sculptor who combined Italian Baroque forms and motifs with Gothic stylistic elements (style known as Churrigueresque).

Cist tomb
Made of stone slabs, sometimes with figurative relief decoration. Common in the Bronze Age in central and eastern Europe, the cist tomb may be considered a forerunner of the sarcophagus. The "soul hole" in the front slab was probably intended for votive offerings.

Cloister
Courtyard with colonnade in a monastery, the arcades decorated with carvings or paintings of religious subjects. The most aesthetically pleasing and architecturally impressive cloisters date from the Romanesque and Gothic periods.

Collarino (or neck)
In the classical orders, that section of the column where the shaft is connected to the capital by means of a cincture and an astragal. In Romanesque architecture it is usually to be found around the middle of the shaft, and is common as a form of decoration on small, slender ornamental columns.

Colonial style
A style developed by Europeans in their colonies. Of special note, that of the southern States of America, in which adapted Renaissance and neoclassical elements are combined and developed according to personal taste. Some forms of colonial style attempted to copy "Old World" models, and so in its own way the style is historicist. Thus, for instance, stone models were imitated in wood; ship's carpenters made doric columns in the form of ship hulls on vertical ribs; egg and dart motifs were improvised with individual pieces turned on a lathe. Even stronger than the claims

Onion domes

of ostentation, however, were the essential practical considerations of making buildings habitable. Many are free imitations of European models.

Colonnade
Line of columns bearing either arches or an entablature, generally an ambulatory around an inner area, though often also connecting two separate architectural units. Occasionally simply freestanding. Popular in Baroque and Classicism.

Colonnette
In Gothic architecture, a slender pilaster which continues on up in the vault rib.

Columbarium
In early Christian times, a sepulcher with niches in the walls for cinerary urns (also a single such niche). So named because of the restrictions of space, which meant that the urns had to be placed close together.

Column
Vertical, round support for an entablature, arch, or other similar structure. Varies in shape according to style or order, and even then considerable variety exists within individual styles. The shapes of columns are major determining features of style (see **Greece** and **Rome** chapters for discussion of the "orders").

Concrete
Water, sand, crushed stone or gravel, and cement powder to bond the mixture. There are various methods of obtaining the correct mixture: with shovels and spades, on a wooden floor, or mechanically (with a concrete mixer) for work on a larger scale. The mixture is poured into moulds while still wet, to harden into the right shape. Concrete is also used for prefabricated building components. Greater resistance to traction and flexion is achieved by the insertion of metal rods into the mixture (reinforced concrete).

Confession
In liturgical parlance, the tomb of a confessor (one who confesses to Christianity in spite of persecution but without suffering martyrdom) or martyr. Usually situated under the high altar.

Coptic style
Early Christian style combining Egyptian, Hellenistic, Syrian, and Byzantine elements. The Copts are Christian descendants of the ancient Egyptians, and their spiritual center is Alexandria.

Corbel
A structural block having one end embedded in a wall and the other projecting out to support a cornice, arch base, etc. In the Corinthian order the modillions (brackets supporting the upper part of the cornice) are in effect small corbels. False corbels sometimes feature on buildings for purely ornamental purposes.

Corinthian order
Ornamental principle of ancient architecture, the most characteristic feature being the acanthus leaf capital. Further details in the **Greece** and **Rome** chapters. Hellenistic styles are mostly based on the Corinthian.

Cornice

The top (usually distinctly shaped) of a wall or any elevation, base structure, gable, pediment, or window (illustrated below). A cornice added on separately is described as "false" (such a feature is technically somewhat questionable).

Cosmati (Maestri)

The name commonly given to marble workers and decorators of the twelfth, thirteenth and fourteenth centuries in Rome and southern Latium, derived from the name *Cosma* which was very popular among them.

Cross

One of the oldest of all symbolic ornamental motifs. Especially as a Christian symbol, there are numerous forms of cross. **A** Greek; **B** Latin; **C** saltire or St Andrew's; **D** Tau or St Anthony's; **E** double with crossed arms; **F** fork; **G** Maltese; **H** potent; **J** triple or Papal; **K** patriarchal or double or of Lorraine; **L** Russian. Illustrated below right and opposite. The St Peter's Cross is the Latin cross upside down (recalling the Apostle's form of martyrdom). Jerusalem cross illustrated on p. 233.

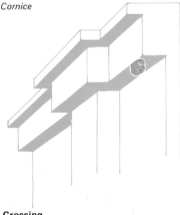

Cornice

Crossing

In a cruciform church, the area of intersection of the center nave and the transept.

Crown

Top section of a building. May take various forms: cornice, battlements, etc.

Crypt

In a Christian church sunken or wholly subterranean chamber, usually sited underneath the choir, where a martyr was buried. In Romanesque architecture it expanded considerably, to cover most of the area of the (raised) sanctuary, becoming a chapel in itself. Rare in post-Gothic architecture.

Cupola

(Italian, "dome.") Dome raised on a square, polygonal, elliptic, or circular base. In the case of four-sided base structures, the transition to a circle at the base of the actual dome was achieved by means of pedentives (an inverted concave triangle of brick springing from each corner and all meeting at the top).

Curtain wall

Technique introduced in the United States in 1950–55, whereby non-load-bearing prefabricated panels are attached to the outside of a structural framework of (usually) steel or reinforced concrete. Provides extra thermal and sound insulation.

Cuvilliés, François de (1695–1768)

French architect and interior designer of the German Rococo. Worked at the court of Bavaria. Principal works include; the Residenztheater (restored after World War II); and the Amalienburg in the Nymphenburg park (both in Munich).

Decorated style

Period of English Gothic (c. 1270–1350) characterized by lavish ornamentation.

Dentil

Small rectangular block – one of a row – under the bed moulding of an Ionic cornice.

Desornamentado

A style of the Spanish Renaissance (under Philip II) characterized by extreme formal austerity.

Deutsches Band

Zigzag frieze common in German brick architecture.

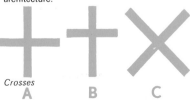

Crosses
A   B   C

D   E   F

G   H

J   K   L

Crosses

Dientzenhofer
Family of Franco-Bohemian Baroque architects: Christoph (1655–1722), Johann (1663–1726), and Kilian Igniz (1689–1751).

Dipteral temple
(From the Greek *dípteros*, "double-winged.") Temple featuring two rows of columns around the cells.

Directoire
In art history, period of French Neoclassicism, so named after the Directory that governed revolutionary France from October 27, 1795, to November 10, 1799. Chronologically the style (or rather "fashion") cannot be clearly separated from the Louis Seize style that preceded it and the Empire style that followed.

Doric order
See **Greece** and **Rome** chapters.

Dosseret (pulvin)
Crowning element of a pillar or column; usually with sloping sides, it forms a base structure for an entablature or arch.

Duomo
(Italian for "cathedral.") Derived from abbreviation of ecclesiastical Latin *Domus Dei* ("house of God").

Early English
First phase of English Gothic (*c.* 1175–1270).

Echinus
(From the Greek *echinos*, "curl.") Circular convex moulding between the abacus and rings of a Doric capital.

Eclecticism
The combining of features of various styles remote both in time and space in order to create something new. Of major importance in architectural thinking in nineteenth-century Europe.

Effner, Joseph (1687–1745)
German architect at the court of Bavaria. Principal works include: wings of the Nymphenburg Palace (1716–18), and parts of Schloss Schleissheim (1719–26) (both in Munich).

Egg and dart
Moulding (convex, semicircular in section) featuring a line of olive, pearl, or bean shapes alternating regularly with an inverted lancehead shape. Typical of Ionic order. Illustrated on p. 232.

Eiermann, Egon (1904–1970)
German architect who contributed to the formation of International Style.

Elgin Marbles
Collection of whole sculptures and fragments from the Parthenon, now in the British Museum, London. So named in memory of Lord Elgin, the British ambassador in Athens who acquired them from the Turks and sent them to London.

Elizabethan
The age of Queen Elizabeth I of England. Stylistically, the final stages of English Gothic, and the flowering of the Renaissance in England.

Emblem
Representational figure having certain ethical, social, liturgical, or political associations, used as a form of ornamentation. Heraldic crests evolved from emblems.

Empire
French Neoclassicism under the Emperor Napoleon, as a style, 1800–30. Characterized by functional, restrained use of Hellenistic and sometimes (somewhat adapted) Egyptian ornamental motifs.

Encrustation
Technique of decoration, whereby pieces of coloured stone are set into the actual building stone. Much in vogue in antiquity and in Byzantine art, it was also common in later periods, particularly for floors.

English garden
Emerged in the second half of the eighteenth century; differs from the more geometrically ordered Baroque garden by its "landscape" effect.

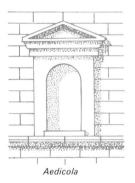

Aedicola

Entasis
(The Greek for "effort," "tension.") The bulge in the Doric column shaft, generally about a third of the way up. Sometimes seems more pronounced than it is in reality.

Epistyle (architrave)
(From the Greek *epistúlion*, "that above the column.") Greek nomenclature for the lower section of the entablature.

Erdmannsdorf, Friederich Wilhelm von (1736–1800)
German Rococo and early neoclassical archi-

tect. Works: Schloss Wörlitz (1769–73); rooms in Sanssouci and the Berliner Schloss (1786–88).

Erwin, later known as Erwin of Steinbach (?–1318)
Magister operis (from 1283 to his death) of Strasbourg cathedral. As has recently been proven, he in fact only designed the west front, with its striking lancet windows above the rose window.

Exedra
In Greek and Roman architecture, a spacious semicircular room by the atrium, completely open on the peristyle side. Early form of the apse.

Extrados
External surface area of an arch or vault.

Faience
Pottery from the Italian town of Faenza (*Faience* being the French version of the name), where ceramic ware was first produced in the fourteenth century. The paste – a mixture predominantly of limestone, kaolin, and quartz – is either modelled on a wheel or poured in liquid form into plaster moulds. It is then fired at around 1200–1300° C and glazed, according to various methods. The individual pieces are then decorated with vitrifiable paints and fired again at about 100° C.

False dome
Dome achieved by means of ever smaller stone rings rising up one on top of another.

Fischer, Johann Michael (1691–1766)
The leading exponent of southern German Baroque architecture. His buildings – churches and monasteries – are characterized by simplicity of line externally, and lightness and brilliance of structural and decorative imagination internally. Main works Benedictine church at Zwiefalten; the abbey of Ottobeuren (considered his masterpiece); St Michael's church, Berg am Laim (Munich); and the abbey of Rott am Inn.

Fischer von Erlach, Johann Bernhard (1656–1723)
Austrian Baroque architect, elevated to the nobility as architect to the Imperial Court. Main works: the Karl Borromäus Kirche; the Hofbibliothek (court library); and the Spanish Riding School (all in Vienna).

Flamboyant

(French, literally "flaming.") A style prevalent during the latter stages of French Gothic, similar to English Late Decorated. Window tracery featuring elaborate flame-like patterns.

Fluting

Vertical grooves running down the shaft of a column. Sharp-edged and rounded in section in the Doric order, they are semicircular in section and separated by fillets in the Ionic.

Flying buttress *see* Buttress

Foil

In Gothic and Moorish architecture, the small decorative arc or space between the cusps of a window or arch. Thus according to the number of foils, an arch may be twin-foil, trefoil, quatrefoil, or multifoil. Illustrated on p. 236.

Foliage, carved

Sculpted stone decoration on the edges of spires, gables, etc. in the shape of sinuous, wavy leaves; a common form of late Gothic ornamentation especially. Illustrated above right.

Fontana, Carlo (1634–1714)

Baroque architect, pupil and collaborator of Bernini's – fusing the techniques of his master with those of Borromini. Author of various writings including *Templum Vaticanum*. Originally from Brusada (in the Canton of Ticino), he worked in Rome.

Fontana, Domenico (1543–1607)

Architect and *stuccatore* (plasterer) in Rome and Naples. He organized large-scale architectural ventures, and amongst other things supervised the transport of the obelisk now in St Peter's square. His masterpiece is the Royal Palace in Naples.

Forum

In the Roman world, an open area, rectangular in shape, forming the main square of a town, and serving both as a marketplace and for political assemblies. Surrounded by public buildings and temples, it had a distinctly religious atmosphere. According to the classical canon, the width of the form had to be two thirds the length, and its surface area was in proportion to the number of inhabitants in the town.

Carved foliage

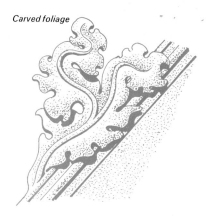

Fresco

Technique of wall painting. The paints are without bonders and are applied to the thin final layer of wall plaster (*intonaco*) while it is still wet (hence the Italian name *affresco – a fresco*, "while fresh"). The lime from the *intonaco* mixes with the sulphurous anhydride of the atmosphere and forms a layer of calcium carbonate which fixes the colours. Fresco generally lasts better than paintings on dry plaster (*a secco*).

Frieze

An ornamental band, usually horizontal, on a wall. Sometimes painted, sometimes sculpted, the ornamentation may be either abstract or figurative. Often characteristic of a particular style. **A** Romanesque round-arch frieze; **B** Norman and Gothic interlacing arch frieze; **C** denticulated frieze; **D** zigzag (Norman dogtooth). Another typically Norman feature is that in which each roundheaded decorative arch is overlapped by several others. Illustrated on p. 232.

Front steps

Open structure incorporating a flight of steps leading to the entrance of a house. A sort of no man's land between house and street. Common in Balkan towns, Holland and in the northern United States. Illustrated on p. 246.

Gable

A sharp-pointed structure surmounting a Gothic door or window. Triangular-topped end elevation of a building; any such vertical triangular section formed by the end of a ridged roof, stretching from the level of the eaves to the ridge. The "step gable" illustrated on p. 232

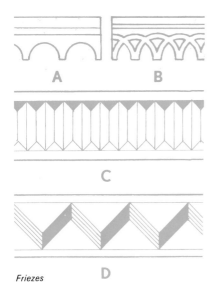

A   B

C

D

Friezes

French Gothic cathedrals sometimes have up to three galleries one above the other. The royal gallery of a Gothic church is a blind arcade with statues of kings, generally situated above the main door.

Egg and dart

Geison
(Greek term.) The cornice projecting above the frieze on an ancient temple.

Geometrical style
Characterized by a predominance of curved or broken lines recalling geometrical figures. Most prehistoric architecture is geometrical, concise and simple, though built without absolute precision.

Germanism
Forms of ornamentation of northern European origin (guilloches, snake motifs, etc.) that feature in Byzantine and Romanesque art, cropping up later also in historicist styles.

Giant order
Columns, pillars, or pilasters rising two or more floors up an external elevation. Commonly used by Palladio and his followers.

is a typical feature of Renaissance architecture in the Low Countries and northern Germany.

Gallery
A long, often narrow room or passage connecting two or more rooms. In early Christian basilicas the gallery (probably for women) ran above the side aisles, with arches giving onto the main nave. In Romanesque and Gothic church architecture there are often external galleries, serving both a stylistic purpose and

Gilly, Friedrich (1772–1800)
German architect based in Berlin, a pupil of Von Erdmannsdorf. Schinkel's teacher. None of his works survive. Many of his designs anticipate north German Neoclassicism, the most remarkable being that for the Prussian National Theater (1800). Gilly was also responsible for first restoring – and thereby saving – the Marienburg.

Gloriette
(French term.) Pavilion or kiosk, usually circular and open in a garden or park, topping a mound or on high ground, commemorating some person or event.

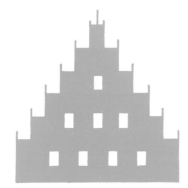

"Step gable"

for ease of maintenance. Greater ornamental value was achieved by rows of tiny arches.

Golden section
Certain strikingly harmonious proportions (governed by a precise mathematical formula) to be found in the reciprocal relation of the

Jerusalem cross

various parts of many buildings, in the articulation of façades, and even in decorative motifs. For greater detail see the **Renaissance** chapter.

Gothic
The great period of European art stretching from the middle of the twelfth century to the end of the Middle Ages (in some countries as late as the sixteenth century). For the origins and connotations of the word see the **Gothic** chapter.

Gothick
Punning designation of that style in which Gothic ornamentation is applied (sometimes to ridiculous excess) to buildings and furniture of later periods.

Goujon, Jean (1510–68)
French Renaissance sculptor and architect who worked in Rouen and (mainly) Paris. Principal works include: the nymphs on the Fontaine des Innocents (1549); decoration of the Louvre (1540–62); four caryatids in the Salle des Antiques in the Louvre (1550).

Graffito
Technique of wall decoration whereby layers of different coloured plaster are applied one on top of another and then carved away according to the particular design. The sections of each colour thus revealed then together form a decorative pattern (sometimes also a figurative design). The under layers tend to be darker than the upper.

Groin (cross) vault
The intersection of two barrel vaults at right angles to each other.

Gropius, Walter (1883–1969)
German architect, founder of the Bauhaus in Weimar (see **Neue Sachlichkeit** chapter). Main works include: the Fagus works, Alfeld (Hanover), in collaboration with Adolf Meyer (1910–11); the Bauhaus, Dessau (1925); the Harvard University Graduate Center (student residential complex), Cambridge, Mass.; and the Selb porcelain factory.

Guarini, Guarino (1624–83)
Late Baroque architect who worked principally in Turin for Charles Emmanuel II of Savoy. A geometrician and theorist of perspective, he created some remarkable decorative perspective effects in his buildings. Author of *Architectura civile* (1737), which had a considerable influence on eighteenth-century concepts of style. Main works in Turin (from 1668) include: the church of S. Lorenzo; the Chapel of the Holy Shroud; and the Palazzo Carignano.

Guild
The word used to denote all the craftsmen (together with their apprentices) engaged in building a church. Still occasionally used today in a similar sense. The members of the guild often had to keep certain building techniques secret. Some of the guilds still existed in the nineteenth century.

Guilloche
Ornamental motif, either painted or carved, composed of two or more intertwined rope-bands; found above all in classical architecture. First emerging with the Ionic order, it then became very popular with the Romans – either sculpted, in stucco, or in mosaic. In the Byzantine period and during the Dark Ages it underwent some curious transformations, achieving major stylistic importance in the early Middle Ages. Illustrated on p. 250.

Half-timbering
A method of building in wood. The walls consist of a framework of beams (mostly in square sections), constituting the load-bearing structure. The in-fill panels are generally of wattle and clay, though in later building brick was also used. Illustrated on p. 248.

Hall
Originally the inner courtyard (Greek, *aulé*) in a Greek house; later a large room intended for solemn assemblies.

Hallenkirche (hall church)
Differs from the basilica design in having both nave and aisles of equal height. Feature of German brick Gothic.

Hellenism
In art history, pertaining to the stylistic concepts that appeared in the age of Alexander the Great (c.330 B.C.) and continued through to the end of the Roman Empire (the reign of Hadrian). Great wealth of ornamentation, subtly balanced and adorned capitals, and naturalistic artistic expression.

Herm
Rectangular stone pillar surmounted by a male head (probably, at first, the god Hermes) and frequently inscribed. In classical times poets, scholars, and heroes were honoured with herms.

Hildebrant, Johann Lucas von
(1668–1745)
Austrian Baroque architect. A pupil of Carlo Fontana, he worked in Franconia and mainly in Vienna. Main works: the Belvedere and Kinsky Palace, Vienna; the new Schloss Mirabell, Salzburg; and the great staircase at Pommersfelden.

Hirsau, reform of
Originated with the Benedictine abbey of Hirsau (Baden-Württemberg, W. Germany). Finished in 1065, this then became the center of a school of architects who evolved new shapes for Romanesque churches, better suited to the Gregorian liturgy, which they were championing ("greater choir" for the singers, "lesser choir" for the non-singers, both usually before the crossing; no apse; and towers forming part of the façade). The new ideas spread through central and southern Germany in the tenth and eleventh centuries.

Historicism
A trend that became fashionable in the second half of the nineteenth century. A mixture – sometimes a mere jumbling together – of stylistic elements from the past. Most attention was paid to the façade, and it is noteworthy more for its technical achievements than for its aesthetic contribution.

Holl, Elias (1573–1646)
German architect employed by the city of Augsburg. Studied in Italy, where he came under the influence of Palladio – though he never shared Palladio's fondness for the Giant order. Main works: the Arsenal (1602–7) and town hall (1615–20) in Augsburg.

Hollar, Wenceslas (1607–67)
Copper engraver in Prague, pupil of Merian,

worked in Strasbourg, Frankfurt, and London. Made numerous engravings of "views" of cities.

House urns
Cinerary urns in the shape of a house or casket, common in the early Iron Age in northern Germany and Etruria (modern Tuscany). Urns of this sort give a splendid picture of what certain types of house must have been like.

Hugenottenmanier
Name given by German historians of architecture to a neoclassical/Baroque style intro-

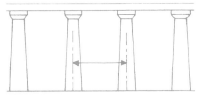

Intercolumn

duced into Germany and Flanders by the Huguenots on their expulsion from France.

Hypaethral temple
Temple with an opening in the roof to let in light.

Illusionistic effects
Usually achieved by structural or painted false perspectives giving an illusion of greater space. During the Renaissance these architectural "tricks" were generally three-dimensional (plastic), while the Baroque on the whole used the two-dimensional medium of painting. One example of false perspective is the apse of Bramante's S. Satiro in Milan.

Impluvium
Square pool in the middle of the atrium of a Roman house, for collecting the rain water that came through the hole in the roof (*compluvium*).

Impost (springer)
Projecting cornice or stone on top of a pillar or some other kind of support, from which an arch springs.

Inlay
An ancient technique of ornamentation – the

use of strips of different coloured rare woods (and often also ivory, mother-of-pearl, and tortoise-shell) to decorate a plain wooden structure. The art of inlay enjoyed a revival with the advent of the Baroque.

Intercolumn
The distance between columns, measured from the centers of the shafts. Illustrated opposite.

Intrados
The interior surface of the curve of an arch (window, vault, etc.). Usually at right angles to the exterior wall surface, and on a generally more modest scale than an embrasure.

Ionic order
Architectural style originating in Ionia, the most characteristic feature of which is the scroll capital and fluted column shaft (see **Greece** and **Rome** chapters).

Jerusalem cross
Illustrated on p. 233.

Jesuit style
A certain type of Baroque found particularly in Latin American church architecture. Usually elaborately decorated by craftsmen of Amerindian origin.

Jones, Inigo (1573–1652)
Architect and stage and costume designer; creator of "the English Classic" – English Neoclassicism. He studied in France and then Italy, where he was influenced by Palladio. Main works include: the Queen's House, Greenwich (1617–35); the largely destroyed Palace of Whitehall (Banqueting House); St. Paul's Covent Garden. Many of his buildings have been destroyed by fire.

Jugendstil
The German version of Art Nouveau, so styled after *Jugend*, the review which championed it.

Keystone
The wedge-shaped stone (voussoir) in the top center of an arch (illustrated on p. 226). In groin and ribbed vaults its shape varies, and where there is complex ribbing it is often richly sculpted.

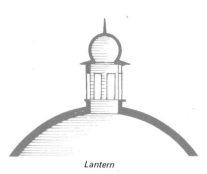

Lantern

Kiosk
Oriental summerhouse, especially common throughout the Ottoman Empire. Designed as arbours for gardens and parks. Usually polygonal or round, with pierced walls. Often domed, or with a steep pitched roof supported on columns.

Klenze, Leo von (1784–1864)
German architect under Ludwig I of Bavaria (from 1816). His work is mainly of neoclassical inspiration, though sometimes Romanesque and Byzantine elements are used, creating a somewhat eclectic style. Main works: the Glyptothek, the Alte Pinakothek, the Propyläen, and the Allerheiligen-Hofkirche (all in Munich); and near Regensburg, a doric *Ruhmeshalle*, or hall of fame, known as Walhalla.

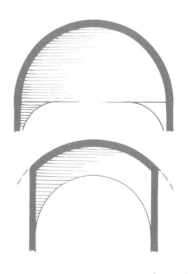

Kubba

Knobelsdorff, Georg Wenceslaus von
(1690–1753)
Prussian Rococo architect and painter, court
architect and friend of Frederick the Great.
Main works: Schloss Rheinsberg (alterations);
the Berlin opera house; the Charlottenburg and
the Schloss in Potsdam; and Sanssouci,
Potsdam. During the building of Sanssouci
(1745–47) his friendship with the king was
broken.

Knorpelwerk or **Knollenwerk**
(German, literally "gnarled work.") A form of
ornamentation (carvings or stucco) in fashion
in the 17th century. Weird, exuberant decoration, often featuring human faces with
bloated noses, bulging eyes, and wild straggling beards. Examples in France, Germany,
and Holland.

Knotted column
In Romanesque architecture, a relatively rare
form of double column with "knotted" shafts –
i.e. featuring ornamental stone knots in the
middle. Found in cloisters and porticos, and
sometimes as window mullions.

Kubba
In a mosque, underground burial chamber of a
ruler or important preacher. Illustrated on p.
235.

Kymation
(Greek, diminutive of *kúma*, "wave.") In
Greco-Roman architecture, double-curved
moulding in the form of stylized leaf, usually as
decoration on a temple cornice, but found also
on base structures, funerary monuments, etc.

Lambris
(French, "panelling.") Decorative cladding on
internal walls – either stucco, wood, or marble.
Sometimes covers the whole wall, sometimes
only the bottom part. Used especially of
Renaissance buildings.

Langhans, Carl Gotthard (1732–1808)
Early German neoclassical architect. His masterwork is the Brandenburg Gate in Berlin.

Lantern
Crowning feature of a dome, much loved by
Renaissance and Baroque architects. Like a
small round or polygonal box, it in turn is
crowned by either a miniature dome or spire,
conceived in proportion to the main dome.
Illustrated on p. 236.

Le Corbusier *pseudonym of* **Charles-
Edouard Jeanneret** (1887–1965)

Foils

French architect. A highly intelligent and
inventive theorist, his thinking contained five
main theses: 1) construction on piles (pillars
holding the building above the level of the
street); 2) roof gardens; 3) individual floors
structurally independent of each other;
4) "horizontal" windows; and 5) totally bare
façades allowing complete freedom of articulation. He worked in many different countries, and his main works include: housing
"units" in Marseilles, Nantes, Berlin, and
Meaux (near Paris); the design for the Indian
city of Chandigarh, begun in 1951; the chapel
of Notre-Dame-du-Haut, Ronchamp, in the
Vosges (1950–55); the Tokyo Museum of
Western Art (1957–59); designs for the
Olivetti center at Rho (1962–64) and the new
hospital in Venice completed in 1966.

Ledoux, Claude-Nicolas (1736–1806)
Engraver and (later) architect, precursor and
inspirer of French Neoclassicism. He built
many *hôtels* in Paris, notably that for the Prince
Montmorency (1769), and a pavilion for
Madame Dubarry (1772). His masterwork is
the salt works at Chaux, around which he
designed an ideal city (this design was never
realized).

Le Nôtre, André (1613–1700)
French garden "architect," creator of the
Baroque park. Main work: the park of
Versailles, on which many later similar projects
were based.

Leonardo da Vinci (1452–1519)
Italian painter, sculptor, architect, scientist, and
inventor; worked in Florence, Milan, Rome,
and then at the end of his life in France for
Francis I. His depth of thought, artistic sensitivity, and originality and practicality (he was
actively involved in designing fortifications)
place him among the greatest of Renaissance
geniuses. His importance as a scientist and
engineer was confirmed by the discovery in
1965 of the collection of drawings now known
as the *Codices Madrid*.

Loggia
An area such as a portico, like a room with (frequently) a vaulted roof and at least one side open. Arcaded loggias are sometimes found on upper floors above palace ambulatories and monastic cloisters.

Lotus pier
Egyptian column in the shape of a stylized lotus flower.

Louis Quatorze
Period of French Baroque (1650–1720), with grandly conceived and richly decorated architecture. Reached its peak of excellence during the reign of Louis XIV.

Louis Quinze
Late phase of French Baroque, under Louis XV (1723–74), contemporary with German and Austrian Rococo. The Rococo style proper never became popular in France.

Louis Seize
Transitional period in the France of Louis XVI (1774–92), stylistically a not always convincing blend of light Rococo "froth" and neoclassical clarity of line.

Lunette
(French, "small moon.") A small arched aperture set in a larger vault, or a semicircular window (for instance, above a door).

Maderno, Carlo (1556–1629)
Architect, pupil of Domenico Fontana, with whom he then collaborated. Worked in Rome and Frascati. His most important work is the extension of St Peter's, Rome (the nave and west front, which prefaces the Italian Baroque). Maderno favoured pronounced plinths, cornices, and mouldings. Other works include; S. Andrea della Valle; the Palazzo Mattei; and a design for the Palazzo Barberini.

Madrasa
Moslem theology school attached to a mosque.

Maiano, Benedetto da (1442–92)
Early Renaissance sculptor and architect, worked mainly in Florence; one of the leading exponents of the Brunelleschian style. The Palazzo Strozzi and the portico of S. Maria delle Grazie (Arezzo) are attributed to him. His greatest sculptures include: the pulpit in S. Croce, Florence; the altar in S. Fina, in the Collegiate church of S. Gimignano; the tomb of Mary of Aragon, Monte Oliveto (Naples); and S. Domenico, Siena.

Majolica
A type of painted and glazed pottery, similar to faience in mode of production and style of decoration. Often used in buildings to cover floors and walls.

Mandorla
Rhomboid or ovoid ornamental motif, reminiscent of an almond. Often features as a halo round the head of a saint, conveying a certain sense of the supernatural. Common in medieval miniatures.

Mannerism
The tendency in art to imitate models, leading to arbitrary exaggeration of figurative elements and contrasts of light and shade to create an emotional effect, and somewhat forcing the stylistic conventions of the Masters. As an art historical term it is generally used of the period between about 1530 and the end of the sixteenth century.

Mansart, Jules-Hardouin (1646–1708)
French architect under Louis XIV. Much influenced by classical styles. Gave his name to the mansard roof (pitched in such a way as to allow space for one or more rooms – not merely attics – "in" the roof), although this design had already been used in the Middle Ages and had been brought back into vogue by François Mansart (Jules's great uncle). Main works:

Tracery

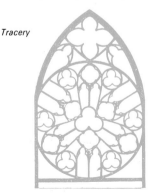

dome of the Hôtel des Invalides (1706); and the Place Vendôme and the Place des Victoires in Paris, which reflect his grandiose urban planning schemes.

Marble

Smooth-grained crystalline limestone, either white or a single colour, or a combination of the most varied colours (i.e. monochrome or polychrome). Used extensively in all ages for both sculpture and building. Each age seems to have had its favourite colour. Thus, for instance, the ancients were most fond of delicate bluish tints; the Baroque favoured polychrome and variously veined types – especially for altars while Neoclassicism tended always to use white. Some of the most famous marbles include; Carrara (pure white); Pentelic

Meander

(bluish-white, sometimes greyish-white); Paro (large-grained, white); Peloponnese (black); Tenedo (red); and *portoro*, from Portovenere (black with golden-yellow veining).

Mausoleum

Monumental tomb, named after Mausolus, satrap of Caria (fourth century B.C.), who built a vast tomb at Halicarnassus which was one of the seven wonders of the world. The Mausoleum is thought to have been a four-sided structure, having a tall base surmounted by an Ionic colonnade, on which stood a seven-meter (twenty-three-foot) high pyramid of twenty-four steps.

Meander

Winding ornamental motif, the name of which derives from the river Meander in Asia Minor. Illustrated above.

Medallion

In architecture, a round or oval ornamental feature (mostly in stucco) on walls or pillars. May serve to frame bas-reliefs or paintings.

Megaron

Central room of the Mycenaean palace, and core of the Hellenic house. In its final form it incorporated a vestibule, an anteroom, and the main room itself (i.e. the megaron proper), to which there was only one door.

Menhir

Prehistoric monument found in France, particularly Brittany, and the British Isles. Consists of a long slab of irregularly shaped stone standing vertically in the ground, carved with decorative motifs or significant symbols. The menhir may be seen as a very early form of stele.

Merian, Matthäus (1593–1650)

Swiss engraver. His reputation and importance for architectural historians are assured by his 19-volume *Theatrum Europaeum* and 16-volume *Topographien*, containing over two thousand maps and views of seventeenth-century towns.

Metope

In a Doric entablature, the square between two triglyphs.

Mezzanino

In English, mezzanine. Italian term for a secondary service floor between the ground and first floors. Often also squeezed in below the roof cornice. Very common in Baroque and neoclassical buildings.

Michelangelo Buonarroti (1475–1564)

Sculptor, architect, painter, and poet. Worked in Florence, Bologna, and Rome. Described as "the father of the Baroque." The stylistic keynote of this genius's work is the blending of tense vigour and sublime harmony. Main works include: the statue of David in front of the Palazzo della Signoria, now in the Accademia, and the Medici tombs (Florence); the Sistine Chapel frescoes, the *palazzi capitolini*, work on the new St Peter's, including the design of the dome, and the statue of Moses intended for the tomb of Julius II, which remained incomplete, later to be destroyed (Rome). He supervised the realization of only a few of his designs – e.g. the Biblioteca Laurenziana in Florence, and the layout and buildings of the Piazza del Campidoglio in Rome (conceived as the ideal center of the *Urbe*).

Michelozzo (1396–1472)

Early Renaissance sculptor and architect, worked in Florence and Milan. Succeeded Brunelleschi in overseeing the building of the *duomo* in Florence. Main works: cloister and library of S. Marco; the Palazzo Medici-Riccardi; and the courtyard of the Palazzo Vecchio (all in Florence).

Mies van der Rohe, Ludwig (1886–1969)

German architect who worked with Behrens, and Gropius. Last director of the Bauhaus, which had to close down in 1933. Main works include: German pavilion for the Barcelona World Exhibition of 1929; Farnsworth House, Plano (Illinois); the Illinois Institute of Technology, Chicago; the Seagram Building, New York; and the Lafayette residential area in Detroit.

Mihrab
Arabic for the niche inside a mosque, always orientated towards Mecca. In architectural terms the mihrab may be seen as a derivation of the Byzantine apse.

Mimbar
The preaching platform (usually wood) inside a mosque.

Minaret
(From the Turkish *minare*.) A tower-like structure, very thin and tall, from which Moslems are summoned to prayer by the *muezzin* five times a day.

Minoan civilization
So named after the legendary King Minos. Cretan civilization of the 3rd and 2nd millennia

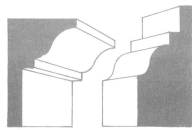

S. moulding

B.C. For greater detail see the **Antiquity** chapter (**The Aegean**).

Module
Basic unit of measurement in Greek architecture: the diameter of a column at the lower scape. The proportions of the other parts of the building were arrived at by multiplication or division of this dimension.

Modulor
System of measurements and ratios developed by Le Corbusier, based on the average height of a human being (conventionally 1.829 meters, (6 foot). The theory proceeds by division in golden sections proportional with the dimensions of the human body.

Monastery
A building or complex of buildings and adjacent ground enclosed within walls and housing a community of monks. Features cloister, church, chapter house, garden, and (usually) library and school. The first Order for the enclosed life was drawn up by St Benedict of Norcia, founder of the Abbey of Montecassino (529).

Stonemason's monograms

Monopteron
(From the Greek *monópteros*, "having one wing.") Vitruvius's name for a round temple (with usually conical roof on a single ring of columns – rare in antiquity, and used by neoclassical architects mostly for parks and gardens).

Moorish
Islamic architectural and decorative style in Spain. As ornamentation, generally used for filling blank wall space, often using several symmetrical planes. Much copied during the Renaissance and Baroque periods.

Mosaic
Technique of wall, floor, and vault decoration, with the advantage of being extremely durable. Fragments of different coloured stone (mostly cut into tiny cubes, *tesserae*, and sometimes glass, are arranged in a bed of putty or cement so as to form a pattern or figurative design. A "Florentine fresco" uses minute chips of stone applied according to the demands of the pattern or cartoon, without any form of jointing.

Mosque
Moslem place of prayer and public worship. Originally a simple courtyard, only later did it acquire a roof (mostly domed). There are three

main types of mosque: the jamic, which has a large courtyard surrounded by a *liwan* (portico); the *madrasa*, which has a school attached to it; and the tomb-mosque, which houses the tomb of some exceptionally devout person.

Moulding
Any shaped element of decoration – either convex or concave. The illustration on p. 239 shows two types of S moulding.

Mozarabic art
Widespread in Spain. Typically features Moorish forms of ornamentation on proto-Romanesque structures.

Mudéjar
A style combining Moorish and Gothic elements, popular in Spain in the fourteenth century. Typical features are horseshoe arches, stalactite vaulting, and richly decorated majolica panels.

Mycenaen civilization
Preclassical Greek civilization, named after its most important center, Mycenae, together with Tiryns, also constitutes its most important archeological site. Flourished from about the middle of the 2nd millennium B.C. to c.1120 B.C.

Narthex
In the old Christian basilica, a portico (or hall) abutting on the outside of the main façade. Place of assembly for catechumens and penitents.

Nave
In a church, the central area between the west door and the crossing (hence not including the choir or apse). Either side of the nave are the aisles.

Neo-Baroque
The ostentatious historicist style that emerged as a reaction against the "cold impersonality" of Neoclassicism towards the end of the nineteenth century. The neo-Baroque tends to relish overloaded sculptural and painted interior decoration.

Neoclassicism
A style inspired by those of ancient Greece and Rome. Emerging in the latter half of the eighteenth century, it gave way to Roman-

ticism at the beginning of the nineteenth century. See **Neoclassicism** chapter.

Neo-Gothic
Second half of the nineteenth century, movement of revival of Gothic architectural and decorative tastes.

Nering, Johann Arnold (1659–95)
German architect (probably of Dutch descent), who worked in Berlin and Frankfurt under Frederick III. Main works (in Berlin): the Arsenal; design for the Friedrichstadt quarter, in which over 300 houses were built to his plans.

Neumann, Balthasar (1687?–1753)
Engineer, captain of artillery, and Baroque architect. Important both for his structural innovations and his artistic sense. Main works: the bishop's Residenz, Würzburg; the great staircase at Schloss Bruchsal – also that at Schloss Brühl; the Vierzehnheiligenkirche; and the abbey church of Neresheim.

Neutra, Richard (1892–)
Austrian architect and art critic; worked in the United States, notably in California, where he built houses, industrial premises, and schools. Main works: Lovell House (1929) and the residential area of Channel Heights (1944), both in Los Angeles. Author of various writings, including: *Biologisches Bauen* (The biology of building); *Wenn wir weiterleben wollen* (If we wish to survive); and *Survival through Design*.

Niemeyer, Oscar (1907–)
Brazilian architect who has quite deliberately turned away from traditional building patterns towards a "Mannerist *Neue Sachlichkeit*" combining monumentality and precision. His main – and most controversial – works are some of the buildings in the new Brazilian capital of Brasilia (inaugurated in 1960).

Nuragh
Ancient Sardinian cone tower in massive masonry, with "terraced" roof.

Nymphaeum
Originally, in antiquity, a shrine dedicated to the nymphs; then in Hellenistic and Roman times a square or circular structure, sometimes with an apse, featuring niches and an architectural "prospect" with columns. During the Renaissance and the Baroque it was a monu-

mental fountain surrounded by elaborate theatrical-set effects, usually featuring mythological figures.

Obelisk
(From the Greek *Obeliskos*, diminutive of *obelos*, "spear: long, pointed object"). In ancient Egypt a symbol of the sun god, consisting of a limestone pillar in three sections one on top of the other – two pyramid trunks and one small pyramid or *piramidion*. The shadow cast by the obelisk also served to show the time of day. It was from this that the classic monolithic square obelisk (similarly crowned with a miniature pyramid) of the Middle Kingdom derived. Such obelisks stood at temple entrances, almost always in pairs, in celebration of the reigns of individual pharaohs.

Stonemasonry

A

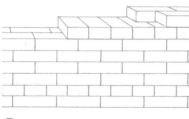

B

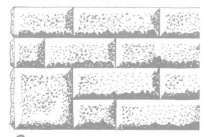

C

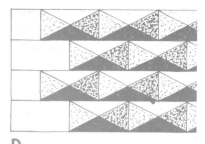

D

Oculus (eye)
Round or oval window (in the Baroque, usually a blind window) as a form of external wall decoration.

Onion dome
Typical feature of southern German Baroque towers – often with a double bulb. Common also in Russian architecture. Both the Russian and German types derive (though quite independently) from the Orient, and resemble each other. Illustrated on p. 227.

Oratory
Chapel set apart for private prayer and worship, one of the very earliest forms of Christian building. Attached to churches or monasteries, they were usually reserved for members of religious communities. Later, frequently built in an upper story of a church or monastery.

Ottonian art
A style found in Germany and Lombardy under the Ottonian dynasty (tenth and eleventh centuries): essentially eclectic – combining Carolingian, Byzantine, and vaguely classical elements – it achieves a courtly, aristocratic elegance. Its most notable contribution in architecture was the Westwerk. Outstanding miniatures, fusing Carolingian and barbarian traditions.

Palladio, Andrea (1508–80)
Renaissance architect, originator of the "Palladian" style – Roman architectural forms used in a severe, yet grand way. Main works include: the "Basilica" and Teatro Olimpico in Vicenza; the Villa Capra (commonly known as the Rotonda), outside Vicenza on the Monti Berici; and the Redentore and S. Giorgio Maggiore in Venice. Author of *I quattro libri dell'architettura* (The four books of architecture).

241

Palmette
Ornamental motif consisting basically of an uneven number of foils or petals fanning out around a stem. Popular among the most ancient civilizations of the East and in the Cretan-Mycenaean area, the palmette continued to be used until the advent of Neoclassicism.

Papyrus column
Egyptian column in the shape of a papyrus plant.

Parler
Fourteenth- to fifteenth-century family of architects and sculptors (German Gothic). The founder of the "dynasty" was Heinrich (probably from Cologne), who built the cathedral of Schwäbisch-Gmünd. His son Peter (c.1330-99) is the best known. He worked in Bohemia, and is responsible for the cathedral of St Vitus in Prague and the church of St Barbara in Kutná Hora.

Patio
Inner courtyard like a small cloister: typical feature of Spanish and Latin American architecture.

Pavilion
(From military Latin *papilio*, after *papilio*, "butterfly.") A four-cornered tent originally. Nowadays, a small building in a park or garden, either ornamental or for recreation. Usually open.

Pediment
The triangular ornamental structure over a doorway or the projecting center section of any elevation. Often incorporates a coat of arms or symbolic figurative decoration (usually sculpted).

Pendentive
Inverted concave triangle supporting a dome on a square or polygonal base structure.

Pergola
A frame structue in a garden, supporting climbing plants and forming a shady walk. More elaborate pergolas consist of columns carrying a light trellis frame. A typical feature of classical and Renaissance architecture.

Peripteral temple
(From the Greek *peripteros*, "with wings – columns – all around.") Temple with a single row of columns surrounding the cella.

Peristyle
Arcaded courtyard in a Greek house (also later in Roman houses). Often laid out as a garden, or leading into a garden.

Perpendicular
Late phase of English Gothic, from c.1350 to the latter half of the sixteenth century. Characterized most strikingly by spacious windows with strong vertical emphasis.

Perrault, Claude (1613-88)
French architect under Louis XIV. His masterpiece is the east elevation (the colonnade) of the Louvre, which he designed in competition with Bernini.

Pilaster
Decorative vertical strip standing out slightly from a wall, usually in the form of a half pillar, either smooth or fluted.

Pillar
A support shaft, differing from a column in being square, polygonal, or "multifoil" in section. Slender pillars, generally of marble, sometimes appear for purely decorative purposes.

Pinakothek
(From the Greek *pinakotheke*, "store, collection of pictures.") In Athens, a large room with vestibule adjoining the left wing of the Propylaea where votive panels were kept. Nowadays the term is used in some languages for "picture gallery."

Piranesi, Giovanni Battista (1720-78)
Architect and engraver who worked principally in Rome. Of his few buildings only S. Maria del Priorato (on the Aventine) survives. His greatest achievement is his great output of etchings. Already popular during his own lifetime, these etchings are mostly of remains of ancient Roman monuments. His graphic work includes: *Varie vedute di Roma* (Various View of Rome); *Antichità romane* (Roman Antiquities); *Le carceri* (The Prisons); and *Grottesche* (Grotesques).

Pisano, Andrea (c.1295-1349)
Italian Gothic sculptor, goldsmith, and architect, who worked in Orvieto, Pisa, and Florence. Main works: bronze doors in the

south elevation of the Baptistery in Florence; and marble reliefs for the lower section of the *campanile* of Florence cathedral.

Pithos
Greek vase of huge dimensions (up to two meters/six feet high) shaped like an inverted cone, used for storing food, or for containing corpses (in a crouched position).

Plinth (or socle)
(From the Greek *plinthos*, "brick.") Base for a column, pillar, or statue.

Pluteus
Parapet or wall made of carved marble slabs. Enclosed the *Schola cantorum* in early Christian basilicas.

Poelzig, Hans (1869–1936)
German architect who worked – and taught – in Breslau, Dresden, and Berlin. A prominent exponent of *Neue Sachlichkeit* both at the beginning and end of his career, he nevertheless had considerable artistic inventiveness, as is displayed in his work on the Berlin Grosses Schauspielhaus in Berlin. More typical works are the Poznań reservoir and the I.G. Farben administrative offices in Frankfurt.

Polygonal masonry (pelasgic or cyclopean)
An ancient style of masonry in which enormous blocks of irregularly-shaped, roughly hewn or completely unhewn stone are piled on top of each other without mortar.

Polystyle pillar
A pillar composed of several shafts "bundled" together. Most notably a feature of Gothic church architecture.

Pöppelmann, Daniel (1662–1736)
German architect at the court of Augustus II, the Strong in Dresden. His masterpiece is the Zwinger in Dresden – a complex of porticos and pavilions in a garden, forming a grand Baroque "folly": a perfect backdrop to his patron's glittering court.

Portico
A structure having at least one side colonnaded, often decorative or monumental, but sometimes serving as a covered walk or market area. In classical architecture it featured at the entrance to buildings, generally with a pediment surmounting the columns.

Renaissance and neoclassical styles revived this latter form.

Prandtauer, Jakob (1658–1726)
Austrian Baroque architect, along with Fischer von Erlach the leading architect of religious buildings in Austria at the time. His masterpiece is the Benedictine abbey of Melk, which, however, was only completed after his death.

Presbytery (sanctuary)
In a church, the east section of the choir, often separated off and slightly raised.

Projection
Projection of any architectural feature in relation to the adjacent section of the building: for instance, cornice, moulding, door and window frames, balcony, exterior stairs, etc.

Pronaos
(From the Greek, "temple hall.") In a Greek temple, the area between the cella and the columns in front (temple *in antis*).

Propylaeum
(From the Greek *propúlaia*, "standing before the gate of a temple.") The grand main entrance steps and colonnades to a temple. The most famous Propylaea are those of the Acropolis at Athens which were designed by Mnesicles.

Prostyle
(From the Greek *próstulos*, "with columns in front.") A Greek temple with a row of columns at the front not terminating in *antae*.

Pulpit
In a church, a raised platform in the main nave, usually abutting on a pillar or a wall. With a parapet wall (which became richly ornamented in the early Middle Ages) and often a baldacchino (which also functioned as a sounding board), the pulpit is where the preacher stands to speak. The first pulpit in Italy was that in Ravello cathedral (*c*.1150).

Raphael (Raffaello Sanzio) (1483–1520)
Painter and architect, worked in Rome 1508–9, continuing the work on the new St Peter's on the death of Bramante (in fact substituting a Latin-cross plan for Bramante's Greek). Other buildings by him are the Palazzi Caffarello and Branconio dell'Aquila, the church of S. Eligio degli Orefici, and (in Florence) the Palazzo Pandolfini. His most

important painted works include the frescoes in the Vatican *Stanze* and *Logge*, the Sistine Chapel, and the Villa Farnesina.

Rayonnant
Style of Gothic, mid thirteenth to early fourteenth century, with window tracery and ornamentation resembling rays of light. Most striking examples occur in rose windows and the pediments and gables over church doors.

Refectory
Communal dining hall in a monastery, usually reached via the cloister, and situated opposite the church. Often of very considerable size, it sometimes had painted decoration on the upper part of the walls (where the tall windows were set) and the ceiling.

Régence
Short period of French art contemporary with the Regency of Philippe d'Orléans (1715–23). *Régence* architecture was supple and elegant, in reaction against the austerity of *Louis Quatorze*, and anticipating the graceful, almost whimsical *Louis Quinze* style.

Relief
A form of three-dimensional art in which the figures or motifs project from a flat background surface – either slightly (bas-relief, low or light relief) or more emphatically (heavy relief). In

Example of Rocaille

Egyptian reliefs the figures are carved into the background surface.

Renaissance
Both a style and movement in the arts and a whole manner of life and conception of living, fundamentally determined by Humanism. The word *rinascita* (re-birth) was first used by Vasari in 1550. See **Renaissance** chapter.

Rocaille
The French equivalent of Rococo – ornamentation (either plaster or carved) featuring wave-like lines and snail and conch shell forms, sometimes almost sculptural in execution, and generally asymmetrical. Illustrated below left.

Rococo
Style of building and ornamentation that emerged towards the end of the Baroque. The word stems from *rocaille*, the main decorative motif, and appeared for the first time in the 1842 supplement of the *Dictionnaire de l'Académie Française* as applying to the style that evolved under Louis XV and during the early part of Louis XVI's reign. The Rococo abounds in exuberant curves and curls – often becoming almost excessive.

Romanesque architecture

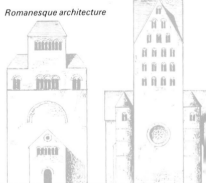

Roentgen, David (1743–1807)
German cabinet maker, creator of his own style, midway between Rococo and Neoclassicism. Roentgen furniture tends to have slender legs, makes use of rare woods and is often inlaid. Much sought after in Germany, France, and England.

Romanesque
Includes all styles of art between c.1000 to the end of the thirteenth century. Main characteristics: round-headed arches, barrel vaults, very thick main walls, rectangular ground plans, richly varying columns and capitals, and decoration on arches. Evokes a sense of stillness and austere strength, without being in any way gloomy. Illustrated above.

Romanticism

Early nineteenth-century movement of European spirituality, literature, art, philosophy, and political thinking. (Some authorities date its beginnings to the final decades of the eighteenth century). The hallmark of Romanticism is the rejection of rigid laws and conventions in a new spirit of freedom, of both thought and creative activity, more in harmony with human nature. It was in painting and poetry – and later

Rose window

music – that this new cultural sensibility was most dramatically expressed. It brought about a re-evaluation of the Middle Ages, Gothic art, and popular song (poetry as a genre was hailed as intrinsically superior to prose), and prepared the way for historicism (i.e. the rediscovery and adoption of artistic motifs and styles of past ages, and research into old cultures).

Rood screen

In Baroque churches, the finely wrought gate dividing off that part of the church reserved for the Divine Majesty (*dóxa*) from the main nave.

Roof, shapes of

A single pitched; **B** saddle or ridged roof; **C** tent-roof; **D** hipped roof; **E** half-hipped roof; **F** mansard roof. Illustrated on p. 249.

The illustration on p. 249 (below) shows a somewhat unusual multiple pitch roof: this form originated in the Inn–Salzach area, on the German–Austrian border, in the sixteenth century. Rather than a simple symmetrical ridged roof, it consists of a row of shallow double pitched roofs concealed behind a false pediment.

Rosette

Ornamental motif in the shape of a rose, found in an endless variety of stylized forms from antiquity through to our own day, in virtually every age.

Rose window

Round window with tracery in the west front of Romanesque and Gothic churches, above the main doors. Illustrated left.

Russian architecture

Rotonda

Used buildings, and sometimes even whole urban districts or complexes, that are almost an exact circle. The Pantheon in Rome is known as *La Rotonda*, as is also the Palladian Villa Capra outside Vicenza.

Ruins

Remains of a building, or of several buildings, destroyed by the processes of time of the violence of man. Attitudes towards old ruins have varied in different times. Sometimes they were used merely as convenient stone quarries; more enlightened ages (already in the Renaissance, for instance, and even more so in the neoclassical era) regarded them with immense respect, and endeavoured to restore and preserve them.

Russian architecture, style of
Russian church architecture derived from Byzantine models and Eastern stylistic elements, developed in a consistent manner with scrupulous respect. The interior is divided into the tabernacle area (the *bema*) and the area for the congregation by means of the *iconostasis*, a wall with three doors (the center door is "holy," and may only be used by bishop, priest, or if need by a deacon); the ornamentation is Eastern in origin, although Baroque features do occur – most notably in the onion domes (often gilded) on the bell towers. This distinctively Russian style survived only in icons after the eighteenth century. From then on almost all architectural stimulus came from Germany, Italy, and France. Illustrated on p. 245.

Rustication
Exterior masonry of irregular and roughly pitted stone.

Saarinen, Eero (1910–61)
Finnish architect who worked with his father Eliel in the U.S. Main works: the General Motors Center, Warren (Michigan); and the T.W.A. terminal at Kennedy airport, New York.

Sacristy (vestry)
In or attached to a church, usually leading in to the choir, and generally also with a door leading outside. Room where church vestments and ornaments are kept. The priest dons his vestments for the liturgy here, and sometimes relics and votive offerings are also kept in this "annex." Originally conceived as a replacement for the diaconicon and prothesis of the early Christian basilica, the sacristy in time became a totally autonomous structure, like a chapel, with magnificent furniture and decorations of its own. The sacristy in modern churches is now essentially functional.

Sarcophagus

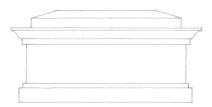

Sanctuary
General word for a consecrated spot. In Greek temples, the "sanctuary" was an inner room (*áduton*) within the cella. For the ancient

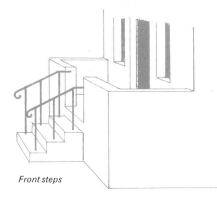

Front steps

Greeks and Romans it was also used of sacred groves or an enclosed temple area. In Christian churches it designates the section of the chancel east of the choir, where the altar stands (the presbytery). It can also be used synonymously with shrine, to denote a church dedicated to a popular saint in the area where he or she lived and performed miracles.

Sandrart, Joachin (1606–88)
German writer on art, painter, and engraver. His reputation rests above all on his book *Teutsche Akademie der edlen Bau-, Bild-, und Malerkünste* (German Academy of the Nobel arts of Architecture, Design, and Painting, 1679–1683), which represents an important contribution to art history, especially painting, with regard to the seventeenth century. His model for this work was Vasari's *Lives*.

Sarcophagus
A tomb, often decorated with reliefs, placed in full view in a crypt or some other such funerary edifice (a sarcophagus is, however, never interred). Usually of stone, sometimes of bronze, it often has a sculpture of the dead person on the lid. The original Greek *sarkophágos* actually means "which eats flesh." The Greeks believed that one of the properties of granite was that it could consume the perishable parts of the body, leaving the bones untouched. Illustrated left.

Schinkel, Karl Friedrich (1781–1841)
German neoclassical architect and painter, pupil of Gilly, worked in Berlin. His first works are clearly classical in inspiration, while his later buildings and designs become increas-

ingly neo-Byzantine and neo-Gothic. Main works include: the Altes Museum, the Neue Wache,and the Schauspielhaus (all in Berlin). See also the **Neoclassicism** chapter.

Schlüter, Andreas (1660?–1714)
German sculptor and architect – though less successful in his latter capacity. He is known above all for his monumental sculptures. Main works include: the Berlin arsenal (*Zeughaus*), for the façade of which he carved more than a hundred keystones; and the bronze equestrian statue of Frederick III in Königsberg (modern Kaliningrad).

Scrollwork
Style of decoration known as *Rollwerk* in German. Appeared in the mid sixteenth century in Flanders and Holland, and soon spread to Germany. The ornamentation resembles small parchment scrolls, somewhat stylized. Such scrolls and spiralling curves were especially popular during the Rococo period, on cornices, doors, furniture, and architectural mouldings. Illustrated on p. 226.

Semper, Gottfried (1803–79)
German historicist architect, one of the creators of the modern style of theater building; worked first in Dresden, then from 1849 in London, Vienna, and Zurich. His masterpiece was the Opernhause in Dresden, which was destroyed by fire in 1869.

Serlio, Sebastiano (1475–1554)
Bolognese architect and theorist of architecture, who worked as a painter of "prospects" in Pesaro, then in Rome, Venice, Thiene, Fontainbleau – where François I entrusted him with the building of the château – and finally Lyons. He is famous in particular for his *Sei Libri dell'architettura di Sebastiano Serlio bolognese*. He anticipated the so-called Palladian (or Venetian – as used by Sansovino) window; a three-bay window, the side bays being flat on top, the center one being arched.

Shaft
The main section of a column, between the capital and the base.

Sheraton, Thomas (1751–1806)
English cabinet maker and theorist of furniture making, second in importance only to Chippendale. His furniture has great simplicity of line, and is basically neoclassical in inspiration. His tables tend to stand on pedestal legs.

Sima
In a temple, the end feature of the entablature on the pediment or the side elevations, serving to channel rain water into the guttering.

Skidmore, Louis (1879–1962)
American architect, founder of the SOM studio (so named after the initials of Skidmore, Owings, and Merrill), in which over a thousand architects worked. Main works include: the Oak Ridge atomic complex (Tennessee, 1943); Lever House in New York (1951–52); and the Chase Manhattan Bank in New York (1957–61).

Socle
The slightly projecting base of a wall, pillar or column. Often merely protective or decorative.

Soufflot, Jacques (1713–80)
French architect who blazed the trail for Neoclassicism in France. His masterpiece is the Parisian church of Ste-Geneviève, now the Panthéon. He studied at the French academy in Rome, and made several trips to Italy later. He was the first person to measure the dimensions of the temples at Paestum.

Spherical (spheroidal) dome
A hemispherical dome with neither a central opening (or eye), nor a lantern, and without ribs. Sometimes depressed, sometimes elevated. Common in late antiquity and in the East. Illustrated on p. 225.

Stavkirke

247

Spire

Pyramidal or conical structure surmounting any vertically inclined base. A typical feature of Gothic.

Splay (splayed jamb)

The oblique slant of a door or window jamb (vertical sidepost supporting the horizontal lintel above), especially common in Romanesque and Gothic architecture.

Spur

A piece of ornamentation at the base of a Romanesque or Gothic column, linking the plinth and the first astragal (or semicircular ring moulding) at the bottom of the shaft. Shaped like a leaf, a small animal, or sometimes a human head.

Squinch

A small half dome in the upper corner of two walls at right angles to each other, serving to support a dome on a polygonal base structure.

Stalactite

Reminiscent of a natural stalactite, and a feature of Moorish architecture (in Arabic, *muqarna*). Formed by superimposition of quarter-spherical mouldings one on top of the other. Can serve as pendentives.

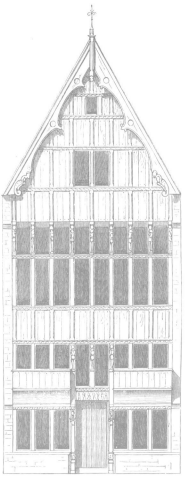

Half-timbering

Stavkirke

Norwegian early medieval wood church. The walls consist of vertical timbers, and the roof has several stories, like a pagoda, each roof "story" being steeply pitched. Illustrated on p. 247.

Stele

A stone slab standing upright in the ground to mark a grave or, in some cases, as a votive offering or a memorial. Funeral steles were erected in Egypt already in the Old Kingdom.

Stoa
Greek word for "portico" – a place for strolling and meeting people.

Stonemason's monogram
Mark or series of marks establishing identity, similar to the "stamp" on a brick. Mostly impossible to decipher, they represent a sort of coded monogram. Illustrated on p. 239.

Stonemasonry
A coursed gable; **B** garden wall bond or English bond; **C** smooth rustication; **D** diamond-pointed rustication. Illustrated on p. 241.

Stucco
A moulding material made of ground fired plaster mixed with crystallized plaster combined with a glue solution. Working with stucco demands great skill, because once it is shaped and has dried, it is extremely hard to "correct." The technique comes originally from the East, but has been used in Europe since the early Middle Ages. Stucco is ideal not only for plain decoration but also for figurative compositions.

Stucco lustro: applied with a heated trowel, then carefully smoothed and polished with wax.

Temple in antis

Stucco marmorizzato: a means of achieving polychrome ornamentation. The "marbled" effect is produced by mixing together dollops of previously coloured stucco. This technique – very popular in the Baroque period, especially on altars – permits a maximum of colour differentiation.

Stylization
Geometrical simplification of natural shapes.

Stylobate
In classical architecture, the upper part of the stereobate (i.e. the platform base on which columns stand).

Swag
Ornamental motif of interwoven leaves, flowers, fruits, and ribbons, in various materials (paper, tinfoil, cloth, or, more permanently, wood, stone, or plaster; the motif may also simply be painted on a flat surface), hanging like an inverted arch. For both interior and exterior decoration.

Examples of roofs

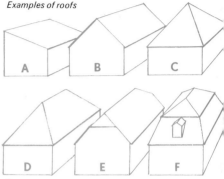

Synagogue
(From the Greek *sunagogé*, "assembly.") Jewish place of prayer; nowadays often a community center as well as a place of worship. In medieval iconography "synagogue" was the name given to a blindfolded female figure representing Judaism (which would be contrasted with another, triumphant, female figure representing the Christian Church). This motif was introduced as part of the anti-Semitic propaganda put about after the crusades.

Multiple pitch roof

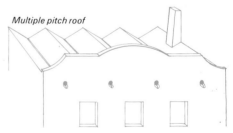

Tablinum
In ancient Roman houses, a reception or dining room.

Telamon (atlas)
An architectural support in the form of a male figure. The word "atlas" derives from the Titan of that name. The telamon reapppears in the ornamentation of Baroque, and later historicist façades.

Temple "in antis"

Small rectangular temple with pronaos between the two extended *antae* of the cells. Very early form of Greek temple. Illustrated on p. 249.

Tympanums

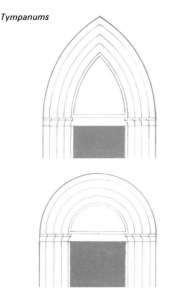

Tower

A tall vertical structure with a relatively small square, polygonal, or circular ground plan, either freestanding or an integral part of some other building (as in a castle). The shape of the tower often allows one to guess the style of the larger, lower structure already from a distance. Not uncommonly, however, such towers in fact date from a different period, and so can lead one to false conclusions. A feature of Italian towns is the *torre comunale*, or civic bell-tower, which summoned the inhabitants to

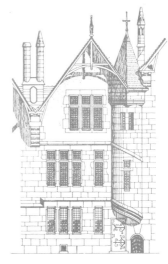

Tower

assemble together or to prepare for battle. Most of these towers were built during the period of the medieval communes.

A typical feature of Gothic buildings is a circular tower containing a spiral staircase, half projecting from an exterior wall (see illustration above).

Tessenow, Heinrich (1876–1950)

German *Neue Sachlichkeit* architect (though not an absolutely rigid adherent to this school). Worked in Berlin and Dresden. Built mostly residential buildings, but also some schools. His masterpiece is the garden city of Hellerau near Dresden, with the Festspielhaus (1912).

Tholos

Circular Greek building, often with an external ring of columns, sometimes with a similar ring also inside.

Tiepolo, Giambattista (1696–1770)

The greatest fresco painter of the Italian Baroque. Worked in Venice, Vicenza, Udine, Würzburg, and Madrid. Main works include: the Villa Valmarana (Vicenza); the Würzburg Residenz (the "imperial hall" and staircase); and the Palazzo Labia in Venice.

Torus (tore)

Convex moulding serving as a base or plinth.

Guilloches

Tracery

The ornamental development of structural elements in Gothic architecture, notably in windows. Excluding carved foliage, the trefoil, and the quatrefoil, almost all Gothic ornamentation takes the form of tracery – a sort of "abstract art" ranging from the barest early developments of the mullion, to the exuberant complexity of the late *flamboyant* and Decorated styles. Illustrated on p. 237.

Tracery window

Window with several lights divided by mullions supporting arches. Typical of Romanesque and Gothic.

Transept

The transeveral section of a church, intersecting the nave to form a cross shape. Similar in design to the main nave.

Triforium

Tribune

Raised platform in a semicircular recess in a Roman basilica, where the praetors, assessors, and other authorities sat. The placing of the bishop's throne in the apse of the early Christian basilica would seem to derive from the Roman tribune.

Triforium

Gallery running above the aisles of a church. Above the main arches and usually just below the sloping side roof, it opens onto the main nave (mostly by means of triple-lancet arches – hence the name "triforium"). It has no windows looking outside. Illustrated left.

Triglyph

Four-sided panel with three flutes (glyphs). Alternates with metopes in Doric architecture.

Trunnion

Any protrusion or side projection of any size.

Tympanum

In an arched doorway, the (often triangular) space between the intrados of the arch and the door lintel. Renaissance buildings in Holland and northern Germany sometimes feature stepped tympanums. Illustrated opposite.

Ulrich von Ensingen (1350–1419)

German architect in charge of the building of Ulm cathedral from 1393 to 1417, and from 1399 also responsible for Strasbourg cathedral. After his death his son Matthäus took over at Ulm, to be succeeded in turn by his grandson Moritz.

Vasari, Giorgio (1511–74)

Painter, architect, and art historian. Worked in many towns, but most importantly in Florence and Rome. As a painter he worked in the Tuscan-Rome mannerist style, never producing anything of outstanding merit. As an architect he was more successful, with magnificent "scenic" effects. His masterpiece is the Palazzo and church of the Cavalieri di Santo Stefano in Pisa. Above all, however, he is known for his *Lives* of Italian artists from Cimabue to Michelangelo (*Le vite de' più eccellenti pittori, scultori e architettori*, 1550).

Vault

Form of roofing, curved and requiring special support structures. May be almost "monolithic" (the most ancient types), made of cement-like conglomerate, or ribbed so as to concentrate the load on the four vertices of the vault base.

Barrel vault: semi-cylindrical vault over a rectangular building. Illustrated below.

Panel vault: a technique of the "After Gothic." Rather than being supported by ribs, the vault is composed of cellular panels which exert pressure on each other in such a way as to be self-supporting. Illustrated above right.

Groin (cross) vault: intersection of two barrel vaults. In the case of ribbed vaults, the rib structure is built before the actual vault surface. Illustrated center right.

Fan vault: late Gothic, especially in England. A common form of vault in which the support comes from radiating fans of complex, highly decorative ribbing. Illustrated below right.

Reticulated vault: late Gothic, with elaborate ribbing forming a kind of basket pattern.

Mirror vault: the ceiling of a room, flat in the middle and vaulted only round the edges. Common in Baroque and Rococo buildings. Usually supported by the ceiling joists or the roof rafters.

View (prospect)

A *genre* of picture that first emerged in the seventeenth century, achieving its greatest heights in the eighteenth century, with the Venetian townscape painters. A realistic portrayal of an architectural complex, a square, a row of houses, or a landscape. The standard "view" was virtually a documentary record; however, there was also a vogue for "views" of imaginary buildings and invented scenes.

Vignola, Jacopo Barozzi, known as
(1507–73)

Architect and writer who worked in Bologna, Rome, Mantua, Piacenza, and other lesser centers. In 1565 he was given charge of the work on the new St Peter's basilica. Main works include: Pope Julius III's villa (now the Etruscan Museum), the small domes on St Peter's, and the Chiesa del Gesú (all in Rome); the Palazzo di Caprarola (Viterbo); the Portico

dei Banchi (Bologna); and S. Maria degli Angeli (Assisi). Author of the *Regola delli cinque ordini d'architettura* (Rule of the five

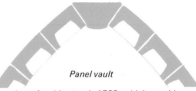

Panel vault

orders of architecture), 1562, which considerably influenced Baroque architecture.

Groin (cross) vault

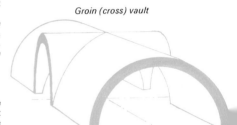

Villard de Honnecourt (thirteenth century) French Gothic architect. His book of drawings and comments has been invaluable to our understanding of Gothic construction techniques.

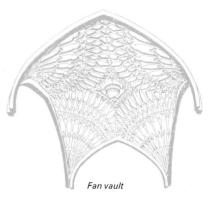

Fan vault

Vitruvius Pollio
Roman architect, probably lived in the Augustan Age. Author of a ten-volume treatise (*De architectura*) written probably around 25 B.C.

Barrel vault

and dedicated to the Emperor Augustus. Rediscovered in the fifteenth century, *De architectura* became the chief source of inspiration for Renaissance architecture.

Volute
Serpentine or S-shaped ornamental motif; the distinguishing feature of the Ionic capital. There are no volutes in medieval architecture. Taken up again in the early Renaissance, it became a vital feature of Baroque decoration. Illustrated below.

Wedge motif
Carved decorative motif on any surface (also in a frieze). On a wood surface a triangular-bladed tool is used, on stone a chisel.

Volute

Westwerk
German term for an enclosed entrance portico at the west end of a church, as evolved in the Carolingian age. Towers were then added to lend the *Westwerk* greater architectural emphasis. See also the **Romanesque** chapter.

Wooden architecture
The oldest examples of wooden structures are the huts built by primitive peoples with curved and interwoven branches and wattle, straw, or mud in-fills. In northern regions, where there

were many forests, some of the most ancient types of house were built in wood, four-sided, using roughly hewn tree trunks, which were either fastened or carpentered together at the four corners. Chinese wooded architecture, with its grace of line and high standard of technical achievement is in a class of its own.

Wren, Christopher (1632–1723)
Architect to Charles II. Worked mostly in London, his major task being the rebuilding of the fifty-one churches destroyed in the Great Fire of 1666. He also produced an urban plan for the whole City, but this was never realized, largely due to the hostility of property holders in the area concerned. Main works include: St Paul's cathedral, London; St Stephen Walbrook, London; Greenwich Hospital; the east wing of Hampton Court; and the Monument commemorating the Great Fire in Pudding Lane.

Wright, Frank Lloyd (1869–1959)
American architect, pupil of Louis Sullivan, who introduced fundamental structural and stylistic innovations, based on a totally new conception of space. Main works include: the Prairie Houses; Fallingwater, at Bear Run (Pennsylvania, 1936); and the Guggenheim Museum in New York (1959, designed in 1946).

Zimmermann, Dominikus (1685–1766)
German architect and interior designer (a master of stucco), who worked in Swabia and Upper Bavaria. Considered the most important exponent of southern German Baroque. Built many village churches, developing a highly personal style. Main works include: the shrine (Wallfahrtskirche) at Steinhausen; the Frauenkirche at Günzburg; and the Wallfahrtskirche at Wies (Steingaden).